Sharing the Good News
with Roman Catholic Friends

Sharing the Good News
with Roman Catholic Friends

By Daniel R. Sánchez, D.Min., D.Phil.
Rudolph González, Ph.D.

Church Starting Network
www.churchstarting.net

SHARING THE GOOD NEWS
WITH ROMAN CATHOLIC FRIENDS

Requests for permission should be addressed in writing to: Church Starting Network, 7240
Briardale Dr., Cumming, Georgia, USA 30041 or contact us at the web site given below.

For more information about this book and other resources and training materials, or to contact
the authors, please refer to the Church Starting Network web site: www.churchstarting.net

Except where otherwise noted, Scripture quotations are taken from the *Holy Bible, New
International Version*, (New York: International Bible Society, 1984),. Used by permission. The
"Practical Section" in Chapter one quotes Scripture verses from *The New American Bible, Saint
Joseph Edition,* (New York: Catholic Book Publishing Co., 1970).,
Used by permission.

Cover Design by
Cynthia Mackey
Cleveland, North Carolina

Library of Congress Cataloging-in-Publication Data

Sánchez, Daniel R., 1936 —
Sharing the good news with Roman Catholic friends / Daniel R. Sanchez and Rudolph D.
González. Includes bibliographical references.
ISBN # 1-894933-33-8
1.   Catholics.   2. Witness bearing (Christianity).   3. Catholic Church
I. Title.   II. González, Rudolph D., 1953 —

BX6329.R6 S52
248.5

Printed and bound in Canada.

ACKNOWLEDGMENTS

We want to expresses our most sincere gratitude and indebtedness to people without whom the writing of this book would not have been possible. We want to thank Dr. José Borrás and Dr. Bartholomew F. Brewer, two former Roman Catholic priests whose example, encouragement, and commitment to "share the truth in love" have inspired us in our work. We also want to thank persons whose scholarly research and writing have enlightened us immeasurably in our task. Among these are James McCarthy, Paul G. Schrotenboer, Eric D. Svendsen, and James R. White. We are also truly indebted to administrative assistants Lisa Seeley and Georgette Lodwick who have assisted us greatly in the preparation of the manuscript for this book. We also owe a great debt of gratitude to our respective wives Carmen B. Sanchez and Virginia L. Gonzalez for their encouragement, sacrifice, and patience as we labored to complete this book. We also want to express our gratitude to Lisa LeBlanc and Ken James for the excellent job they did of reading our manuscript and providing valuable editorial suggestions. We also want to acknowledge the contribution of the persons whose testimonies we utilized in the vignettes at the beginning of the chapters. Their willingness to open their hearts and minds to the Lord and His Word, despite traditional and social pressures is an inspiration to us all. As the inhabitants of ancient Berea (Acts 17:11), these new believers listened to the message with great eagerness, and every day studied the Scriptures to see if what their religious leaders said was really true. We thank them all. Above everything, *to God be the glory!*

PREFACE

The greatest thing we can ever do is to lead someone to a personal *experience of salvation in Jesus Christ*. This has profound implications for *this life* and for *eternity*. This task, however, becomes challenging and complicated when people already have a socio-religious tradition that has many of the wonderful elements of Christianity, yet fails to point to Christ directly as the only means of salvation. With heavy hearts, we must point out that there are many nominal Christians among Protestants, Eastern Orthodox and Roman Catholics who fall under this category. Others have addressed the need for evangelization among the first two groups.[1] In this book, we will focus on nominal Christians who identify themselves as Roman Catholics.[22] While it is acknowledged that there are other Catholic groups which may believe differently, this book primarily refers to *Roman* Catholics. Henceforth, the term "Catholics" will be used to refer to Roman Catholics.

Many of them are sincere, devoted, and loving people who, in varying degrees, give intellectual assent to basic doctrines of the Catholic Church and participate in its liturgical rites.[3] However, they have not responded in repentance and faith to Jesus Christ as their personal Savior and Lord and do not have a lifestyle that demonstrates a sense of freedom from the guilt of sin, relief from the fear of judgement, and joy in their relationship with God.[4] As a result of this, they often feel confused and alienated when they face the trials and tribulations of life and either have a false hope or do not have a sense of assurance when they think about their eternal destiny.

Our purpose in this book is not to analyze all of the teachings and practices of the Roman Catholic Church.[5] We will, however, be very diligent in comparing its teachings with that which the Bible teaches regarding salvation. We simply cannot afford to gloss over vital biblical doctrines upon which the eternal destiny of people hinges. While we acknowledge that we have common concerns regarding the pressing moral issues of our day,[6] we want to be extremely careful to not lose sight of our highest priority, which is to share the message of salvation that produces a radical change in the lifestyle of believers and progressively conforms them to the likeness of Christ. We will, therefore, follow the biblical injunctions to *"speak the truth in love"* (Ehesians 4:15) and to always be prepared to give an answer to those who ask about the hope that is within us, but to do it "with *gentleness* and *respect*" (1 Pet. 3:15-16). In other words, we are not going to practice *"sloppy agape,"* but *"tough love"* (Gal. 4:16). We agree with James White that: "Christian love cannot be separated from Christian truth. True love rejoices with truth and true love *tells* the truth."[7] This love, therefore, compels us to go to the Word of God, learn what it teaches about salvation, and hold it as the standard by which we evaluate our religious experience, regardless of our religious affiliation. In this book, therefore, we will examine the issues that relate to an *understanding* of the biblical doctrine of salvation, the *spirit* in which it should be communicated, and the most appropriate *methods* that should be utilized to lead people to a personal experience of salvation in Jesus Christ.[8]

There are several groups of people whom we will seek to help with the material in this book. First, we want to help Evangelical Christians who want to share the gospel of salvation with their dear Roman Catholic relatives and friends, but feel unprepared because they know little of the Church's teachings and practices. To address this need, we will utilize Roman Catholic sources to acquaint our readers with the teachings of the Church, especially those regarding salvation. Second, we want to help those who were formerly Roman Catholics and are now Evangelical Christians. This group often makes the mistake of thinking that if they can just convince Roman Catholics that they are wrong in everything they believe, they will automatically become receptive to the gospel message. In their zeal related to their new found faith, former Roman Catholics, at times, witness to their relatives and friends in a spirit of *condemnation*, *anger*, and *impatience*, which turns out to be counter productive. To help this group, we will share time proven approaches that they can use to witness to their loved ones in a spirit of *love* and *wisdom*. The third group that we will try to help with this book is nominal Christians among Roman Catholics who have not had a personal experience of salvation in Jesus Christ and are sincerely seeking to know the truth about their eternal destiny. With them we will respectfully explore the question: "If what you are counting on to give you peace with God here on earth and get you into heaven is not what the Bible teaches, would you want to know it?"[9]

One of the unique characteristics of this book is that it will not only seek to analyze the principal teachings of the Roman Catholic Church regarding salvation in the light of Scripture, as several excellent books have done recently,[10] but it will also endeavor to equip readers to communicate the message of salvation utilizing strategies that are *biblically sound* and *pragmatically effective*. These strategies are based on the sixty years of cumulative experience, that we as authors have had, in ministering to people with a Roman Catholic background. This book, therefore, will address the *principal doctrines*, *pertinent cultural factors*, and *relevant historical issues* that will enable readers to witness to their Roman Catholic friends in an *informed*, *appropriate*, *cordial*, *confident*, and *effective* manner.

PREFACE

The format for the first five chapters has the following segments: (1) Introduction: Case Study, (2) Bible Studies, (3) Learning Activities, and (4) Practical Instruction. The case studies, based on the actual experience of people, contain valuable information on the pilgrimage that people go through as they come to a personal, saving relationship with Jesus Christ. Through the Bible Studies, we will establish a solid biblical foundation for the concepts that will be shared in each chapter. The lessons learned in these studies will be invaluable in knowing how to prepare the ground for the effective seed sowing of the gospel. In the Learning Activities, we will share appropriate approaches and methods to lead nominal Christians to a personal faith in Christ by eliminating unnecessary obstacles in the establishment of meaningful relationships and effective communication. In the Practical Instruction sections, we will seek to help readers have a clearer understanding of the teachings and practices of the Roman Catholic Church. This will enable the reader to converse more confidently about that which the Bible teaches in contrast with some of the teachings of the Roman Catholic Church. In the last four chapters of the book, we have included case studies as well as a series of lessons dealing with *evangelization*, *discipleship,* and *congregational* strategies that can be utilized to help believers grow in their new life in Christ.

This book can be used in a variety of ways. First, an individual reader can read the Bible Studies, do the Learning Activities, and devote time to the Practical Instruction sections. The individual reader can also utilize selected sections of this book for evangelistic Bible studies and for discipleship. Second, this book can be used in a variety of settings (e.g., retreats, training series in churches) to train groups to witness to and disciple relatives, friends, and other interested persons. Specific instruction for the group study format are found in the table of contents section of this book.

ENDNOTES

[1] Others have written about nominal Christians among Protestants and Orthodox groups. See Thailand Report: Christian Witness to Nominal Protestants, and Christian Witness to Orthodox. Lausanne Committee for World Evangelisation.

[3] See No. 10, Christian Witness to Nominal Christians Among Roman Catholics (Wheaton: Lausanne Committee for World Evangelism, 1980), 7.

[4] For an excellent book on the assurance of salvation, see Donald S. Whitney, *How Can I Be Sure I'm A Christian?* (Colorado Springs: NAVPRESS, 1994).

[5] For a survey of different approaches see James Leo Garrett, Jr., *Baptists and Roman Catholicism*(Nashville: Broadman Press,1965). Some Roman Catholics divide Evangelicals into three categories: (1) Lunatics, (2) Sophisticated - Intolerant, (3) Informed - Conciliatory. See Philip St. Romain, "Catholic Answers to Fundamentalism," (Ligouri,MO: Ligouri Publications, 1989), audio cassette presented by Father Juan Vargas, C.SS.R.

[6] Some even suggest that we now have so many social concerns in common with our Roman Catholic friends that we ought to forget about any doctrinal differences and concentrate our efforts jointly on the political arena tocombat the evils of modern day society (e.g., abortion, pornography, etc.) The implication is that the moral issues on which we agree are more important than the doctrinal differences that divide us. For a discussion that explores laying aside some of the doctrinal differences to engage in joint efforts see Charles Colson and Richard John Newhaus, *Evangelicals and Catholics Together: Toward a Common Mission* (Dallas: Word, Inc, 1995), 18. For an opposing view see, James G. McCarthy, *The Gospel According to Rome* (Eugene: Harvest House, 1995), 7.

[7] James R. White, *The Roman Catholic Controversy*(Minneapolis: Bethany Publishers), 1996, 17.

[8] Our biblically based conviction is that the work of atonement was wrought *solo Christo* (by Christ alone). We are adopted as children of God *sola gratia* (by grace alone). Our justification is *sola fide* (by faith alone). Our worship and service is *soli Deo gloria* (for the glory of God alone) Paul G. Schrotenboer, *Roman Catholicism: A Contemporary Evangelical Perspective*, (Grand Rapids: Baker Book House, 1988), 16.

[9] This question has been adapted from William Fay's question in William Fay & Ralph Hodge, *Sharing Jesus Without Fear* (Nashville: Lifeway Press, 1997), 16.

[10] See, McCarthy, White, Schrotenboer op. cit.

Table of Contents

ACKNOWLEDGMENTS

PREFACE

PART 1: Understanding the Gospel Message

1. UNDERSTANDING THE BIBLICAL CONCEPT OF
   SALVATION 19
   Introduction: Lydia's Grief 19
   Bible Study: Jesus And Nicodemus (John 3:1-2) [Part 1] 21
      The Teachings of Jesus Regarding Salvation: (John 3:1-21) 22
      The Levels of Communication Jesus Used 27
   Learning Activity 32
      Levels of Communication
   Practical Instruction 33
      Doctrine of Salvation 33
      Earned or A Free Gift? 33
      Received Through The Sacraments or Experience With Christ? 38
      Mediated Through Church or Through Christ? 42
      Assurance of Salvation? 45

2. LEARNING HOW TO SHARE THE MESSAGE OF
   SALVATION 55
   Introduction: Joe's Discovery 55
   Bible Study: Jesus And Nicodemus (John 3:1-2) [Part 2] 58
      Lessons From Nicodemus: 58
      A "Pilgrim's Progress" Story 58
   Learning Activity 65
      Prepare Your Testimony 65
      Practice Your Testimony 66
   Practical Instruction 70
      Beliefs We Have in Common 71
      Practices That We Have in Common 76
      Values That We Have in Common 76

PART 2: Communicating Thegospel Message .. 79

3. RECOGNIZING OPPORTUNITIES TO SHARE THE MESSAGE OF SALVATION 81
Introduction: Nora's Disappointment 81
    Bible Study: Jesus And The Samaritan Woman (John4:1-29) 84
    Jesus Cultivated A Friendship 85
    Jesus Created An Interest 87
    Jesus Comprehended Her Situation 89
    Jesus Concentrated On Essential Aspects Of Salvation 91
    Jesus Communicated The Message Progressively 93
Learning Activity 97
    1. Don'ts 100
    2. Do's 100
Practical Instruction 103
    Second Vatican Council 103
    Spiritual Obstacles 112

4. ANSWERING SINCERE QUESTIONS ABOUT SALVATION .. 113
Introduction: Janie's Enquiry 113
Bible Study: How Jesus Dealt With Sincere Questions 115
    Learning Activity 117
    Plan of Salvation (practice) .. 117
    Practical Instruction 118
    Responding to sincere questions 118

PART 3. Discipling New Believers 129

5. ENCOURAGING NEW BELIEVER'S PILGRIMAGE 131
Introduction: Pablo's Pilgrimage 131
Bible Study: Saul of Tarsus: A Case Study 133
    Paul Was a Very Devout Person 133
    Paul Had an Encounter With Jesus 135
    Paul Began His Discipleship 137
    Lessons on Discipleship From Paul 139
Learning Activities 140
    Evaluate Your Own Discipleship 140
    Activity 2: Design Discipleship Strategies 140
Practical Instruction 141
    Chapter by chapter 141

Transformed lives 142
A study of topics relating to salvation 142

6. ENABLING THE NEW BELIEVER'S SPIRITUAL DEVELOPMENT 147
Introduction: Pam's Discipleship 147
    The Dimensions Of Discipleship 150

7. ADDRESSING DOCTRINAL ISSUES 157
Introduction: Martha's Decision 157
Discipleship Lessons 160
    1. The Supreme Authority: The Bible Or Tradition? 161
    2. Veneration Of Mary And Of The Saints 171
    3. Catholic Teaching About The Sacraments 189
    4. The Elements Of Catholic Worship 195
    5. Justification 204
    6. Confession 207
    7. Purgatory 209
    8. Head Of The Church 211
    9. Baptism 215

PART 4: Contextualizing Strategies 227

8. DEVELOPING EVANGELIZATION STRATEGIES 229
Introduction: Rafael's Journey 229
Evangelization Strategy Lessons 231
    10. Building Witnessing Relationships 233
    11. Approaches To The Various Types Of Catholics 253
    12. Reaching Our Latin American Friends 259

9. DESIGNING CONGREGATIONAL STRATEGIES 265
Introduction: Maria's New Family 265
Congregational Strategy Lessons 267
    13. Concept Of The Church 270
    14. Biblical Ceremonies For Socio-religious Acts 276
    15. Contextualized Worship Services 285

INSTRUCTIONS FOR THE LEADER 297

BIBLIOGRAPHY 299

PART ONE:

UNDERSTANDING THE GOSPEL MESSAGE

UNDERSTANDING THE BIBLICAL CONCEPT OF SALVATION

Introduction: Lydia's Grief

My efforts to understand the concept of salvation came early in life. I was in the sixth grade in elementary school, when I developed a friendship with a very lovely classmate named Lydia. She and her family were very active in the Catholic Church that was a block away from their home. One day, the tranquility of their family was shattered when Lydia's mother died unexpectedly. Because of my appreciation for Lydia, I decided to attend her mother's funeral. The church was packed with family members, community leaders, and classmates. The ritual, the vestments of the priest and altar boys, as well as the paintings on the walls and icons were very impressive. Throughout the funeral service, however, I kept asking myself: "When is the priest going to give the family words of comfort and assurance that Lydia's mother is in heaven with the Lord? Well, he never did. The priest did recite the passage "I am the resurrection and the life, he who believes in me though he should die, will come to life again," but he did it in a very cursory manner and never applied it to Lydia's mother. Before leading the procession to the front door of the church, the priest made the sign of the cross over the casket with the receptacle carrying the incense. The sight of the smoke and the smell of the incense gave the ritual a mystical quality. Yet, in my heart there was a yearning for a word of comfort and assurance.

At the cemetery the priest said a few kind words about Lydia's mother, recited a prayer, and then departed. With tears streaming down the sides of his face, Lydia's oldest brother knelt by the grave, made the sign of the cross and remained there for a long time. When the time came to leave, Lydia and her brothers and sisters kept on crying and saying: "Goodbye Mommy, we will never see you again!" I cried with them as we departed and kept asking myself, why doesn't anyone tell them that their mother is in heaven and that they can see her again?

Two years earlier, after a period of doubt and confusion, I had received Jesus Christ as my best friend and my savior. I had struggled with two questions: "what is the purpose of my life" and "what will happen to me when I die?" I had not committed any crimes, however, I knew that I had offended God with my thoughts and my actions and I was afraid to die. It was at that time that I started reading the Bible. My hunger for God's word was so great that when my parents would turn off the lights, I would use a flashlight under the covers to continue to read. One night during an evangelistic meeting at church, the evangelist preached a message that pierced my heart. I walked forward, knelt at the altar, asked God to forgive me of all of my sins, and invited Jesus into my life. The change was miraculous. I immediately felt a sense of peace in my heart and the fear of death disappeared. Something within me told me that if I were to die, I would immediately go to the presence of my best friend, Jesus.

On the day of the funeral I began to ask myself, could it be that there is something in the teachings or practices of the Catholic Church that I have missed? In an effort to understand what Lydia was going through, I would put holy water on my forehead, make the sign of the cross, wear a scapular, and review in my mind every thing the priest had said at the funeral. Try as I may, I simply did not find any sense of assurance regarding the salvation of departed loved ones or of people seeking to follow the teachings and practices of the Catholic Church. As a result of that experience, I decided to focus on what the Bible had to say about the salvation of those who place their trust in Christ as their personal savior. With that in mind, let's examine what Jesus said to Nicodemus about eternal salvation.

BIBLE STUDY

Jesus And Nicodemus (John3:1-2) [Part 1]

Jesus' encounter with Nicodemus is a fascinating case study that reveals the great difference that exists between lifeless traditional religion and a vibrant spiritual faith. In spite of his standing as a "Teacher of Israel" it becomes evident in the dialogue that Nicodemus was lacking in real spiritual understanding and did not have a vibrant personal relationship with God. Though trained as a *Pharisee,* someone to whom the average Jew looked up as a spiritual guide, His understanding of the way in which a person is made acceptable to God was truly deficient. This exchange shows that despite his great learning regarding the Law, the spiritual connection was *lacking* in his life.

The fact that Nicodemus came to Jesus at all indicates that the teaching of the Messiah must have had a great impact on his mind. Surely he must have heard something that gripped him; he could not easily dismiss the words of this Galilean teacher. There are indications later in the gospel that Nicodemus was willing to give Jesus the benefit of the doubt (John 7:50-51). On the other hand, the fact that he came by night suggests that he was not willing to be seen with him openly, much less be identified as one of His disciples, at least not yet. Nicodemus must have felt himself riding on the proverbial "horns of a dilema" and all because he chanced to give Jesus an honest hearing. Nicodemus is to be commended because he came to talk with Jesus despite risking his place of prominence in Israel.

Jesus' dialogue with Nicodemus is an important component in the overall narratological structure of John's gospel. Coming relatively early in the gospel, it functions much like the Sermon on the Mount in Matthew's gospel (Matt 5-7)—it is a programmatic statement. From the outset, this brief dialogue reveals the spiritual nature of salvation, a theological premise that will remain constant throughout. Thus, whenever a subsequent reference is made to spiritual worship, it is this discussion, which lays the seminal ground for our understanding. [2]

Overall, the encounter reveals how deficient Nicodemus' understanding was with regards to the spiritual nature of salvation. Ironically, Jesus' message is incomprehensible to this learned "teacher of Israel." It is evident from his questions (v.4, 9) that despite the vast storehouse of his religious tradition he has difficulty understanding the concept of the new birth. Nicodemus never answers with a theological counter-punch. Although Nicodemus sought out Jesus, perhaps to debate, it was the Lord who held class and did all the teaching that night. We might well ask how this formidable theologian could be so utterly impotent.

It should be understood that in John's gospel Nicodemus represents Israelite religion, thus, the Lord is overpowering while addressing him. Here we have an exposure of a religion of dead works. Despite what we might "feel" for this good man, his brand of religion posed a mortal threat to all its adherents. Jesus challenges the best champion of Israelite religion and reveals for the first time in this gospel the superior faith of the Spirit.

Jesus' discussion with Nicodemus focuses essentially on the topic of salvation. The story's primary purpose in the gospel is to pit two competing theologies and to show which one is superior. In it we see the superior power of Jesus' message. Thus, in keeping with John's program, the aim of this Bible study is to prepare the reader to understand the spiritual distinctiveness of biblical salvation. We advance the kingdom of God no further if all we do is offer people one lifeless religion in exchange for another. Through this study, the reader will understand where the power of the gospel lies (Romans 1:16-17). Knowing what makes the gospel powerful unto salvation will equip readers to share their faith with assurance. Note the following lessons Nicodemus learned.

The Teachings of Jesus Regarding Salvation: (John 3:1-21)

Salvation is a *spiritual* experience.

The context for the meeting between Jesus and Nicodemus is important. Note that from His first Passover visit to Jerusalem, Jesus walked into the city and asserted His authority over the religious establishment (John 2:13-17). Unlike the synoptic gospels, which tend to downplay His messianic stature until later in the gospels, here Jesus is much more proactive in laying down His messianic claims.[3] The background for understanding Nicodemus' interest in seeking out Jesus is clear; Jesus had responded somewhat enigmatically to the request of the religious leaders for a sign that would confirm His authority in commandeering the temple precinct (2:18-22). Still, while He did perform many signs on behalf of the common people (v. 23), John notes that Jesus remained reserved, unwilling to trust the people fully (vv. 24-25). There is every reason to believe that Nicodemus saw miracles, but were they truly "signs" that corroborated Jesus' claim to be from God? After all, why would a man sent from God treat God's religious representatives with such reserve?

Nicodemus' decision to visit Jesus under the cover of night has been discussed earlier and will not be revisited. Suffice it to say that we must take Nicodemus' initial statement to Jesus as an honest appraisal of the Lord. He is consistently shown to be an honest religious figure throughout John's gospel (John 7:50-51; 19:39-42). Thus, based on what he had seen from Jesus over the span of the Passover feast he truly believed that Jesus held the *imprimatur* (approval) of God's divine favor and impressive rabbinic credentials (3:1-2).

Nicodemus' flattering introduction did not stop Jesus from looking beyond human pleasantries to the core problem this man represented. Jesus responded to his opening remarks by saying, "unless a man is born of water and the Spirit, he cannot enter the kingdom of God" (v. 5). From the beginning of the discussion, a telling reality comes to the surface. Nicodemus does not understand what Jesus is saying. Nicodemus is left dumbfounded. His feeble query is revealing, "How can these things be?" All the while, Jesus moves into a monologue, asserting that Nicodemus is incapable of understanding spiritual truth because he does not "know" nor has he "seen" heavenly things (vv. 10-12). By contrast Jesus' words are true because they are founded on His personal heavenly knowledge (vv. 13-15).

The pattern of heavenly spiritual truth is set in apposition to human earthly knowledge. Jesus explained that a person is born physically of human parents, but is born spiritually of the Spirit (see v. 6). Jesus was aware that Nicodemus had made every effort possible to be a good religious person, but being religious was not enough to enter the kingdom of God. Jesus made it clear that we must have a spiritual transformation so radical that the best way to describe it is to compare it to a new birth.

Application: Have you ever gotten over your head by feigning to know something you knew absolutely nothing about and it becomes painfully obvious to those you tried to impress? For many people, salvation is one of those things that they believe they know: good works, a good life, do wrong to no person, help the needy; these kinds of things are the works that ensure salvation, or so they believe. However, those of us who have come to experience God's saving grace, know personally that no amount of those kinds of works could ever merit God's forgiveness and earn His salvation. Somehow, people need to come to the point where the shallowness and insufficiency of their religious tradition is made painfully known to them. While the Bible teaches this is the work of the Holy Spirit (John 16:7-14), we cooperate with God's Spirit by consistently stressing the spiritual nature of salvation as being solely the work of God.

The implication of Jesus' forthrightness with Nicodemus for witnessing is not to be missed: there is no point of contact between humanly generated religion and spiritual transformation, when it comes to salvation (Romans 8:1-5). Nicodemus' total ignorance revealed that his religion was not vitally connected to God's way of salvation. Some would say that this is cruel, but it is true! What this means for our witnessing is serious. It is not our place to allow a good person's trust in their own works to alter our presentation of the gospel. We must lovingly and faithfully lift Jesus before them as their only hope of salvation (John 3:14-15; 12:32; cf., Colossians 1:24-29; 2:8-14) and trust that in His time the Holy Spirit will draw them to a saving knowledge that recognizes the futility of trusting in works of the flesh (John 3:6; Romans 8:6-7).

Salvation is a *gift*

Recognizing that salvation is a *gift* of God is important. The following syllogism will help: Salvation is a spiritual experience. All lost people are spiritually dead; therefore lost people are incapable of saving themselves. If we remember that all people are sinners and are spiritually dead, then we come to realize why salvation can never be earned. A spiritually dead person is incapable of doing anything "spiritual" and we have already established that salvation is a spiritual work. What is salvation? Essentially, it is the gift of spiritual Life, and this is something only God can give.

Nicodemus was so overwhelmed by the idea of a new birth that he asked, "How can this be?" (v.9). How can all my sins, my mistakes, my habits of the past be erased? How can a person who has lived as long as I have start all over again? How many sacrifices do I have to offer to be totally cleansed of all my sin so that God can accept me?" Jesus answered in a way that Nicodemus could begin to understand. By reminding him of the brazen serpent event (John 3:14-15; cf., Num 21:4-9), Nicodemus was told that sin, like the bite of the fiery serpents of old is a mortal wound about which people can do nothing. Salvation could only come through a divine remedy; the Son of Man was God's gracious remedy to the universal affliction of sin.

John 3:16 is unique in that it is the only verse in John that puts forth the teaching of Jesus as God's gift to humanity.[4] The passage also declares that Jesus was sent to the world (v.17). The two ideas complement each other. One commentator captures the force of the two verbs well: "To 'send' Jesus is more clearly associated with God's will for the world, whereas *"to give"* seems to be used in 3:16 to underscore that the incarnation derives from God's love for the world as well as from God's will."[5] It was God's will to send His Son. His will was motivated by His love for the world. Thus is the nature of God's gift. There is no way that we can earn or deserve it.

Application: The concept of salvation as God's gift is difficult for many Roman Catholics to accept. While they are familiar enough with the language of grace, in practice, their daily piety is driven by religious ritual actions and material sacrifices. Many Roman Catholics feel that good works can't do anything but help to insure their salvation. This is very ironic, since most Catholics will confess that no one can ever be fully assured of his salvation.

The Christian witness needs to have a good understanding of the place and function of "good works" in the life of the redeemed person (Galatians 5:22-26; Ephesians 2:8-10; Colossians 3:10-11). While it is necessary to banish "human works" as helpful to salvation, we must stress the place of "good works" in the Christian's life. Otherwise, many Roman Catholics will feel that we are asking them to go through some cheap verbal trick if works are totally discredited. Remember that when a person comes to faith in Christ as God's unmerited gift, works of righteousness take on a new meaning. No longer are they done with some personal ulterior motive (e.g., to be saved; to save others from purgatory; etc.). Instead they flow from a transformed heart as works inspired and empowered by the indwelling Spirit of God. Saving the baby of Spirit-empowered works while we throw out the bath water of works-based salvation will not compromise the message of salvation.

Salvation is received through *faith*.

The place of faith in the work of regeneration is important to understand. While the substantive "faith" is not used in John's gospel its verbal form " believe" or "believing" is prominent throughout the gospel. Interestingly, John's stated purpose for writing the gospel is "that you may **believe** that Jesus is the Christ, the Son of God; and that **believing** you may have life in His name." (John 20:31) The gospel does not talk about faith as some abstract principle. Instead, it shows cameos of belief (John 4:1-42, 46-54; 5:1-9; 7:31; 8:26-30; 9:35-38; etc.) and unbelief (7:5, 48; 8:48-59; 12:37-41; etc.). In one telling passage, the multitudes inquire, "What shall we do that we may **work** the works of God?" Jesus' responds: "This is the work of God, that you **believe** in Him whom He has sent."(John 6:28-29). Clearly salvation comes by faith apart from works (Ephesians 2:8-9; 1 Peter 1:5; 2 Timothy 1:9; Titus

3:5-6). Towards the end of His public ministry, Jesus makes an important declaration. People will be judged on whether they keep and believe His words (12:46-50). Throughout the gospel, people were given opportunities to see His messianic authority and simply believe. Nowhere is the need to perform religious duties for the sake of gaining salvation mentioned.

It is especially important that Jesus underscored to Nicodemus that salvation is attained through faith alone. Nicodemus was depending upon his observance of the Law and of the prescribed religious practice to save himself. Jesus had to make it clear that whoever *believes* in Him shall not perish but have eternal life. Jesus stresses this point three times (vv.15, 16,19) to Nicodemus.

Application: The Biblical doctrine of faith needs to be clearly understood. Many Catholics see faith and works as integral components and, indeed, so does Scripture. It behooves us, therefore, to know how faith and works are related. Mere intellectual ascent to the truths of the Bible will never save a person (James 2:19). The kind of faith that saves is itself a gift of God (Acts 15:11; John 4:10; Ephesians 2:8) and leads a person to repentance (1 Corinthians 7:9-10). When acted upon, the saved person performs works of righteousness (James 1:22-25; 2:14-26). While Paul reminds us that we stand righteous only on the basis of our faith (Romans 11:20). Hebrews shows, in a sweeping panoramic fashion, the powerful works done by God's people across the ages that possessed faith (Hebrews 11). Roman Catholics need to understand the difference between the gift of faith that enables a lost person to believe and that same gift in the life of a child of God, which empowers him/her to serve (Romans 12:3-8; 1 Peter 4:10-11).

Salvation is a *present possession*.

Salvation as a *present* possession is stressed more strongly by John than other New Testament writers (see, however, 1 Timothy 6:19). In verse 15 Jesus affirms, "Whoever believes, may in him have eternal life." John affirms as much in verse 16, "that whosoever believes in Him should not perish, but have eternal life." Note that both the believing and the having are synchronic events. The stress on salvation as a present reality is meant to underscore its instantaneous and abiding quality. There is an assurance mediated at the point of conversion that God alone confirms through the Spirit (Ephesians 1:13-14; 1 John 1:1-4; 5:10-12), transforming us into heirs "in Christ" (Galatians 3:23-29; 4:4-6). Salvation, however, is not just a present reality; it is eternal. Most commentators recognize the rich theological significance of the word "eternal." It means more than merely the assurance of never ending life. Eternal life is life in communion with God, who alone abides in eternity (Deuteronomy 33:27; Psalm 90:1-2; 1 Peter 1:3-5).

Application: Roman Catholic doctrine does not recognize the possibility of salvation as a *present* and *assured* possession. Most Catholics believe that their eternal fate is tied up with living a life that, on a balance, tilts to the good and away from the bad. Because they continually weigh the good against the bad in their lives assurance is never guaranteed. The question of "sainthood" is a revealing illustration of how far the average Catholic feels about his/her eternal state. While evangelical Christianity acknowledges the sainthood of all believer's based on the finished work of Christ, Roman Catholicism reserves the title of sainthood only for a select number of individuals, and only after an extensive ecclesiastical investigation that can take decades or longer. The point is that your Roman Catholic friend will not consider himself to be a saint.

Knowing that we have salvation, however, frees us up from trying to earn it on the basis of flawed works. The Roman Catholic desperately needs to understand this. We can impress this upon the person by asking them to take seriously God's promises in scripture. In the end, his faith must be founded on God's immutable promises (1 Corinthians 1:9; Hebrews 10:23; 2 Peter 1:3-4; 3:13) and not human persuasion.

The Levels of Communication Jesus Used

In the previous section we stressed the theological command that Jesus manifested over Nicodemus. It is important to remember that while he needed to point out the deficiency of Nicodemus' religion, Jesus did not treat this ruler of Israel with disdain. To the contrary, it is evident from later passages in John that Nicodemus did not harbor a bad impression of Jesus, and in the end was willing to identify with the crucified Savior openly (19:39-40). This could hardly have happened if Jesus had not treated him with dignity. The Lord did not belittle him, even if his religion was shown to be wanting.[6] As the following study shows, communication took place at all levels.[7] Remember the importance of communication skills, for God has chosen the foolishness of preaching to reach the lost for Christ. Note the following progression:

The contact began with a *Face-to-Face* conversation

The conversation between Jesus and Nicodemus began where most conversations begin, at a face-to-face level (vv. 2-3). Nicodemus initiated the conversation by stating a popular perception. Jesus was a teacher from God, validated by the number of signs He had performed. It is important to note that canonically, recognizing that Jesus was a teacher with *bona fides,* while flattering, was far from a complete understanding of His unique person and ministry.[88] The synoptic gospels all record Jesus' question about the masses' assessment of His person as well as that of His disciples (Matt 16:13-16; Mark 8:27-29; Luke 9:18-20). From the response of the disciples to Jesus as the Christ it is evident that recognizing His prophetic office was insufficient.

Jesus was not just a teacher sent from God. John the Baptist recognized the sacrificial nature of His person and ministry (John 1:29,36).

Jesus did not deny the man's assessment, even though it was deficient. This part of the conversation helped Jesus to assess the condition of the night visitor. Though very short, Nicodemus' initial opening statement suggests that the conversation started off on the right foot. There is no hint of an adversarial spirit. Certainly, Nicodemus showed a basic respect for Jesus and it is certain that Jesus was motivated by the most altruistic of reasons, to reach him for eternal life.

Application: Friendships usually begin by trading pleasantries and taking the time to build a basis for genuine relationships. This can only happen when you show a genuine desire to know people, their family, their job, interests and hobbies, and so on. Relational evangelism is not simply about enduring the initial getting acquainted stage to gain some information about the "target" for the sake of pressuring him to receive Christ. Most people can sense when our interest is mixed.

However, face-to-face conversation helps us form preliminary impressions, which can be helpful in praying with discernment for the person. But, these initial opportunities are two-way streets. Your life as a believer in Christ should be firmly cemented at this early time, lest your newfound Catholic friend fail to see the life of Christ in you (Matt 5:13-16).

The conversation entered into a *Mind-to-Mind* interaction

Immediately after Nicodemus initiated the conversation, Jesus began to reveal spiritual truth. Again, remember that John probably left out much of the actual conversation. This is common throughout the New Testament.[9]

In the dialogue we see that Nicodemus did not totally dismiss the idea of the new birth. Unlike many religious leaders who passed judgment on Jesus (5:16-18; 7:1; 10:31-33), Nicodemus retained an open mind throughout. He did, however, express his honest misgivings about the possibility of a new birth (vv.4, 9).

28

Jesus took the time to deal with these questions. He explained that He was talking about a *spiritual* birth. He then cautioned Nicodemus against letting his intellect hinder his search: "You should not be surprised at my saying, 'You must be born again.'" (v. 7). That Jesus was willing to interact at an intellectual level with Nicodemus is further reinforced by the illustration He offers. "The wind blows where it wishes and you hear the sound of it, but do not know where it comes from and where it is going; so is everyone who is born of the Spirit" (v.8). Here, Jesus used a metaphorical analogy to help Nicodemus understand the nature of the spiritual birth by making reference to the wind, which he experienced every day.[10] In fact, Jesus may have gone further in helping Nicodemus. In Aramaic (the language Jesus likely used) the word for "wind" and "spirit" is the same (*ruah*). Thus, by illustrating the nature of a "spiritual" experience with "wind" phenomena the language itself made the analogy all the more forceful. As Nicodemus suspected, Jesus was in true rabbinic form.[11]

Application: Many Roman Catholics are unfamiliar with words and phrases believers take for granted. Terms such as "born again" continue to be grossly misunderstood in society in spite of decades of use and popular books written on the subject. Also, remember that common theological language can also have a different meaning to a Roman Catholic. Christians need to be aware of this potential barrier to effective communication. Sharing the gospel may require us to seek *clarity* and *common ground* in language. Theological concepts will need to be clearly defined and redefined, and defined yet again. The gospel is not "spiritual" in the sense that it contradicts all human reason. While Paul tells us that the gospel is foolishness to Jews and Greeks for different reasons (1 Corinthians 1:21-31), the gospel has a logic that can be understood when certain presuppositions are embraced. For example, if the person is made to realize that humanity lives under the fallen state of spiritual death then the offer of salvation as seen in special revelation (the Bible) makes sense. Or, if we come to see that all human works are indeed tainted by sin we begin to see why Jesus, as the only sinless and spotless atonement for sin, is our only hope of salvation. Both of the preceding examples can be illustrated from human experience. Reasonable analogies to human experiences can help the truth of the gospel "dawn" on people's understanding. Jesus' utilization of the brazen serpent is an example of this, for this was an experience in the history of Israel with which Nicodemus was familiar. These analogies provided bridges of communication.

UNDERSTANDING

The conversation climaxed in a *Heart-to-Heart* exchange

Finally, Jesus turned the conversation to the darkest event of history, His eventual death. The suffering and death of Jesus has been called His *Passion,* and for good reason. Jesus talked to Nicodemus about the depth to which obedience to God's will would compel Him to go. He told him that He was going to die (John 3:14) while making it plain that His sacrifice was motivated by divine love. Jesus assured Nicodemus that those who believe in Him would have everlasting life (v.15). At this level, Jesus communicated what was closest to His heart (see Phil 2:4-8).

The apostles, in their writings, also exhibit great passion in the proclamation of the gospel.[12] This point can hardly be emphasized enough. The gospel is not some abstract thesis that calls for nothing more than intellectual assent. It must be communicated from heart to heart.

Application: For many people (Roman Catholics and non- Catholics alike) their religion becomes rote and meaningless. Often religion is practiced out of a sense of duty and tradition, but with no sense of its vital importance. If you are going to share the gospel, don't just deliver the message. Invest yourself and your emotions in the giving. Often, if you get to the point where you can communicate at the heart to heart level with people regarding their experiences (e.g., grief, victories, transitions), communicating the good news of salvation will be a natural consequence. Remember Paul's letters of commendation:

You yourselves are our letter, written on our hearts, known and read by every body. You show that you are letters from Christ, the result of our ministry, written not with ink but with the Spirit of the living God, not on tablets of stone but on tablets of human hearts. (2 Corinthians 3:2-3)

Conclusion

An aspect that was not covered in the study is the repeated mention of judgment in this account (John 3: 17,18,19). While verses 3-15 stress that because of God's love Jesus has made salvation a present reality to anyone who believes, verses 16-21 present the reverse side of the coin. People stand presently judged (condemned) by their rejection of Jesus. Thus, the added imperative of life's uncertainties should make us aware that every time we talk about the gospel to a lost person, his eternal state hangs in the balance. The Bible says nothing of other opportunities to come to saving faith after this life.

Thus, it is important that we ask ourselves, "At what level are we communicating with those who need to hear the gospel?" Knowing what we know about the precarious state of the lost, what are we willing to do, and how far are we willing to go to cultivate real friendships and to exhaust our communication opportunities to present the gospel honestly and lovingly?

LEARNING ACTIVITY

1) Levels Of Communication

LEVEL	NAME	STRATEGY
Face to Face		
Mind to Mind		
Heart-to-Heart		

Use the chart to do the following:

1. Place the names of people you want to witness to and indicate the level at which you are presently communicating with them.

2. Under "Strategy" write out briefly what you should do to get to the next level (if you are not at the heart to heart level).

3. Share this with prayer partners and spend time in prayer, asking the Lord to help you improve your communication skills with ` these people.

4. Begin looking for opportunities to deepen your level of communication with them.

PRACTICAL INSTRUCTION

The Doctrine of Salvation

Even though Catholics and Evangelicals use the terms "salvation" and "justification," it is important to know that the meanings they assign to these terms are vastly different. In this segment, we will compare the Catholic Church doctrine of salvation with that which the Bible teaches about salvation.

Is Salvation Earned or Is It A Free Gift?

The Catholic Church Teaches That Salvation is Earned

The Roman Catholic Church teaches that eternal life is made possible by the grace of God and is a merited reward earned by the good works that a person does. *The Dogmatic Theology for the Laity* states:

> It is a universally accepted dogma of the Catholic Church that man, in union with the grace of the Holy Spirit must merit heaven by his good works... we can actually merit heaven as our reward ... Heaven must be fought for; we must earn heaven.[13]

This echos what the Council of Trent affirmed:

> To those who work well to the end and keep their trust in God, eternal life should be held out both as a grace promised in his mercy through Jesus Christ to the children of God, and as a reward to be faithfully bestowed, on the promise of God himself, for their *good works* and *merits*.(italics mine)[14]

The Dogmatic Theology for the Laity, quoted above, affirms that the good works are done "in union with the grace of the Holy Spirit," but it adds that heaven can be a *reward* that is *merited* by the person. Likewise, the Council of Trent mentions the *grace* of God and the *merits* of Christ in the justification of a person, but it adds the good deeds done by a person as essential for meriting and increasing grace and obtaining eternal life. It is clear that a person's good deeds or works are considered essential for attaining salvation. The Catholic Church's insistence that good deeds are not optional in a person's salvation is reflected in the Council of Trent's decree that people who do not hold this view should be "anathema."[15]

James McCarthy states:

> Eternal life, according to the Church, is a truly merited reward. It is merited condignly, not congruously. It is not a free gift which God graciously gives apart from anything man has done to earn it.[16]

McCarthy further clarifies the terms used by Roman Catholic theologians. "Congruous" means "an undeserved merit due to the graciousness of God." "Condign" means "a well deserved merit."[1717] McCarthy, op. Cit. McCarthy cites Thomas Acquinas, *Summa Theologica*, Pts. 1-11, q. 114. Art. 3.

The Catholic Church teaches that eternal life is attained condingly. That is to say that it is through good works that a person merits salvation.[18]

James White adds:

> If it is asserted that Christ's work is dependent upon the actions of humankind and that pendent upon works (whether these be penance, baptism, whatever), this is works salvation... It is not necessary that God's grace or mercy be absent in salvation for a teaching to be branded a 'works salvation.' The key issue is whether these works are necessary and determinative to salvation.[19]

According to Roman Catholic doctrine, salvation is based on the atonement of Christ but attained as a *reward* for the *good deeds* that a person has done. How does this compare with what the Bible teaches about salvation?

The Bible Teaches That Salvation Is A Free Gift

The references listed in this section have been taken from the Catholic Bible, *The New American Bible, Saint Joseph Edition*.[20] This has been done for two reasons. First, we want to erase any doubt people might have regarding the version of Scripture that is utilized. In other words, we do not want people to say: "Well, that's what the Protestant Bible says." Second, we want Evangelicals to feel confident in utilizing a Roman Catholic version of the Bible in sharing the good news of salvation with their friends. In most instances the New Testament verses that are used will be clear and compelling. In a few instances, as we will point out, it will be useful to utilize the original Greek language to clarify meanings.

Salvation Is Freely Given By God

"Yes, God so loved the world that he gave his only Son that whoever believes in him may not die but have eternal life" (John 3:16 NAB).

"The wages of sin is death, but the gift of God is eternal life in Christ Jesus our Lord" (Romans 6:23)

"I give to them eternal life and they shall never perish" (John 10:28).

"If death began its reign through one man because of his offense, much more shall those who receive the overflowing grace and gift of justice live and reign through the one man's obedience, Jesus Christ" (Romans 5:17).

"I am the Alpha and Omega. I will give to drink without cost from the spring of life-giving water" (Revelations 21:6).

In all of these Scripture verses, either the noun "gift" (Charisma) or the verb "give" (didomi) is used. The clear meaning of these verses is that salvation is a gift of God. If it is a gift, it cannot be earned or merited. Otherwise, it ceases to be a gift and becomes a reward. The Bible teaches unequivocally that eternal life is an unmerited, free gift of God. Since this is so, there is no room in the Bible for a "works salvation." The good works that a Christian does are not to attain salvation, but as a result (the fruit) of the salvation that has been received.

Salvation Is Received By Grace Through Faith

"But when the kindness and love of God appeared, he saved us; not because of any righteous deed that we had done, but because of his mercy. He saved us by the washing[21] of regeneration and renewal by the Holy Spirit. This Spirit he lavished on us through Jesus Christ our Savior, that we might be justified by his grace and become heirs, according to the hope[22] of eternal life" (Titus 3:4-7).

"But if the choice is by grace, it is not because of their works - otherwise grace would not be grace" (Romans 11:6).

"I repeat, it is owing to his favor that salvation is yours through faith. This is not your own doing, it is God's gift, neither is it a reward for anything you have accomplished, so let no one pride himself on it" (Ephesians 2:8,9).

"Now that we have been justified by his blood, it is all the more certain that we shall be saved by him from God's wrath" (Romans 5:9).

"I will not treat God's precious gift as pointless. If justice is available through the law, then Christ died to no purpose" (Galatians 2:21).

"All men are undeservedly justified by the gift of God through the redemption wrought in Christ Jesus. What occasion is there for boasting? It is ruled out. By what law, the law of works? Not at all! By the law of faith. For we hold that a man is justified by faith apart from observance of the law" (Romans 3:24, 27, 28).

"Hence, all depends on faith, everything is grace." (Romans 4:16).[23]

"Nevertheless, knowing that a man is not justified by legal observance but by faith in Jesus Christ, we too have believed in him in order to be justified by faith in Christ, not by the observance of the law for by works of the law no one will be justified" (Galatians 2:16).

"Now, when a man works, his wages are not regarded as a favor but as his due. But when a man does nothing, yet believes in him who justifies the sinful, his faith is credited as justice" (Romans 4:4,5).

"It should be obvious that no one is justified in God's sight by the law, for 'the just man shall live by faith" (Galatians 3:11).

These marvelous verses of Scripture make it very clear that we are justified (made right with God) by grace through faith in Jesus Christ. It is because of the grace of God offered through the death on the cross of his Son that our sins can be forgiven. As sinners, there is nothing we can do to merit God's salvation. The Bible clearly states: "The wages of sin is death, but the gift of God is eternal life in Christ Jesus our Lord" (Romans 6:23). As the Apostle points out in Galatians 2:21, if we could have saved ourselves by our good deeds then Christ died in vain. Would God not have spared his Son from dying on that cruel cross if we could save ourselves through the good things we have done? "Saving grace, by definition, excludes the entire concept of human works or merit. No human merit, even that supposedly produced by human works performed in a state of grace, will ever stand before the judgement of God. Only the righteousness of Christ, apprehended by faith, will."[24] (For additional information see Lesson E)

The powerful and compelling testimony of God's Word is that we are saved by grace through faith. God's grace (His unmerited favor) forgives us of all of our sins when we put our faith (trust) in His Son Jesus Christ who died for us on the cross. "Justification is by faith alone so that it can be by grace alone."[25] It is only by putting our entire faith on the completed work of Christ on the cross without any claim to human merit that we can receive salvation as his free gift to us. "Faith abandons all efforts at work or merit and realizes our complete dependence upon God, not just for the provision of a way of salvation, but for the entire action of salvation."[26] Ibid., 150. Of the seven sacraments, the first three (Baptism, Eucharist and Confirmation) are considered sacraments of initiation. The next two (Penance and Anointing of the Sick) are considered sacraments of healing. The last two (Holy Orders and Matrimony) are considered sacraments of service. See McCarthy, op. Cit., 98.

> "Any who did accept him he empowered to become children of God. These are they who believe in his name" (John 1:12)

Is Salvation Received Through The Sacraments Or As A Personal Experience With Christ?

The Catholic Church Teaches That Salvation Is Received Through The Sacraments

The Roman Catholic Church teaches that the Sacraments are necessary for salvation.[27] The seven sacraments are viewed as the "primary means by which God bestows sanctifying and actual grace upon the faithful."[28] McCarthy, op. Cit., 55-57. McCarthy explains that "sanctifying grace" is a gift of the Holy Spirit initially given to individuals through the sacrament of baptism. Actual grace is a supernatural assistance to do good and avoid evil.

GRACE

BAPTISM EUCHARIST CONFIRMATION PENANCE ANOINTING

---//-----//-------//-----//-----//-----

INDIVIDUAL

Catholics define a sacrament as: "a sign instituted by Christ to give grace."[29] Each sacrament is not viewed by the Church as a mere symbolic expression of grace, but as a channel of God's grace. It is through the sacraments that God confers grace. John O'Brien affirms:

> [Christ] likewise established the sacraments which serve
> as so many channels through which the grace and blessings
> of Redemption reach the soul of each individual recipient...
> Christ by his suffering and death gained a vast reservoir. It

37

> is necessary that some means be devised to tap the reservoir
> and carry its riches to our souls. The sacraments are the
> means: channels of divine grace to the souls of men.[30]

One catechism uses a drawing similar to the following one illustrate the sacraments through which grace flows to the individual.

Baptism

According to Catholic theology, "Baptism is the Sacrament of rebirth through which Jesus gives us the divine life of sanctifying grace and joins us to his mystical body."[31] Baptism removes original sin, justifies the person, and makes the person a member of the Roman Catholic Church. Baptism infuses sanctifying grace to the recipient. Baptism is considered absolutely necessary for salvation. The Council of Trent decreed: "If anyone says that baptism is optional, that it is not necessary for salvation, let him be anathema."[32] (See Lesson I for more information).

Eucharist

> "The Holy Eucharist is the Sacrament and the sacrifice
> in which Jesus Christ, under the appearances of bread and
> wine is contained, offered and received."[33] Killgallon, *Life
> in Christ,* p. 175.

Catholic theology teaches that in the celebration of the Eucharist the bread actually becomes the body of Christ and the wine becomes his blood. The Eucharist is considered the central act of Catholicism.[34] Catholics are encouraged to participate in the Eucharist frequently.

Confirmation

The Catholic Church teaches that "Confirmation is the Sacrament through which Jesus confers on us the Holy Spirit, making us full-fledged and responsible members of the Mystical Body. We also receive the graces of the Holy Spirit, especially those that enable us to profess, explain and spread the faith."[35] "The bishop usually administers confirmation."[36] Catholics are usually confirmed at the age of twelve after receiving the prescribed instruction on the doctrines of the Church.

Penance

Catholic theology affirms that "Penance is the sacrament by which Jesus through the absolution of the priest, forgives sins committed after Baptism."[37] Generally, Penance is first received at the age of eight, prior to the First Communion. Subsequently, Catholics are expected to confess their sins to a priest, who in turn proposes a penance and declares absolution.

Anointing the Sick

This sacrament was previously known as Extreme Unction. "The Sacrament of the Sick is the sacrament in which Jesus, through the anointing and prayers of the priest, gives health and strength to the person who is now seriously ill."[38] At times this sacrament is performed to ask for physical healing. When persons are at the point of death, however, this sacrament is given along with Penance and the Eucharist. These are then called the last rites.

Holy Orders

This is the sacrament of Ordination.[39] Through this sacrament, men are incorporated into the episcopate as bishops, the presbyterate as priests, or the diaconate as deacons.[40]

Matrimony

This is the marriage ceremony of the Catholic church. This sacrament "gives the graces needed to live a Christian married life."[41]

The Catholic Church teaches that of the seven sacraments, *five* are essential for salvation (Baptism, Confirmation, the Holy Eucharist, Penance, and Extreme Unction). Even after participating in all these sacraments, however, a person does not have the assurance of salvation, because if he has committed a sin after having gone to confession, he will have to go to purgatory and reside there until he is purged of his sins. What does the Bible teach about the manner in which salvation is received? (See Lesson C for more information on the sacraments).

The Bible Teaches That Salvation Is The Result of a Personal Experience With Christ.

"In support of his testimony, he used many other arguments and kept urging: 'Save yourselves from this generation which has gone astray.' Those who accepted his message were baptized; some three thousand were added that day. They devoted themselves to the apostles' teachings, to the breaking of bread and the prayers" (Acts 2:40-42).

"This is the message he sent to the sons of Israel, the good news of peace proclaimed through Jesus Christ who is Lord of all... To him all the prophets testify, saying that everyone who believes in him has forgiveness of sins through his name....Peter had not finished these words when the Holy Spirit descended upon all who were listening... Peter asked the question a that point, 'What can stop these people who have received the Holy Spirit, even as we have, from being baptized with water?' So he gave orders that they be baptized in the name of Jesus Christ" (Acts 10:36,43, 46-48).

"One who listened was a woman named Lydia, a dealer in purple goods from the town of Thyatira. She already reverenced God, and the Lord opened her heart to accept what Paul was saying. After she and her household had been baptized, she extended an invitation: 'If you are convinced that I believe in the Lord, come and stay at my house. She managed to prevail on us" (Acts 16:14,15).

"The jailer called for light, then rushed in and fell trembling at the feet of Paul and Silas. After a brief interval, he led them out and said 'Men, what must I do to be saved?' Their answer was, 'Believe on the Lord Jesus Christ and you will be saved, and all your household. They proceeded to announce the word of God to him and to everyone in his house. And at that late hour of the night he took them in and bathed their wounds; then he and his whole house were baptized" (Acts 16:29-33).

In these representative verses of Scripture, we see a pattern. First, the people placed their faith in Jesus and then they were baptized. Acts 2 says that those who "accepted the message" were baptized. In the case of Cornelius, it is evident that when he and his household accepted Jesus as their savior the Holy Spirit came upon them. This convinced Peter that they had received forgiveness of sins through the name of Jesus. It was on the basis of this that he baptized them. Acts 16 clearly states that Lydia allowed the Lord to open her heart to accept the gospel as Paul shared it and then she was baptized. The clear indication of Acts 16 is that the Philippian jailer and his family followed Paul's advice and they "believed on the Lord Jesus Christ" and then they were baptized. It is clear that the people mentioned in these passages of Scripture were not saved through the rite of baptism. They were saved because they placed their faith on the Lord Jesus and then they were baptized. Likewise, Cornelius and his family did not receive the sacrament of Confirmation in order to be saved. They believed in Jesus as their savior, received the Holy Spirit, and then they were baptized. Later we will discuss in more detail the concept of the sacraments as taught by the Catholic Church. It is sufficient to point out here that the Bible does not teach that saving grace comes through ceremonial acts (such as the sacraments) but as a result of a personal faith in Jesus Christ. (For a fuller discussion on the sacraments, see Lesson C)

Is Salvation Mediated Through The Roman Catholic Church orThrough Christ Himself?

Catholic Theology Teaches That Salvation Is Mediated Through The Church.

Catholic theologians teach that salvation is obtained through the mediation of the church. Their position is that salvation cannot be attained outside of the Catholic Church.

Based on the experience of Cornelius in the Book of Acts, who was "a devout man and one that feared God," even before being baptized, Catholic theologians assert that people who do not have a Catholic inheritance without it being their fault can attain salvation. This benefit, however, is not reserved for those who do not accept the mediation of the Catholic Church. The Contemporary Catechism explains:

> The Catholic Church teaches that God wants the salvation of all people who are saved in and by means of Christ; to belong to the Church founded by Christ, known

and understood as the community of salvation, is necessary for salvation; those who have this knowledge and understanding and deliberately reject this church cannot be saved.[45]

Catholic theology teaches that salvation is mediated through the sacraments of the church. By virtue of the fact that the sacraments are offered through the Church, it is the channel of salvation for the people. The Church considers itself a "sort of general sacrament" and is viewed as a "sign and instrument of grace which unites men supernaturally to God and to one another."[46]

John O'Brien states:

> The administration of the sacraments was entrusted to the Church to which Jesus gave complete jurisdiction over the deposit of divine truth and over the means of sanctification... The sacraments of the holy Sacrifice of the Mass are the chief channels through which the fruits of redemption, the blessings and graces of God, are applied to individuals.[47]

The Catholic Church does not teach that salvation is obtained in a direct and personal way, but through the mediation of the Church.

The Bible Teaches That There is Only One Mediator

Christ Is Our Only Mediator

> "And the truth is this: God is one. One is also the Mediator between God and men, the man Christ Jesus, who gave himself a ransom for all" (1 Tim. 2:5-6).

> "Jesus told him: I am the way, and the truth, and the life; no one comes to the Father but through me" (John 14:6).

> "I am the gate. Whoever enters through me will be safe. He will go in and out, and find pasture. The thief comes only to steal and slaughter and destroy, I came that they might have life and have it to the full" (John 10:9-10)

"There is no salvation in anyone else, for there is no other name in the whole world given to men by which we are to be saved" (Acts 4:12).

Christ Is Our Only Priest

"My little ones, I am writing this to keep you from sin. But if anyone should sin, we have in the presence of the Father, Jesus Christ, an intercessor who is just. He is an offering for our sins, and not for our sins only, but for the whole world" (1 John 2:1-2).

"But if we acknowledge our sins, he who is just can be trusted to forgive our sins and cleanse us from every wrong" (1 John 1:9),

"Therefore, he is able to save those who approach God through him, since he forever lives to make intercession for them" (Hebrews 7:25).

"Therefore, since we have a great high priest who has gone through the heavens, Jesus, the Son of God, let us hold fast to the faith we profess. For we do not have a high priest who is unable to sympathize with our weaknesses, but we have one who was tempted in every way, just as we are, yet was without sin. Let us then approach the throne of grace with great confidence so that we may receive mercy and favor and to find grace to help us in our time of need" (Heb. 4:14-16).

These verses make it abundantly clear that Christ is the all sufficient mediator and priest, therefore we should go directly to him for our salvation and our sanctification. At times Roman Catholics present the argument that Jesus is the judge and that Mary is the merciful mediator. Others state that it is easier to go to a priest because he is more likely to understand their situation. While these statements may reflect impeccable human logic, they are absolutely wrong because they are unbiblical. Notice that Hebrews 4 states categorically that Christ is the all sufficient mediator and priest. No one can understand us better and be more merciful than Christ because no one else has died for our sins and no one else is at the right hand of the Father interceding for us. We should, therefore, not spend time looking for other mediators but approach Christ with great confidence, for we have the assurance that if we sincerely confess our sins to him, he will gladly forgive us.

Can People Have The Assurance of their Salvation?

The Catholic Church Teaches That People Cannot Be Sure of Their Salvation

The Catholic Church defines salvation as "the freedom from sin, reconciliation with God by means of Christ and the union with God in heaven forever."[48]

Although we agree with that excellent definition, the truth is that the Catholic Church does not teach the assurance that the believer has of being with God in heaven forever. In spite of the fact that a person has received all of the sacraments, the person does not have the assurance of salvation from the judgement to come because the Catholic Church teaches that salvation is not an event but a process. This process involves frequent reception of the sacraments and cooperation with sanctifying grace, which is received at baptism. This sanctifying grace, however, can be lost through committing serious and deliberate sins. This makes it necessary for a person to continue to replenish grace (called actual grace which is temporary) through the sacraments (especially Penance). It is not, therefore, until he dies and is purified by the fire of purgatory, that a Catholic can be sure of entering heaven. The Contemporary Catholic Catechism says:

> "Good men who die in grace might have to be purified of all sin and imperfection before they gain the eternal joy of heaven. No one of us, no matter how attached to Christ and the Christian life, would feel ready to enter heaven as he is. The manner of purgation, the time, the place or the length is shrouded in mystery. God simply has not made these revelations to us."[49]

The Catechism uses primarily two verses of Scripture to support the existence of purgatory. The first of them is Revelation 21:27, which says: "No unclean thing shall enter it." The explanation is that if a person commits a sin after having confessed and dies, such a person is not ready to go to heaven directly and therefore has to go to purgatory to purge away his sins. The other passage is from 2 Maccabees 12:43-46, in which Judas Macabaeus orders an offering to be taken so that there may be offered in Jerusalem a ". . .sacrifice to be offered for the sin of the dead." These were Jewish soldiers who had died on the battlefield trying to liberate Israel. It is important for us to understand that this was in a Jewish context, not a Christian one. The New Testament does not teach that doctrine. The Catechism admits that "reason more than the Scriptures leads the Church to believe in purgatory of the dead." Nevertheless, the church teaches the concept of purgatory, which contributes to the insecurity that many Catholics have with regard to their salvation. Many think that they will have to go to purgatory before going to heaven. This is seen clearly in the commentary of Catholic writer, Nevins:

> "If one studies the lives of the canonized saints, one realizes that, despite a life of heroic holiness, none of them claimed to be saved, but continued working toward salvation until the moment of death, which came with the hope in the mercy and justice of God." [50]

How can the Catholic Church affirm that saving grace is received at the moment of baptism, yet teach that in this life a person cannot be sure that he or she will go to heaven?

In *The Gospel According to Rome,* McCarthy explains:

> Though Catholics can obtain justification in an instant through baptism, they can lose it just as quickly through mortal sin. In the same day, a Catholic can wake up justified, lose the grace of justification through mortal sin, and be justified again through the sacrament of penance. For some Catholics, the cycle is repeated hundreds of times during a lifetime, yet only the state of the soul at the moment of death ultimately matters. [51]

The Catholic Church teaches that a person's sins may be forgiven, yet, he will have to face the temporal punishment for his sins. Hardon explains:

> One of the distinctive features of Catholic Christianity is the notion of temporal punishment due to sin. Behind the notion is the belief that a person's guilt before God may be remitted without necessarily the debt of the penalty for having broken a divine law. Venial sins carry with them only temporal punishment, either in this life or in purgatory; mortal sins carry the penalty of eternal punishment, which is always remitted with the remission of guilt, but unexpiated temporal punishment may be due. It is made to God through the merits of Christ "by the penances sent from God and

patiently endured, or those imposed by the priest, or by the penances voluntarily undertaken, such as fasts, prayers, almsgiving, or other works of piety." [52]

Due to the teachings of the Catholic Church regarding the sacraments, the distinction it makes between *venial* and *mortal* sin, and the notion that sin may be forgiven, yet temporal punishment is due, a person must continually work toward his salvation. If a person is baptized and then commits sins, he needs to go to confession to have these sins forgiven. If a person after going to confession commits a venial sin and dies, he will have to go to purgatory before going to heaven. However, if a person commits a mortal sin and dies without confession, that person will go to hell. That uncertainty keeps a person guessing and hoping that he will do enough good deeds to merit saving grace and that he will not have any unconfessed sins at the time of death otherwise, he will either go to hell or to purgatory before making it into heaven.

The sad thing is that people do not have the assurance of their salvation even after having observed the practices of the church with great devotion, and this has implications for the present life as well as the one to come. Lacking in their lives is the joy of their salvation and the living hope of eternal life.

The Bible Teaches That We Can Be Sure of Our Salvation

"I solemnly assure you, the man who hears my word and has faith in him who sent me possesses eternal life. He does not come under condemnation, but has passed from death to life" (John 5:24).

"I have written this to you to make you realize that you possess eternal life—you who believe in the name of the Son of God" (1 John 5:13).

"I give to them eternal life, and they shall never perish. No one shall snatch them out of my hand" (John 10:28)

"In him you too were chosen; when you heard the glad tidings of salvation, the word of truth, and believed in it, you were sealed with the Holy Spirit who had been promised. He is the pledge of our inheritance, the first payment against the full redemption of a people God has made his own, to praise his glory" (Ephesians 1:13,14).

"But if we walk in the light, as he is in the light, we have fellowship with one another, and the blood of his Son Jesus cleanses us from all sin" (1 John 1:7).

"This Son is the reflection of the Father's glory, the exact representation of the Father's glory, and he sustains all things by his powerful word. When he had cleansed us from our sins, he took his seat at the right hand of the Majesty in heaven" (Hebrews 1:3).

"When you were dead in your sins and your flesh was uncircumcised, God gave you new life in company with Christ, He pardoned all our sins. He canceled the bond that stood against us with all its claims, snatching it up and nailing it to the cross" (Colossians 2:13,14).

We see in these and other verses (Acts 10:43; Ephesians 1:7; 1 Peter 3:18; 1 John 5:11-13) the assurance which Jesus gives that if we accept Him as Savior and Lord, salvation is our present possession. The first two verses use the verb "possess" in the present tense. The Bible does not say that those who put their trust in the Lord will possess or hopefully might possess eternal life in the future. In the third and fourth verses we are assured of Christ's commitment to our salvation. We have Christ's assurance that we will not be snatched out of his hand. We also have the Holy Spirit, who has sealed us. He is the pledge (our engagement ring) of our salvation. In 1 John 1:7, we have the assurance that as we walk in fellowship with Jesus his blood continues to cleanse us of all sin. This truth is also affirmed in Hebrews 1:3, which clearly states that Jesus "provided purification for sins." In Colossians 2:13,14, we have the assurance that the debt of our sins, as well as their punishments, were canceled out by the sacrifice of Christ on the Cross. That is why he was able to say to the penitent on the cross: "I assure you, this day you will be with me in paradise" (Luke 23:43). This makes purgatory totally unnecessary.

Donald Whitney explains:

"Assurance of salvation is a God-given awareness that He has accepted the death of Christ on your behalf and forgiven you of your sins. It involves confidence that God loves you, that He has chosen you, and that you will go to heaven. Assurance includes a sense of freedom from guilt of sin, relief from fear of judgment, and joy in your relationship with God your Father."[53]

Some Catholics have the impression that Evangelicals "have an over-simplistic certainty of salvation, achieved instantly upon acceptance of Christ as Savior."[54] They cite Matt. 7:21 ("Not every one that says to me Lord, Lord shall enter the kingdom of heaven.") to support their argument. Some believe that we commit the sin of presumption when we state that we are sure of our salvation.

In explaining our assurance of salvation, we need to make sure that we stress that this certainty is based on the promises of Christ (e.g., John 5:24) and not on our own merit. Further, we need to stress that salvation is not just a matter of making a public profession of faith. It must result in ongoing discipleship which follows the teachings of Christ (Romans 8:1). In other words, genuine salvation expresses itself in genuine discipleship. The good works that a person does will be the result of this salvation and not the means to attain it (Romans 11:6).

Conclusion

The Catholic Church teaches that salvation is mediated, sacramental, and uncertain. In contrast, Evangelicals base their concept of salvation on the Scripture verses just reviewed as well as numerous others. These verses teach that we can be certain of our salvation, that our salvation is personal (we can go directly to Christ, our Mediator), and that salvation is by grace through faith in Christ and not through sacraments. Professor Borrás makes this point when he says:

> We have to explain that salvation is something personal and that we belong to the church of Christ because we are believers, not the other way around. It is not the church that begets members through the Baptismal Sacrament but the Lord who adds to the church, one by one, those who have been saved through the Holy Spirit.[55]

In the next chapter, we will share some approaches that can be utilized to explain God's plan of salvation to our Catholic friends who have not received Christ as their personal savior. It is important, however, to point out at the outset that leading people to a personal faith in Christ involves more than simply sharing "the facts of the gospel." Salvation is not just mental assent to a set of beliefs. It comes about as the result of a personal and spiritual experience with the living Christ. This means first of, all that we need to pray that the Holy Spirit will work in the hearts of our friends, as well as, in ours as we seek to share the biblical teaching regarding salvation. It also means that we need to share a testimony of our own experience of salvation and how this has changed our lives. For nominal Christians who consider themselves Catholics, the idea of salvation does not include an abiding relationship with the living Christ, but the observance of a set of rules and a vague notion that more good deeds than bad ones will somehow get them toheaven. Even some Catholics who attend church regularly and receive the sacraments do not have a personal relationship with Christ, the confidence that their sins have been forgiven, and the assurance of going to heaven when they die. For them salvation is a long and uncertain process. This is why the biblical gospel is the good news of salvation in Jesus Christ. This should motivate born again Christians to share the gospel with those who have not heard it or do not understand it.

ENDNOTES

1   The authors have been personally acquainted with each of the persons described in the vignettes that are presented at the beginning of each chapter. In order to safeguard their privacy, the names in these case studies have been changed.

2   A similar case can be seen in Acts and speaking in tongues. Acts 2:1-13 gives the full interpretive key for reading later and less detailed accounts of the same phenomena (e.g., 8:14-17; 9:17-18; 10:44-48; et al).

3   Note that John gives two accounts of Jesus' cleansing the temple, the first being at the beginning of His ministry (2:14-18).

4   Many Bible students believe verses 16-21 are not Jesus' words but rather John's interpretation of the Lord's message to Nicodemus. Regardless of who the speaker is their message offers an important elaboration. Marcus Dods, *The Gospel of St. John, TEGT*(Grand Rapids: Wm. B. Eerdamsn, 1961), 716-717.

5   Gail R. O'Day, *The Gospel of John, NIB* (Nashville: Abingdon, 1995), 552.

6   Jesus sometimes employed a severe attitude to those who sought Him out, but he did it with a view to bringing out the quality and sincerity of their search (e.g., Mark 5:25-34; Matt 15:21-28; John 2:1-5).

7   The four levels of communication in the following outline are taken from G. Campbell Morgan, *The Great Physician,* (London: Marshall, Morgan, & Scott, 1963), 74-79.

8   The synoptic gospels all record Jesus' question about the masses' assessment of His person as well as that of His disciples   (Matt 16:13-16; Mark 8:27-29; Luke 9:18-20). From the response of the disciples to Jesus as the Christ it is evident that recognizing His prophetic office was insufficient.

9   Most sermons, speeches, and dialogues are stylized and shaped by the theological considerations of the inspired writer..The accounts, while shortened summaries, are not fictitious.

10   The distinction between a metaphor and simile lies in the use or absence of a connective such as "like, as, seems," etc. While similes make explicit connections they are implied in metaphors. See Robert H. Stein, *The Method and Message of Jesus' Teachings,* (Philadelphia: Westminster, 1978), 14, 15.

11   Ibid., 1. Stein notes "Teacher" was used 45 times of Jesus in the four gospels.

12   Examples include Paul's impassioned plea to the Galatians (Galatians 4:12-20), his demonstration of affection to the Thessalonians (1 Thessalonians 3:5-10).

13   Matthias Premm, *Dogmatic Theology for the Laity* (Rockford, IL: Tan Books, 1967), 262.

14   Council of Trent, session 6, "Decree on Justification," chapter 16.

15   Council of Trent, session 6, "Decree on Justification," canon 32.

16   James G. McCarthy, *The Gospel According to Rome,* (Eugene: Harvest House Publishers, 1995), 101, 102.

17   McCarthy, op. Cit. McCarthy cites Thomas Acquinas, *Summa Theologica*, Pts. 1-11, q. 114. Art. 3.

18   McCarthy further explains that there are three forms of merited reward: an increase of grace, eternal life, and an increased glory in heaven, Op. Cit., 98-100.

19   James R. White, *The Roman Catholic Controversy* (Minneapolis: Bethany House Publishers, 1996), 131.

20   *The New American Bible, Saint Joseph Edition,* (New York: Catholic Book Publishing Co., 1970)

21 We have inserted the phrase "washing of regeneration" because in the Greek the word "loutpou" (which means washing) has been used in place of the word "baptismatos" (which means baptism).

22 In place of the phrase "in hope of eternal life" we have utilized the phrase "according to the hope of eternal life" because the Greek uses the word "kata" (which means according to).

23 Here we have used a translation from the Greek to point out the relationship between faith and grace more clearly. *Novum Testamentum Graece* , (New York: American Bible Society, 1957), 899.

24 James R. White, *The Roman Catholic Controversy*(Minneapolis: Bethany House Publishers, 1996), 150-151.

25 Ibid., 151.

26 Ibid

27 Michael A. McGuire, *Baltimore Catechism No. 1*, (New York: Benzinger Brothers, 1942), p. 36.

28 McCarthy, op. Cit., 55-57. McCarthy explains that "sanctifying grace" is a gift of the Holy Spirit initially given to individuals through the sacrament of baptism. Actual grace is a supernatural assistance to do good and avoid evil.

29 Killgallon, *Life in Christ*, p. 155.

30 John O'Brien, *The faith of Millions* (Huntington, IN: Our Sunday Visitor, Inc., 1974), 142.

31 Killgallon, *Life in Christ,* p. 160. See also Baltimore Catechism No. 1, pp. 87-88.

32 Council of Trent, Cannon 5 of the Decree Concerning the Sacraments.

33 Killgallon, *Life in Christ,* p. 175.

34 McCarthy, op. Cit., 333.

35 Killgallon, *Life in Christ,* p. 167.

36 McGuire, *Baltimore Catechism,* p. 90.

37 Killgallon, *Life in Christ,* p. 187.

38 Killgallon, *Life in Christ,* p. 198.

39 William J. Cogan, *Catechism for Adults,* (Youngston, Arizona: Cogan Productions, 1975), p. 59.

40 McCarthy, op. Cit., 335.

41 Ibid.

42 *Saint Irenaeus, Adversus Haereses,* II, 24, 1.

43 Origen *Homili in Jesu Nave,* 3, 5.

44 John A. Hardon, S.J., *The Catholic Catechism* (New York: Image Books, 1981), 234.

45 *Contemporary Catholic Catechism,* 251; 15. Foy a. Felician, *Catholic Almanac Catechism,* No. 1 (New York: Benzinger Brothers, 1942), 36. A. McGuire, *Baltimore Catechism,* (Huntingyon: Our Sunday Visitor, 1977), 380.

46 Walter M. Abbott, *The Documents of Vatican II* (New York: America Press, 1966), 15.

47 John O'Brien, *The Faith of Millions* (Huntington: Our Sunday Visitor, Inc. 1974), 142.

48 Roy A. Felician, *Catholic Almanac* (Huntington: Our Sunday Visitor, 1992), 326.

49 Williams, *Contemporary Catholic Catechism,* p. 251.

50 Albert J. Nevins, M.M., *Answering a Fundamentalist* (Huntington: Our Sunday Visitor, 1990), 67.

51 McCarthy, op. Cit., 104.

52 Hardon, *The Catholic Catechism,* 490.

53 Donald S. Whitney, *How Can I Be Sure I'm A Christian?* (Colorado Springs: NavPress Publishing Group, 1994), 12.

[54] Albert J. Nevins, *Answering A Fundamentalist* (Huntington: Our Sunday Visitor, 1990), p. 13.
[55] José Borrás, "Catholicism Today and Our Mission Task," *Baptist Witness in Catholic Europe,* (Rome: Baptist Publishing House, 1973), p. 109.

CHAPTER TWO

LEARNING HOW TO SHARE THE MESSAGE OF SALVATION

Introduction: Joe's Discovery

During the 1980 Winter Olympics in Lake Placid, New York, some students came from several Evangelical seminaries to assist us with the awesome task of sharing the good news of salvation with people who came from all over the world. In order to prepare for this historical event, we set up a coffee house where we could invite people in for dialogue as we enjoyed refreshments. We also trained may volunteers in addition to our seminary students. Among the seminary students who came was Joe O'Brien. When I first met him I commented that it was great to have someone with an Irish background with us because there are not many Irish people in our Evangelical churches. He laughed and said, "I used to be a Catholic. In fact, I was studying for the priesthood when I had a life-changing experience with Christ." When he said that, I invited him out of the cold and the falling snow into our coffee house. I was very interested in learning what his experience had been.

Once inside the coffee house, while we were drinking hot chocolate, I asked Joe about his religious pilgrimage. He told me that he grew up in a typical Irish Roman Catholic home in the northeastern part of the country. He went to parochial school, served as an altar boy, and upon graduating from college enrolled in a Roman Catholic seminary. One day when he was sitting on a park bench an "old man" came by, sat next to him, and started a conversation. He asked Joe: "Do you mind if I share with you the most interesting experience of my life." Joe thought, "If I let him do this maybe he will be happy and he will leave me alone." So Joe told him that this would be alright. The man started out by telling him that he used to be very religious, that he followed the teachings of the church as much as he could hoping that his good deeds would outweigh his bad ones and somehow he would someday make it to heaven. He added that despite all of this, he did not really feel close to God, there was a void in his life and a gnawing fear that in the end he might not be good enough to go to heaven. He added that he shared this with a fellow worker who, in turn, gave him a New Testament and asked him to read it. As he started to read he began to find portions that spoke directly to his needs and pointed to the possibility of knowing Jesus directly in a spiritual way. After much reading in the Gospels, he came to the point when he prayed to Jesus, asked him to forgive him of his sins, and invited him to guide his life. "This," the 'old man' said, "resulted in a complete change of my life." He added: "Now I know that Jesus has forgiven me of my sins, that he is with me in every experience of life, and that I will be ready to meet him in heaven when I die, not because of any good thing I might have done, but because he died on the cross to make my salvation possible."

The "old man" then asked Joe: "Is it OK if I show you in this Bible (New Testament) how you can have an experience like this with Christ? Joe again thought: "Maybe if I let him do this, he will let me be." When Joe gave him permission, the "old man" proceeded to use a marked New Testament in which he had written questions and underlined the verses that could be used to answer such questions as: "Why did Jesus Come,? Why don't we have this abundant life,? and How is this life made possible?" As he did this, he helped Joe go through verses that explain how a person can receive the gift of salvation. He then asked Joe: "Would you accept this portion of the Bible as a gift from me?" Joe, once again thought that for sure this man would leave, so he agreed to receive it. The man thanked Joe for receiving his gift and said to him: "Would it be OK with you if I pray for you before I leave?" Since it was the man's final request, Joe agreed to let him pray. The man started by praying the Lord's Prayer, which Joe could follow easily. However, the man then prayed for Joe specifically mentioning his name and asking God to bless him and to lead him in his desire to know Him better. When the man finished the prayer, Joe turned his back on him so that he could not see Joe's tears. Joe told me: "It broke me up. Never in my life had anyone prayed for me by name and asked God to bless me."

Joe then took the New Testament and left. In his room, he read the questions again and reviewed the answers. Each time, however, he would put the New Testament down and say: "This is interesting, but it is not what the Church teaches about how a person is made right with God. We receive salving grace through the sacraments." Throughout the succeeding days, Joe would read the verses and would struggle with their meaning. One day, he was so overcome by the message of these verses that he knelt by his bed and prayed: "Oh God, if what I am reading is true, then I repent of my sins and I want to ask Jesus to come into my life." Joe then began to experience the presence of Christ as he had never experienced it before. He felt at peace with God and a sense of assurance about his future. There were, however, many teachings of the Catholic Church that were different from what he was reading in the Bible. What made it difficult was that there were many leaders in the Catholic Church whom he appreciated and admired because of their sincerity and dedication. When he would ask them questions, however, they would point to the teachings of the Catholic Church and would not deal with the Scriptural portions that related to these doctrines. After months of Bible reading, soul searching, and dialogue, Joe decided that he could no longer continue studying for the priesthood. He felt the strong conviction that the Word of God had to be the final authority in all doctrinal matters.

BIBLE STUDY

Lessons From Nicodemus:
A "Pilgrim's Progress" Story

Introduction

As our first Bible study showed, Nicodemus' encounter with Jesus (John 3: 1-21) provides a valuable lesson in understanding the nature of salvation. Canonically, that is within the gospel of John itself, John successfully places Jesus against the best and most noble representative of Israel's religious tradition and is able to show the spiritual bankruptcy of his traditions. In this story we also see the diversity and progression of communication that took place. Far from a perfunctory or condescending "dumping" of information, both Nicodemus and Jesus treated each other with respect and dignity. Nicodemus took "the road less traveled" and in contrast to his religious comrades, showed sincere deference to Jesus. For His part, Jesus answered Nicodemus' questions honestly. The exchange was intellectually challenging and affective. It lead to a heart to heart talk.

Unlike many characters which only appear once in the gospel, Nicodemus appears at three pivotal points (Chaps. 3, 7, 19). John's decision to bring Nicodemus to the narrative in such a sequential fashion is a stroke of inspiration. By doing this, he portrays him as a flesh and blood individual. The screen they are cast upon is somewhat flat; the issues become immediately present, as does the resolution for good or bad. While there is evidence that many go through a time of personal struggle, as we shall see, their issues, like in a 30 minute TV program, are quickly resolved. Nicodemus, however, by "resurfacing" is seen as one who lives in a more dynamic context. John has in effect given us an opportunity to see Nicodemus holistically by casting him with the backdrop of his personal struggle (Chap. 3), the struggle of balancing a growing commitment to Jesus and societal pressures (Chap. 7), and finally allowing us to see his commitment in action by coming to grips with the crucified Jesus (Chap 19). Nicodemus is the extrapolation of what we only see in germinal form in the lives of many of the people mentioned in the gospel of John.[1] Thus, there are implications in the life of Nicodemus as it unfolds in the gospel for existential decisions, societal challenges, and decisions with costly ramifications. Along the way, Jesus had declared, "And I, if I be lifted up from the earth, will draw all men to Myself" (John 12:32).

It is important to note that Jesus had foretold His crucifixion to Nicodemus (3:14) and in the end, this religious leader is there at the foot of the cross (19:39-40). The apostle John has chosen Nicodemus as a test case, to show us how this pilgrimage towards the Savior often happens in life. This lesson allows us to view Nicodemus' progress towards his open identification with Jesus as a process that underwent five phases.[2]

Nicodemus Began at the Point of *Discovery*

It goes without saying that if Jesus had never visited Jerusalem, Nicodemus' impressions about Him might have been shaped by second hand information or misinformation, gossip, innuendo, superstition, so on and so forth. This religious leader of Israel, however, had an opportunity to see Jesus at work from a distance (John 2:23) and also to speak with him personally (3:1-21). He had an ideal vantage point to evaluate the man's integrity. Did His teaching match the quality of His actions? Knowingly or not, Nicodemus' awareness of the Galilean took him on a road to discovery. Along this road, he discovered several truths with which he would have to wrestle and come to some decision. By seeing him at work performing miracles Nicodemus discovered that Jesus came from God. He was convinced that no one could perform miraculous signs if God were not with him (v. 2). By hearing Him speak Nicodemus discovered that to see and enter the kingdom of God (v. 3, 5), a person needed to be born again, that is, to be born spiritually.

At this early point in his life, Nicodemus discovered information that could not easily be discounted. Since he had already concluded that Jesus was endowed with favor from above, His words and teachings had to be taken seriously.

Application: The gospel is heavy with content. Too often, gospel presentations are shallow stories that do not really convey the essence of saving truth. It behooves us to understand the nature of the *Kerygma* in the preaching of Paul and Peter as occurs in many of the New Testament letters. While I am not suggesting that every gospel presentation should be a full course in Theology 101, I do insist that a Biblical presentation of the gospel should include a basic number of facts with which as people discover them, the Spirit can work in the life of the person to bring about saving faith.[3]

Nicodemus Moved on to *Deliberation*

Hearing truth and really understanding its meaning are two very different things. Nicodemus not only took the time to listen, he also wanted to comprehend fully. Knowing that God had sent Jesus, he found it hard to understand what Jesus was saying. Thus, he asked, "How can a man be born when he is old?" (v. 4) and "How can this be?" (v. 9)

It is obvious, from the conversation, that Nicodemus was thinking in physical rather than spiritual terms. Jesus' teaching was very different from what he had been brought up to believe. His religious tradition said that salvation was attained through observing the Law, but Jesus was talking to him about salvation through faith in the Son of God (v. 16). His tradition gave emphasis to personal responsibility in keeping even the minutest detail of the law and the six hundred plus ordinances stipulated in rabbinic tradition. Jesus, however, emphasized the need to trust Him as God's only way to gain salvation. The two approaches could not be more contradictory. Trust in self or trust in Jesus, which way was right? It was not easy for Nicodemus to understand. He had many questions.

Application: Evangelical Christians who sincerely want to reach people with the gospel need to think soberly about the way they present the message. While we should not omit an aspect of God's plan of salvation because it is offensive to people's sensibilities, we can do alot to make the message clear. Keep in mind that the gospel is never given in a vacuum. People will hear your presentation, but the voices from his or her religious tradition echo in their minds as well. In opting for the gospel it often comes down to a struggle between what they have been taught over the years and what they are being presented as God's sure message. While it is easier to see retrospectively, it is rarely easy to "just let go." Remember that spiritual truth, which may seem so "obvious" to us, is utterly foreign to the lost. There is nothing wrong in presenting the same truth in various ways to help drive the point home. It goes without saying that there are no "stupid" questions. We should be ready to answer all questions regardless of their nature. If it takes ten attempts to bring clarity to the discussion, so be it.

Nicodemus Made a Personal *Decision*

The question as to when Nicodemus came to faith in Christ is difficult to answer. Nowhere is his conversion clearly stated. However, the fact of his salvation is clearly implied by his willingness to identify with Jesus at the crucifixion. Nicodemus must have made his decision sometime between his encounter with Jesus on that dark night and the day the Lord died. This aspect of Nicodemus is enigmatic to say the least, but there is a reason. Already, there is an indication of a time lapse that takes place with some of the people

Jesus meets. In two cases (e.g., the lame man at the pool of Bethesda, Chap 5:1-15; the man born blind, Chap 9:1-38) Jesus performs an initial miracle (5:1-9; 9:1-7). The person is left to stand before religious authorities and/or family with less than perfect knowledge (5:10-13; 9:8-34). Then Jesus returns sometime later to finish the job of salvation (5:14-15; 9:35-38). It's as if John wants us to know that any kind of "encounter" with Jesus brings with it the possibility of difficult social and family repercussions. There is evidence that like, Nicodemus, some of the people that came across the challenging message of salvation also had a time of struggle. It is for this purpose that Nicodemus is shown with more detail, and yet annoying uncertainty. Nicodemus functions as a paradigm of the person who takes Jesus' message seriously. It may take time to process it all. Family and friends who don't understand often weigh in. In the end, one's decision for Christ is a very intimate event that happens in the deepest recesses of the heart. From John's point of view, it is not nearly as important to know when Nicodemus fully surrendered to God's grace. It is important to know that eventually his faith in Jesus turned him from a "twilight follower" to one who walked in the full light of the truth.

Application: It goes without saying that the act of regeneration is something that happens in the presence of God. The miracle is not disclosed to us. Only God knows the actual moment of conversion. Nevertheless, it is incumbent upon us to plead earnestly for people to act on their free will and make a commitment to Jesus as their Savior (Matt 11:28; Acts 2:38-40; 2 Cor 5:20; Heb 10:22-24). Salvation is not given automatically, but it is a gift one must accept. It is also important to be discerning. Often, decisions are made in the hearts of people, unknown to the believer working with the person, and perhaps not fully understood by the person either (Rom 8:26; cf., 1 Cor 2:6-13). While God takes note immediately, it may take us some time to come to the realization. Like newborn babies, new converts do not understand the jargon of salvation and may not know how to express what God has done in their lives. Christians should be sensitive to the work of the Spirit in people's lives. We do this, by asking diagnostic questions, by really hearing the person, and by looking for the obvious fruit of the Spirit that accompany salvation.

Nicodemus Experienced *Dissonance* from Society

The fact that Nicodemus made a decision to receive Jesus did not guarantee that things would be easy for him. In John 7, we notice that his peers were enemies of Jesus. In verse 48, they asked, "Has any of the rulers of the Pharisees believed in him?" In verse 51, Nicodemus made a veiled attempt to defend Jesus by asking, "Does our law condemn a man without first hearing him to find out what he is doing?" Notice, however, that he did not challenge their statement that "a prophet does not come out of Galilee" (v. 52) nor did he answer the question, "has any of the Pharisees believed in him?"

Like the lame man at the pool of Bethesda and the man born blind, Nicodemus received a great deal of dissonance from those who surrounded him. What they said contradicted or questioned the things he heard from Christ. Nicodemus desperately wanted to continue to believe, but being a faithful follower is not always easy in a world that rejects the gospel.

Application: Nearly every person who comes to faith in Christ out of a Roman Catholic background experiences first hand the "ache" of dissonance. Like most religions in the world, Roman Catholicism is more than a set of religious beliefs. This religion is steeped in promoting "holy contracts" with social acquaintances and family, that when broken are tantamount to treason. For many family members, conversion to any faith away from the Catholic Church is unforgivable. Ultimately, many new believers succumb to the pressures brought upon them by family, friends, and the parish priest. Evangelical Christians should anticipate that it will be necessary to help new converts during the initial difficult days. This may include working through issues of social responsibilities and how a Christian can remain in fellowship with God and honor social/cultural institutions.[4]

Nicodemus Followed Jesus in *Discipleship*

In John 19:39-40, we notice that Nicodemus, along with Joseph of Arimathea, took the body of Jesus from the cross, prepared it for burial, and tenderly placed it in the tomb. Undoubtedly, as Nicodemus saw the body of Jesus on the cross, the words of the Master echoed in his heart, "even so must the Son of man be lifted up" (John 3:14).

Nicodemus gave every evidence that he had became a disciple. First, he was willing to spend a very large amount of money on the ointment to prepare the body of the Master (v.39). Second, he was willing to touch a dead body (of the Lord), which would cause a Jew to be ceremonially impure. Third, he was willing to do this publicly. This gives evidence that Nicodemus reached a stage where he was willing to profess his faith in Jesus openly. He may have initiated his search under the cover of darkness but faith in Jesus Christ is not something that can be concealed for long (John 8:12; 1 John 1:5-7).

Discipleship is a costly lifestyle. The New Testament has much to say about the nature of the new life "in Christ." While Paul uses the language of "taking off" the old man and "putting on" the new man (Col 3:1-17), Peter speaks of discipleship as a process that begins with spiritual infancy and progresses to maturity (1 Pet 2:1-5). Discipleship is life-long; it never ends this side of eternity (Phil 3:12-17). Discipleship is the daily decision to allow yourself to be conformed to the likeness of Christ in thoughts and in actions (Rom 8:28-29; 12:1-2; Gal 2:20; Phil 3:8-11).

Application: The decision to walk in discipleship is sometimes instantaneous. Often, however, the person struggles with the implications of discipleship for the new lifestyle. Keep in mind that many of the practices and habits of the Roman Catholic are deeply ingrained behaviors that may take time to overcome. There is evidence that believers in Christ continued to perform the activities of their former unregenerate lifestyle (1 Cor 5-6; 8; 1 Thess 4:1-8). While they are encouraged to make progress in their daily behavior, nowhere are these individuals treated as apostates or false brethren. John's first epistle (1 John 1:5-10) can be helpful in working with new believers. The passage acknowledges the presence of sin in the life of the redeemed, but the stress is placed on being continuously transformed through confession to Christ. A believer may sin, but is not overpowered by a sinful lifestyle. The Christian eliminates sinful habits as these become known to him/her through the work of the Holy Spirit. Thus, fellowship with God is maintained. Incidentally, this "cure" is not just for new converts coming out of blatantly sinful lifestyles. The process outlined here is to be followed by all Christians regardless of time in Christian service and pay grade.

Finally, working with new believers who have yet to work through all the detrimental entanglements of their former life may, in the end, prove to be a test of our love and patience as well. We must avoid the extremes of pharisaical legalism, on the one hand, and on the other hand, helping them to rationalize their situation and thus becoming enablers of continued sin.

Conclusion

What do we learn from the experience of Nicodemus? There are people (mainly those who do not grow up in Evangelical homes) who go through similar stages in their pilgrimage toward discipleship. They go through discovery, deliberation, decision, dissonance, and discipleship. This has implications for the way we share the gospel with them. We must be patient and answer their questions (how can this be?). We must also offer them our friendship to help them through the periods of dissonance and continue to share the Word of God with them until they confess openly that they are disciples of the Lord.

Dialogue: This dialogue reveals Nicodemus' pilgrimage.

Nicodemus	Prospect
1. Heard about Jesus, (John 3). Believed him to be a "Rabbi". No one could do these things unless God be with Him. - Jesus shared with him God's salvation plan. - We are not told that he recieved Christ. On that first visit,he had many questions.	Has positive view of Jesus as an "extraordinary teacher." Hears the gospel but due to past traditions needs time to think through these things.
2. Tried to defend Jesus (John 7). No evidence that he identified publicly with Jesus (vv.48,52). He did not answer the question "have you believed?"	He is a "secret" follower of Jesus like Joseph of Arimathea (John 19:38). He fears cultural ostracism.
3. Identified publicly (John 19:36-40) a) Invested in (ointment) b) Helped prepare (body) c) Violated one of the (rules) of touching a dead body	He identifies fully with Jesus and is willing to pay the price.

LEARNING ACTIVITY

Prepare Your Testimony

One of the most powerful tools in witnessing is to share our testimony. People will generally listen when we share the difference Jesus has made in our lives. Share your testimony with humility, brevity, and clarity. Avoid using "church talk" and use language that people can understand.

Paul's Testimony

When the apostle Paul (Acts 26) shared his testimony, he generally used the following outline:

1. What my life was like before knowing Jesus.
2. How I came to know Jesus.
3. How Jesus helps me face life today.
4. How you can know Jesus too.

Nicodemus' Testimony

Another way to share your testimony is to follow the outline from the Bible Study on Nicodemus:

1. **Discovery** - How I discovered that Jesus died to save me.
2. **Deliberation** - Questions which came up as I tried to understand how to invite Jesus into my life.
3. **Decision** - How I decided to invite Jesus into my life
4. **Dissonance** - Doubts I had and pressure I was under after I decided to become a follower of Jesus.
5. **Discipleship** - How the Lord helped me to overcome these doubts and pressures and what my life is like now that I have a personal relationship with Jesus.

Timothy's Testimony

If you have grown up in an Evangelical family, your testimony may be more similar to Timothy's. Paul says to Timothy: "and that from a child you have known the Holy Scriptures, which are able to make you wise unto salvation through faith which is Jesus Christ" (2 Timothy 3:15). It is obvious that Timothy learned the Scriptures as he was growing up and then came to a point when he put his faith in Christ Jesus as his personal savior. That is why he became "wise unto salvation." If your experience was similar to Timothy's your testimony can follow a similar pattern.

1. How I Grew Up Hearing the Scriptures at Home
2. How I made a Personal Decision to Receive Christ.
3. How Jesus Has Spared Me From Many Downfalls
4. What Jesus Means to Me in My Daily Life

Slice of Life Testimony

Some testimonies may not begin with the description of a conversion experience but with a life experience in which the presence of Jesus Christ has made all the difference in the world. These types of testimonies are most effective when the person you are seeking to reach with the love of Christ is going through a similar experience. Some of these experiences are:

1. **Grief** - loss of a loved one, illness, anxiety
2. **Transition** - in personal life, at work, in the family, in the community
3. **Joys** - accomplishments, recognitions, reconciliation
4. **Influences** - persons that have influenced their lives

In these instances the best thing to do is to listen to people as they speak about what is in their hearts, to ask questions, and to empathize with their experience. After doing this, you can share with them about a similar experience that you have had and point out how knowing Christ as your personal savior has brought you through these experiences and made all the difference in your life. You can then share with them how Jesus can bless their lives with his abiding presence.

Practice Your Testimony

Use the outline that best fits your experience. Write a brief paragraph under each major heading telling how you came to know Jesus as your personal Savior. After you have prepared your testimony, take time to share it with someone in your group. When you share your testimony with a friend, speak about the doubts and fears that you had and then share, with enthusiasm, the difference that your personal faith in Christ has made in your life.

Preparing to Present the Gospel

Guidelines

There are some guidelines we must follow if we are to lead our Catholic friends to experience personal salvation in Christ.

1. Do not discuss religion. Your main purpose is to lead the person to Christ.
2. Present the gospel with simplicity and sound logic.
3. Distinguish between the official position of the Catholic Church and what each individual believes.
4. As you study the Bible together, let the prospect discover what the Word of God says. Encourage the person to read the verses, to think about their meaning and let the Word of God speak to them.
5. Concentrate only on issues essential to salvation. Don't discuss the wrong issues.
6. Do not ask: "Are you a Christian? (Catholics consider themselves Christians) or "Are you saved?" Your question should be: "What is your personal relationship to Jesus Christ?"
7. Use a Catholic Bible or a version acceptable to Catholics such as a *Good News Bible.*
8. Emphasize that a gift is not a possession until it is received (Romans 6:23; John 1:12)

Marking a New Testament

1. Instructions

One of the best ways to present the plan of salvation to Catholics is to use a marked New Testament. This helps them read the verses straight from the Word of God. It is also helpful to give the New Testament to the prospect. There have been numerous instances where the prospect has not understood the full meaning of the passages until he or she has read them several times over an extended period of time.

    a. On the first page of your New Testament write the question: "What is your personal relationship to Christ?" Then put: "Turn to page _."

b.   After you turn to page __ where John 10:10 is found:

1.   Highlight the verse with a light yellow marker.
2.   Write on the top of the page the question: "Why did Christ come?"
3.   Write on the bottom of the page "Turn to page __" (Where Romans 3:23 is found).

c.   Repeat steps 1-3 for each verse used in the gospel presentation writing the appropriate questions of the gospel presentation (see next page).

d.   Write on the last page of the New Testament:

MY DECISION TO RECEIVE CHRIST

I admit before God that I am a sinner and that Jesus died for my sins. I now open the door of my life to Christ and accept His gift of salvation.

Name:

Date:

2.   Questions

Begin with the question, "What is your relationship to Christ?" Explain by saying, "We are not going to talk about religion; we just want to find out what the Bible says about our relationship to Christ." Lead from there to the questions found in your marked New Testament.

a.   Why did Christ come? (John 10:10)
b.   Why don't we have this gift? (Romans 3:23)
c.   What is the result of sin? (Romans 6:23a)
d.   What is God's gift? (Romans 6:23b)
e.   How did God make this possible? (Romans 5:8)
f.   Can we earn this gift? (Ephesians 2:8-9)
g.   If we could earn this gift (Galatians. 2:21), would Christ have died? (Galatians 3:1-5)
h.   How does this gift become ours? (John 1:12)
i.   How did the dying thief receive this gift? (Luke 23:39-43)
j.   Can we be sure we have this gift? (John 5:24)
k.   Will you open the door of your life to Christ?[5] (Revelations 3:20)

Give your friends the New Testament as a gift. Suggest that they read these portions of Scripture that are highlighted. Let your friend know that you will be praying for him and that you will be glad to converse with him if he has any questions.

Presenting the Plan of Salvation with a Marked New Testament

If the opportunity presents itself and your friend is receptive to hearing what the Bible says about salvation, you can use the same marked New Testament to present the gospel. There are some guidelines, however, that you will want to follow:

1. You need to let your friend read aloud, first the question, then the Scripture verse, and then answer the question aloud. The Bible says that faith comes by *hearing* the Word of God.[6]

2. If your friend does not answer correctly, ask him/her to read it again. It is very important that people discover for themselves what the Word of God says. For example, if you tell your friends that they are sinners, they may respond in a defensive manner. But if they read, "for all have sinned," they will know that this includes them.[7]

3. Ask your friend to pray the prayer of acceptance with you.

If your friend is not ready yet, do these things:

4. Pray for your friend. Begin with the Lord's Prayer.

5. Then ask God to help your friend learn the things that He wants your friend to know. Pray for any need he/she might have. (Suggestion: Make the prayer as personal as possible. You may want to hold hands with your friend.)

6. Ask your friend to sign his/her name when he or she has made a decision to accept Christ.

The A-B-C Plan

Another very simple way to share the plan of salvation is what J. B. Rowell calls the "ABC plan" [8].

"A" "All have sinned and come short of the glory of God."
(Romans 3:23)

"B" "Behold the Lamb of God which taketh away the sin of the world" (John 1:29).

"C" "Believe on the Lord Jesus Christ and thou shalt be saved" (Acts 16:31)

"D" "Come unto me, all ye that labor and are heavy laden, and I will give you rest" (Matthew 11:28).

Using a Tract

There are times when it is handy to use a well-written, brief tract to explain the plan of salvation to a friend or relative. Such tracts as *How To Have A Full And Meaningful Life* can be used during a witnessing conversation or can be given as a gift for the person to read and discuss with you later. In selecting tracts, however, avoid those that are very confrontational or that basically try to prove that Roman Catholic beliefs are totally wrong. These types of tracts offend and alienate people.

PRACTICAL INSTRUCTION

One of the most basic principles of teaching is to begin with what is known and to go from there to what is unknown. Our Lord Jesus Christ used this principle when telling parables. Jesus took these parables from people's everyday life. When Jesus spoke about the sower, about the lost sheep, about the talents and about the widow and the judge, the hearers were familiar with the situations that he was describing and were in a good position to understand the teaching that he was wanting to share with them.

When it is a matter of sharing the message of salvation with our Catholic friends, it is important that we know what we have in common and the things in which we differ. First, what we have in common can serve as a bridge of communication. If we begin with what we have in common, many Catholics feel more calm when dialoguing with us instead of thinking that we Evangelicals are against everything that they believe. Second, if we understand what we have in common (and the doctrines in which we differ), we Evangelicals will avoid the error of accusing Catholics of believing things that they really do not believe. One of the things that bothers Catholics the most is Evangelicals going to their homes and accusing them of "being idolaters, of not believing in Christ, of believing that they will save themselves by their good works instead of by the grace of Christ, etc." There is a certain sense in which this can be said about some Catholics, but, as we will see later, informed Catholics see these doctrines from another point of view and feel insulted when we Evangelicals accuse them of believing things that they do not believe. Third, if we know our differences, we will avoid the error of thinking that the concept of salvation is the same for both groups. Since The Vatican Council (1962-1965), there have been groups of persons who believe that the changes in the mass (the music, the participation of the laity, etc.) indicate that Catholics do not need to hear the message of salvation. To avoid errors, it is important that we know the similarities and differences between Catholics and Evangelicals. In this section we will focus on our similarities in order to establish bridges of communication.

WHAT WE HAVE IN COMMON

Beliefs We Have in Common

The Apostle's Creed

What has come to be known as "The Apostle's Creed" originated probably in the second century as a basic formula of professed faith before a person was baptized. By the fourth century, a similar formula to the one used today began to be used among the Christian Churches of the West. By the eighth century, the present formula began to appear in books on Christian doctrines. This creed is officially recognized by the Roman Catholic Church.

Let us review and evaluate this creed to see how much we agree with what is found in it.

I believe in God the Father Almighty, Creator of heaven and earth; and in Jesus Christ His only Son, Our Lord; who was conceived by the Holy Spirit, born of the Virgin Mary, suffered under Pontius Pilate, was crucified, died, and buried. He descended into hell; on the third day He rose from among the dead; He ascended to heaven, is seated at the right hand of God the Father Almighty, from where he will come to judge the living and the dead. I believe in the Holy Spirit, the Holy Universal Church, the communion of saints, the forgiveness of sins, the resurrection of the body, and life eternal. Amen.[9]

In order to emphasize what we have in common with the Catholic Church, let us give attention to the principle doctrines that are found in this creed.[10]

The Doctrine of God the Father Almighty

The Catholic catechism teaches that God is the Father of all humanity who has created all human beings, has provided for the needs of his children, and has shared his life with humanity. God reveals himself through the universe that he created and by means of his word. In his revelation, God tells us that he is love, that he knows everything, that he is infinite, that he is righteous, that he is immutable, that he is eternal, that he is all powerful, that he is everywhere , and that he is spirit.[11] He is the Spirit without limit. He is all powerful and knows everything. He does not need anything from anyone outside himself, but all things depend on him. Nevertheless, God is interested in and sustains all things which he created. He invites all people to be his adopted children.[12]

The Doctrine of Jesus Christ, the Unique Son of God

The Catholic catechism teaches that Jesus Christ is the God-man who was born of the Virgin Mary in Bethlehem of Judah and who lived in Nazareth where he began his early ministry. When preaching His Good News, Jesus spoke to people about the infinite love of God toward them, about the mystery of the Trinity, about his own divinity, about the church, about love and how to pray. While dying on the cross, Christ paid the price for the sins of humanity and has made salvation possible for all people. After rising from the grave, Christ taught the apostles that he was not only the promised Messiah, but also the eternal Son of God. After his resurrection, Christ appeared to his disciples for forty days, promised them the coming of the Holy Spirit, gave them the commandment to spread the gospel throughout the world, and then he ascended as high priest into heaven, from where he will return to judge the living and the dead.[13]

The Doctrine of the Holy Spirit

The Catholic catechism affirms that the Holy Spirit is the Spirit of the Father and The Son, the third person of the Trinity. As the "Giver of Life," the Holy Spirit enlivens the church and the lives of the believers. The Holy Spirit confirmed the ministry of Christ in his baptism, in his mission of bringing the kingdom of God, in his transfiguration, in his passion, his death, his resurrection, and his ascension. The Holy Spirit is active in the lives of the believers animating, purifying, and strengthening. He gives spiritual gifts and produces fruits in the hearts of Christians. He gives life, unity, and inspiration to the church.[14]

The Doctrine of the Virgin Birth of Jesus

The doctrine of the virgin birth of Jesus is intimately bound with the doctrine of the divinity and deity of Jesus. The Catholic catechism explains that if Jesus were not really human, he could not save us. "Inasmuch he had to be in everything like his brothers, in order to come to be a merciful and faithful high priest in what refers to God, to purge the sins of the people" (Hebrews 2:7). If Jesus were not God, he could not redeem us, because only a holy and immortal God can: 1)free all the human race from sin and death, and 2) give us our part in the fullness of the godly life. The virgin birth is one of the proofs of Jesus' divinity.[15] When describing the part that Mary played, the Catholic catechism explains:

> Matthew describes the virginal conception of Jesus by Mary as the fulfillment of Isaiah's prophecy (Mt. 1:23; Isaiah 7:14). Luke describes the call of God to the Virgin Mary to come through the Holy Spirit, the power of the highest, to be the mother of Jesus, the Son of God (Lu. 1:26-38). . . Early in the Gospel of John, Mary is described as the "Mother of Jesus.". . . Late in his gospel, the "hour" of Jesus has arrived. Mary, at the foot of the cross, is handed over to the beloved disciple by the crucified Jesus (Jn 19:25-27).[16]

In another part, the Catholic catechism cites the Council of Chalcedon (451 A.D.),which says:

> Christ is One and the same Son, Our Lord Jesus Christ,. . . the same truly God and truly man. . . the same in being with the Father with regard to his divinity and one in being

71

> with us with regard to humanity, like us in everything except with regard to sin. The same one, born from the Father before the ages with regard to his divinity, and in the last days for us and our salvation, was born with regard to his humanity by Mary, the Virgin, Mother of God.[17]

The discussions with respect to the divinity and the humanity of Jesus are closely bound to the theme of his virgin birth. In this doctrine in particular, Evangelicals have more in common with conservative Catholics than with some liberal Protestants who deny the virgin birth of Jesus.

The Doctrine of the Church

The Catholic catechism teaches that the church was founded by Christ to continue his saving mission on earth. The church has received the gifts of its founder and, receives the mission to proclaim and to establish the kingdom of Christ and of God among all peoples. The catechism adds that the church has a missionary mandate (Mt. 28:19), whose origin and goal is the Holy Trinity, motivated by the love of God (2 Cor. 5:2) and with the Holy Spirit as the principle agent. The central mission of the "people of God" is the central theme of the four gospels. Mark presents the mission as the proclamation of the Gospel to guide others to faith: "Truly this was the Son of God" (Mar. 15:39). The mission of Matthew emphasizes the teaching of the Christian community (Mt. 28:19-20; 16:18). Luke emphasizes the transforming power of the Gospel to effect conversion through merciful love of God and liberation from the root of sin. In the Gospel of John, Jesus sends the disciples on a mission, just as the Father has sent Him. The church is apostolic because Jesus established it upon the foundation of the apostles (Eph. 2:20) and because it protects and carries on the witness and the teaching of the apostles (Mt. 28:19-20).[18]

The Doctrine of the Resurrection

The Second Vatican Council (1962-1965) gives a summary of the Christians' "faith in the resurrection" by using a series of texts from the Apostle Paul. "...as we are waiting for the blessed hope and the glorious appearing of our great God and Savior, Jesus Christ" (Titus 2:13); "who will transform the body of our humiliation so that it may be like the body of his glory" (Phil. 3:21); "to be glorified in his saints and be admired in all those who believed in him" (2 Thess. 1:10). As Christians, we believe firmly that Christ was resurrected from the dead and lives forever with the Father and the Holy Spirit. "And this is the will of the one who sent me: that every one who sees the Son, and believes on him, will have everlasting life; and I will raise him up on the last day" (John 6:40).[19]

The Catholic catechism explains:

> This notion of "eternal life" is based first solidly in the living God, the source of all life, who revealed himself in the history of salvation in the Old Testament, and especially in his Son, Our Lord Jesus Christ. Second, this notion derives from our faith conviction that we have been redeemed by his Son, who by his resurrection has come to be the giver of life: "Because as the Father raises the dead, and gives them life, in the same way also the Son raises those to whom he wishes to give life" (Jn. 5:21). Finally, this "eternal life" is already "present" and based on Jesus' disciples, whose Christian testimony and works draw others to "believe that Jesus Christ is the Son of God," so that believing "they must have life in his name."[20]

The Doctrine of the Bible

The documents of Second Vatican Council teach the following about the Holy Scriptures:

> In his goodness and wisdom, God chose to reveal himself and to allow us to know   the purpose of his will (Eph. 1:9), making it possible that, through Christ, the word made flesh, a person may have access to the Father in the Holy Spirit and may come to take part in the divine nature (Eph. 2:18; 2 Pe. 1:4). . . Therefore, Christ the Lord, in whom the complete revelation of the Supreme God reaches its fullness (2 Cor 1:20; 3:16; 4:6), commissioned the apostles to preach that gospel which is the source of all saving truth and moral teaching and in that way to impart to them divine gifts. . .This commission was fulfilled faithfully by the apostles who, by means of their oral preaching, by example and by orders, communicated what they had received from the lips of Christ, concerning their coexistence with him and concerning what he did, or concerning what they learned impelled by the Holy Spirit. The commission was fulfilled also by the apostles and apostolic people who, under the inspiration of the Holy Spirit, put the message of

> salvation in writing. . . being that all that was declared by the inspired authors of holy writers has to be accepted as inspired by the Holy Spirit, it is logical to think that one has to accept that the books of the Scriptures teach firmly, faithfully, and without error that truth which God was wanting to be placed in the Holy scriptures for our salvation. Therefore, "all scripture is inspired by God, and useful for teaching, for reproving, for correcting, for instructing in righteousness, so that the persons of God may be perfect, entirely prepared for every good work." (2 Tim 3:16-17).[21]

A note of explanation needs to be given here. In this segment we have focused on the beliefs Evangelicals and Roman Catholics have in common that can be used as bridges of communications. This could well lead to the question that if we have all of these beliefs in common, are there any significant differences left? The answer is that there are many crucial differences. These stem principally from that which the Roman Catholic Church has *added* to the biblical doctrines. One example is the doctrines regarding Mary that the Catholic Church has added such as the Immaculate Conception, the Assumption, and the Coronation of Mary, all of which lack a biblical foundation. In another section we will deal with these differences. The purpose of this segment is to point out the beliefs that we do have in common which can be the starting point in the evangelization process.

Practices That We Have in Common

Due to the beliefs that we have in common, there are certain practices that Catholics and Evangelicals have in common. Some of these center on religious celebrations. Among these are the celebrations of the birth, passion, death, and resurrection of Jesus. Others are family and social celebrations or reunions revolve around the transitions of life, such as: (1) birth, (2) birthdays, (3) weddings, (4) anniversaries, (5) funerals, and (6) memorial reunions These provide opportunities to cultivate friendships and to share the gospel in settings that are cordial and positive.

Values That We Have in Common

A Roman Catholic leader writes:

> If we think about it, there are many moral and spiritual values that we Catholics and Evangelicals have in common.

74

A survey which was made between Catholics and Evangelicals reveals that "the majority of Catholics and Evangelicals feel that pornography is a serious problem, that parents are less willing to discipline their children, that except for financial necessity, women with little children ought not to work outside the home, that divorce ought to be made more difficult, and that abortion is not permitted.[22]

Besides these values mentioned here, there is great concern in both groups over wars and the extermination of groups in different parts of the world, hunger in many countries, sickness (plagues, etc.) in certain regions of the world, the proliferation of drugs, the high rate of illegitimate children, the breakup of many homes, and crime in their communities.

As we can observe, we have many things in common with regard to doctrines (of God, Jesus Christ, the Holy Spirit, the virgin birth of Jesus, the resurrection, the Holy Scriptures), and to certain values related to the society that surrounds us. Later we will talk about the differences that we have, but it is important that what we have in common can be used as a bridge of communication to guide them to a clearer knowledge of the message of salvation.

ENDNOTES

[1.] Nicodemus embodies issues inherent in confessing Jesus in a hostile environment,something John acknowledges as well (John 12: 36-43).

[2.] See David Hesselgrave, *Communicating Christ Cross-culturally,* (Grand Rapids: Zondervan, 1978).

[3.] The Christian witness should prepare beforehand a gospel presentation. Many good methods are available including *The Roman Road to Salvation, The Four Spiritual Laws, The Personal Commitment Guide, Faith, And The Net Evangelism Strategy.*

[4.] Such customs include god-parent/god-child responsibilities, debutante expectations, involvement in baptismal and wedding rites, etc.

[5] Adapted from Rev. Joe O'Connel's, *"Witnessing to Catholics"* unpublished research paper.

[6] Adapted from Fay's suggestions in William Fay & Ralph Hodge, *Sharing Jesus Without Fear* (Nashville: Lifeway Press, 1997), 16.

[7] Ibid.

[8] J. B. Rowell, *How to Lead Catholics to Christ* (n.p., 1966), p. 10.

[9] John A. Hardon, *The Catholic Catechism,* (New York: Doubleday, 1981) , 157

[10] In order to avoid a discussion at this time about the word "catholic," we have used the synonym "universal."

[11] James Killgallon, Gerard Weber, Leonard Ziegmann, *Life in Christ* (ACTA Foundation, 1976), 11-17.

[12] Ibid., 17.

[13] Ibid., 44-76.

[14] Episcopal Commission, *The Catholic Faith Catechism* (Manila: Metro Life Publications, 1994), 288-289.

[15] Ibid., 108.

[16] Ibid., 109.

[17] Ibid., 108.

[18] Ibid., 300-306.

[19] Ibid., 451.

[20] Ibid., 451.

[21] Abbott, *Documents of Vatican II,* 12-19.

[22] George Barna, *"Christian Marketing Perspective"* (Glendale, Spring, 1988), Volume 4, Number 2.

PART TWO:

COMMUNICATING THE GOSPEL MESSAGE

RECOGNIZING OPPORTUNITIES TO SHARE THE MESSAGE OF SALVATION

Introduction: Nora's Disappointment

While serving as a missionary in the Republic of Panama, I was asked to be interim pastor in a church. Typically our Sunday services were the ones with the highest attendance. Wednesday nights, however, had a special meaning for our congregation because we had more time for expository Bible study. A young lady who started attending these Bible studies would always stay after the sessions and ask a number of questions. She told me that she was Roman Catholic and that she had some charismatic friends who had encouraged her to study the Bible. I was pleased that she was showing such an interest in the Bible and that she was searching for spiritual guidance. At times she would have tears in her eyes as she talked about the spiritual truths she was discovering.

One night after the Bible study, she asked me, "What do you Evangelicals think about the Virgin Mary?" In a very authoritative manner, I answered: "In the first place, you have used the wrong terminology, because Mary did not remain a virgin, she had other children after the birth of Jesus. In the second place, you Catholics are totally wrong because you worship Mary and the Bible teaches that that is idolatry." Completely shocked she responded: "That's impossible, our blessed Mother did not have any more children. She is forever a virgin."

With a great deal of confidence, I answered: "Let me show you what the Bible says about Mary." I then opened the Bible to John 2:12, which mentions Jesus's mother, brothers, and disciples. Quickly I flipped to Matthew 12:46, Mark 3:31, and Luke 8:19 all of which refer to Jesus' brothers. I even showed the passages such as Matthew 13:55,56 and Mark 6:3,4 which also mention his sisters. I also pointed out that initially, not even his brothers believed in him (John 7:5). She replied, " But the priest has told us that they were Jesus' cousins not his brothers and sisters." I quickly replied: "Roman Catholic priests have purposely kept people in spiritual darkness just to keep them within the Church. The priest well knows that in the Greek the words for brothers and cousins are totally different and where the Bible refers to the brothers of Jesus it is referring to the children Mary had after having given birth to Jesus." I further pointed out that the Bible clearly states that "Joseph did not know (have marital relations with) Mary until Jesus was born" (Matthew 25:1).

This means that afterwards, they did have normal marital relations. I also stressed that the term "first born" meant that there were other children born to her. Otherwise, why would the term be used?

I further pointed out that the Catholic Church teaches doctrines about Mary that have absolutely no biblical basis. For example, I told her that the Catholic Church teaches that Mary is a mediatrix between people and Christ. Opening the Bible to 1 Timothy 2:5, I read to her the verse that says that "there is one mediator between God and man and that is Jesus Christ." As I spoke, the young lady kept shaking her head and saying "I can't believe this. That's not what the Catholic Church teaches." I answered, "Well, that's the problem with you Catholics, you go by what the Church teaches and not what the Bible teaches." I added: "What you need to do is make up your mind. Are you going to let the Church or the Bible determine what you believe? What you need to do is take a clear stand, turn your back on the teachings of the Catholic Church and start following what the Bible teaches." She again seemed very confused and said that she would have to think about this some more.

My initial emotion was one of satisfaction. I felt that I had really laid out before her what the Bible teaches and what she should do. My elation was later tempered by the fact that *she never came back*. I won the *argument*, but I lost the *person*. As I have reflected on this, I have had to admit that my intention was good, but my approach was wrong. There are several things that I did wrong. First, I was judgmental. I accused her of willfully and knowingly participating in idolatry. Second, I was impatient. I wanted her to understand all of the biblical doctrines at once without allowing time for the Holy Spirit to work in her heart. Third, I focused on her *religious affiliation* and not her *personal relationship* with Christ. By pointing out the errors of Catholic doctrine, I thought that she would see the light immediately and become receptive to the gospel. Fourth, I was insensitive. She was simply not *emotionally* and *intellectually* ready to hear what I pointed out to her about Mary having more children. I did not concentrate enough on leading her to a personal experience of salvation in Jesus Christ. Fifth, I did not make a distinction between the evangelism phase (leading her to Christ) and the discipleship phase (helping her to understand more fully the basic Christian doctrines and their implication to her life). So that you won't make the mistakes I made, let us sit at the feet of Jesus and find out how he shared the good news of salvation with a woman who had a very limited knowledge of Scripture, a confused religious tradition, a vague hope about the future, a pathetic life history, and a profound spiritual thirst; the Samaritan woman.

BIBLE STUDY

Jesus And The Samaritan Woman

Introduction

The essential message of the gospel is the proclamation to the world that God loves fallen humanity enough to give His Son as a ransom for their sin (John 3:16-17; 1 Tim 2:5-6; Heb 9:28; 1 John 2:2). God's genuine love can be no more clearly demonstrated than by offering a way whereby a person in sinful rebellion (Job 13:23; Isa 53:6) is restored to a proper relationship with Him and made to become a child of God (John 1:12; Gal 3:26). The gospel is permeated with the demonstration of God's unilateral and undeserved affection through and through (Rom 5:8; 2 Cor 5:19).

God's love as shown in the gospel provides the proper motivation for those who would proclaim this life-changing message. It is not nearly enough simply to be able to articulate the "steps of salvation" with rote accuracy. Like the Master, the message of God's love needs to be delivered by a loving messenger (2 Cor 6:11-13). As it often turns out, in matters of salvation the messenger is usually the first thing our Roman Catholic friend encounters before his/her ears are ever attuned to the gospel itself (Rom 10:14-15; 1 Cor 1:22-25). For this reason it behooves us to ask how the Evangelical Christian messenger can demonstrate love in sharing the gospel.

In the study that follows we prepare seminar participants to share their faith by focusing on opportunities, challenges, and attitudes that prepare the ground in people's lives for a fruitful harvest. Jesus' encounter with the Samaritan woman offers us a valuable lesson for putting our compassion into action. Christ's example will challenge us to move out of our comfort zones in many ways for the sake of reaching the lost.

Jesus as a Methodological Model

Jesus' encounter with the woman from Samaria (John 4:1-42) is rich in instruction for Evangelical Christians who take their witnessing seriously. This account can help us keep key issues in mind when working with those who have not experienced the new birth and who have questions regarding their relationship with God. The learning possibilities inherent in this story are various in nature. By way of inference, this story brings to the forefront the personal implications that follow from Jesus' outreach beyond the conventions of His geographical and social context. While He was willing to go beyond traditional limits, He was capable of looking with discernment deep within the needy person to identify the universal longings we all have in common. In doing so, He knew how to deal with the life of the lost. Finally, in a progressive four-fold pattern Jesus could begin with a person where they were and move them inexorably to an encounter with Him as their Savior. Jesus' encounter with the Samaritan woman will challenge everyone who wishes to work with people very much unlike themselves. He shows us how to work with people respectfully but decisively. Note the following aspects.

Jesus *Cultivated* A Friendship (John 4:1-6)

By going out of His way geographically

John 4:4 states that Jesus "had to go through Samaria." The gospels show evidence of at least four trips Jesus undertook between Galilee and Jerusalem during His ministry. It is likely he traveled between Judea and Galilee with regularity. To move from one region to the other, however, there stood in the way Samaria, a region viewed with much disdain and acrimony built up over three centuries. In an ironical quirk of fate, travel through Samaria offered the shortest distance linking Jews in the northern areas with those in the south[1]. Nevertheless, traveling through Samaria demanded a heavy social toll that Jews regularly refused to pay. Many Jews simply avoided any contact with Samaritans and traveled back and forth through Perea on the eastern bank of the Jordan. The gospels show that Jesus also used this less controversial route at times (Matt 19:1; Mark 10:1).

Thus, how are we to understand Jesus' decision to travel through Samaria? Was it born of expediency, needing to make it to Galilee a day or two sooner? While some scholars argue that the trip through Samaria was necessary to cut down on travel time and perhaps to avoid confrontation with the Pharisees (John 4:1-3), the use of "had to" (from dei', *dei*) in the text points to a programmatic and theological use in John. Scholars have shown that the term is often used to suggest a "divine necessity." As is evident elsewhere in John (e.g., 3:14, 30; 9:4) Jesus was motivated to travel through Samaria primarily out of a sense of His Father's will. There was no desire to avoid Samaria, nor did he struggle with rationalizing the need to travel via a different route. God would have him travel through Samaria and so he goes. It's as simple as that.

Application: Jesus' travel through Samaria challenges our smugness in predetermining beforehand to know God's will completely (Jas 4:13-17). Because God is sovereign, He may require us to "go the extra mile" in demonstrating our willingness to change for the sake of the lost. Often, this happens by moving beyond our comfortable and well-worn patterns of ministry. Openness to God's authority to direct our path even into uncomfortable situations (e.g. Paul's travel to Jerusalem, Acts 21:7-14) can be a necessary preparation to be used by God to lead people unlike us to faith in Christ.

By going out of His way socially

The social toll for dealing with Samaritans was not insignificant. Various aspects need to be understood. As many scholars note, Jewish and Samaritan hostility dated back to the Assyrian's resettlement of Northern Israel (2 Kgs 17:14-23). The introduction of gentile peoples produced a mixed race of dwellers that scrupulous Jews could simply not accept. Intertestamental history also reveals that Samaritans claimed a religious legitimacy of their own dating back to Moses and the Pentateuch (Deut 11:29; 27:12; Josh 8:23). With both peoples claiming Moses as foundational to their religious identity it is easy to see how Jews and Samaritans would hold each other with contempt. (Neh 4; Ezra 4).

The Jewish historian Josephus recounts the construction of a temple on Mount Gerizim by Sanballat during Persian times[2]. Clearly, for pious Jews who believed the temple in Jerusalem was the sole Sanctuary of Yahweh, the Samaritans could only be seen as apostate heretics. Though John Hyrcanus, the Hasmonean monarch destroyed the temple in 128 BC, Samaritans still worshiped on the site and held to the superiority of their faith. The unbending theological posture of Palestinian Jews during this time gave little room for interacting with Samaritans. Many Samaritans for their part also held negative knee-jerk reactions whenever Jerusalem was so much as evoked (Luke 9:51-56).

Finally, it is also likely that the Samaritan woman indirectly alluded to the fear by some Jews of ritual contamination through any kind of interaction with Samaritans. One commentator captures the woman's underlying issue "There was a trace of sarcasm in the woman's reply, as if she meant, 'We Samaritans are the dirt under your feet until you want something; then we are good enough!'"[3] It is no wonder the Samaritan woman was startled that Jesus spoke to her (v.9). The issue was not that a man should ask a woman for a drink during the hot noon hour (Gen 24:17; cf., Job 22:7), but that a Jew should ever sink to ask a Samaritan for anything!

Application: When Jesus initiated His interaction with the Samaritan woman He did so against the grain of entrenched hatred and suspicion between Jews and Samaritans. History, however, teaches us that all things built by human hands eventually crumble. Human prejudices can fall as well. Reaching out to people of a different faith tradition such as Roman Catholics will expose you to similar circumstances. No one likes to have His or her faith challenged by someone else's beliefs, especially when an air of superiority or arrogance is perceived, deserved or otherwise. Remember that outreach is done to bring people into a saving relationship with Christ. It is not our place to win an argument at the expense of losing the person. As we will note soon enough, Jesus' message transcended the squabble between the Jerusalem and Gerizim factions. Keep in mind that although a Roman Catholic may see the conversation as dealing with the legitimacy of Catholic faith as opposed to "Protestant" faith, it really isn't about such issues at all. Like Jesus, we need to be willing to go out of our way socially in order to witness to Roman Catholics.

Jesus *Created* An Interest: (John 4:7-14)

By recognizing the value of a felt need

At the noon hour, and with the sun near its zenith, the heat of the day was in full force. Arriving at the well of Jacob, a cool drink of water offered much needed refreshment. Water is, of course, one of the absolute necessities of life and ranks among the most basic needs in Maslow's hierarchy of human needs. Someone has said that the human body is composed roughly of 70 percent water. Like air and food, life cannot be sustained without it.

Jesus acknowledged the need we all have when thirst pushes all other concerns aside until it is quenched. In so doing, He used this common point of contact to reveal the need we all have for His life-giving message.

Application: Often, the ability to discern a felt need can only come when we try to "walk in the other person's shoes." This involves learning as much as we can about the person's life experience and his cultural world, taking the time to know him personally and understanding his situation. While "understanding" people who are a lot like us socially is challenge enough, working with people with whom we have little or no apparent points of commonality will test us to the limit. A relatively simple thing, such as being offered something to eat that is not a part of our usual diet, if not handled well, can cause a complete breakdown in the possibility of a fruitful outcome.

Let's face it, many Evangelical Christians are unwilling to embrace their own "Samaria," even when, ostensibly, they commit to going wherever Jesus leads. "Samaritans" have a God-given right to exist as Samaritans and it is not our job to adjust their culture to suit our sensibilities. Many well-intentioned Evangelical Christians will never see the plight of the lost person simply because they refuse to give up some personal comfort.

By relating to a spiritual need

Felt needs are great vehicles for relating the gospel message. John's gospel uses several metaphors related directly to basic human needs (e.g., Jesus as the Bread of Life [John 6:35], living water [John 7:37], Light [John 8:12], etc.). In this case, Jesus does not let the woman's initial cynicism sway Him from making a spiritual connection. His reference to "living water," while understandable as a natural phenomenon, is also tantalizingly spiritual in its import. In the Bible "living water" can literally mean spring water as opposed to water held in cisterns or wells (Genesis 26:19; Leviticus 14:5). However, there is also a symbolic use that hints at God's ability to quench the thirst of the soul (Isa 41:17; 44:3; 55:1). While Jesus' mention of the water he offered was predicated as a "gift of God," the woman only heard what she was capable of understanding in her spiritual state (vv.11-12). Although Jesus insisted upon the spiritual dimensions of His offer, she seems to have misunderstood the gift of water as magical, thus releasing her from any future need of water (v.14). Clearly, the woman did not understand Jesus' teaching, but what is important to note is that through the intervening conversation the woman stayed engaged and went from being a cynical provider of stale water to showing a genuine desire to drink the "living waters" Jesus offered (v.15).

Application: It should be understood that "felt needs" are real issues in survival and quality of life. Perhaps, because they are so basic, it is often hard to look beyond them as bridge analogies that illustrate the greater spiritual need. In reaching out to our Catholic friends, analogies to fundamental needs in life can be helpful tools for introducing them to God's saving grace. People will often readily make the spiritual connection, but there are always individuals who, initially, do not understand. Commitment to share the gospel should have no time limits and should exhaust every possibility to make the gospel clear and understandable. Receiving the gospel is a spiritual exercise and people who have never experienced God's gift are spiritually dead and suffer from a darkened understanding (2 Cor 4:4-6; Eph 2:1; 4:17-18; 1 Pet 4:6). So long as there is genuine interest, the Evangelical Christian witness should not tire, regardless of the slowness of any progress, or of misunderstandings, which regularly are the case. As Jesus spoke to the Samaritan woman about the living water a new possibility eventually began to dawn on her: She could quench the thirst of her soul and experience a different kind of life. As we cultivate a friendship, we are in a better position to create an interest in spiritual matters by helping them see that our need of Jesus is basic and universal. One way to do this is to share our testimony of how Jesus has made a difference in our lives.

Jesus *Comprehended* Her Situation (John 4:16-18)

By probing into her lost spiritual condition

Jesus' probe into the marital status of the Samaritan woman is open to interpretation While some scholars believe Jesus was defending himself against a possible charge of impropriety by discussing an intimate subject matter with a lone woman in public seems unlikely, the gospels are full of instances where Jesus' actions infuriated the "religious and morality squads" of the day (Matt 9:11; 11:19; 12:9-14; Mark 2:16; Luke 6:7; 15:1-2; John 8:1-6; et al.).

Doubtless, His primary reason must have been to prepare her heart for receiving the living water of the gospel. Asking her to produce her husband (v.16) took her quickly to a pathological condition in her life. Often, people attempt to segregate the "spiritual" from the "secular," believing that both spheres of life can operate independent of each other. Jesus, however, saw no such line of demarcation. For Jesus bringing up her marital status was not off limits. The gospel in its power introduces the sovereignty of God into all the affairs of life.

It is important to note that His request to have the woman produce a husband was not presented in a condemning way. Even though the woman was a sinner under the most liberal allowances for marriage and divorce in the culture, there is no judgmental attitude shown towards her.[4] Jesus did, however, exercise "tough love" helping the woman to realize her need of salvation by forcing to the surface her deplorable marital history and reinforcing her need for spiritual transformation.

Application: The decision to probe into delicate moral issues in the lives of those whom we wish to reach for Christ should not be undertaken lightly. While Jesus had all the facts necessary to present the Samaritan woman with the seriousness of her moral lapse, an unbiased understanding of all the facts is not available to us. Still, to the degree that the relationship matures and as comfort levels grow, people will often reveal painful episodes in their life that scream for the healing. Moral failure, so common in our modern culture, is as common among Roman Catholics as among people in general. At critical times such as these it is important to remember that while Jesus did not approve of her lifestyle, there must have been a tone of compassion. When dealing with Roman Catholics, remember that assurance of salvation and the declaration of total forgiveness from sin are not taught in the Catholic Church. Dealing with issues of sinful behavior often tends to point us to the easy but detrimental extremes of judgmental condemnation or non-confrontational permissibility. God requires nothing less than mercy and justice from His servants.

By finding a redeemable fragment of her life

The woman's response to Jesus, while terse, was truthful, "I have no husband." While it is implied that her marital history was well known in the community (see vv. 28-29), acknowledging the immensity of her marital failure is not something she could easily do without further injury to her ego. It is important to note Jesus' approach. While he could have chided her for being deceptive and not completely open with Him, he looked for the positive in her answer.

Paul's instruction to the Philippians may be helpful here. As believers we are told to "dwell" on the more noble and honorable aspects of life (Phil 4:8). The apostle's use of the verb "dwell" basically expresses the idea of *reckoning to,* or *taking into account,* etc. Paul would have us follow what Jesus did in practice; as He looked at the Samaritan woman, he reckoned to her credit what little He could salvage from the spiritual wreck of her life. Jesus was an expert at this. It is said of him in Matthew 12:20 "A battered reed He will not break off, and a smoldering wick He will not put out, until He leads justice to victory." Jesus took the opportunity to commend her basic honesty: " What you have just said is quite true" (v.18). So long as there was a smoldering ember to work with, her conscience was not irreparably damaged and God could still kindle the fire of the gospel in her life (cf., Titus 1:15-16).

Application: It is a well-known and well-worn truism that, like a coin, there are two sides to every story. Painful experiences in life are often the result of external abuse, but personal destructive behavior takes its toll as well. Remember that the gospel begins with an understanding of the fallen nature of humanity (Rom 3:23). The gospel is "good news" specifically because it is God's way of redeeming our life from the clutches of sin and death (Luke 4:18-19; John 10:10; 1 John 3:8). When persons take the gospel seriously it will force them to come to terms with the root causes that wreak havoc in their lives. Honesty and transparency on the part of the person should elicit understanding and mercy from the child of God. Thus, having awakened in her an interest in a new lifestyle, Jesus maintained the dialogue on a positive note. She continued to listen as she sensed that He was willing to see the best in her.

Jesus *Concentrated* On Essential Aspects Of Salvation (4:19-24)

By avoiding discussions of "Religion"

As noted, the Samaritans had a different set of theological beliefs, based in part on their "alternative" understanding of Scripture. Unlike the Jews, who recognized the authority of the Torah, the prophetic books, and the writings (Tanak), Samaritans accepted only Moses' writings (Pentateuch) as inspired. Samaritans believed Moses had identified the proper site for the worship of Yahweh as opposite Mt. Ebal - Mt. Gerizim (Deut 27:1-28:68). They also believed that Abraham had offered Isaac on Mount Gerizim instead of Zion near Jerusalem. Jesus, however, had no intention of taking sides. Like the captain of the Host of the Lord who met Joshua near Jericho, His sword could not be bought, nor taken for granted for that matter (Josh 5:13-15).

It should be stressed that from a Christian perspective both Samaritan religion and the Palestinian Judaism of the first century were equally illegitimate expressions of Yahweh worship (v.21 cf., v.24). For Jesus, both traditions missed the mark. The worship of God was not dependent on a geographical location, something that both religions emphasized. Christ's insistence that true worship was founded on Spirit and truth was a threat to both religions. Stephen, the first Christian martyr, paid with his life for proclaiming that faith in Christ liberated worshipers from ties to physical earthly locations, no matter how significant for their faith (see Acts 7:48).

Application: Opportunities to engage in protracted theological debate can be very energizing, but are ultimately misguided. They rarely lead to decisions for Christ. We need to be able to exercise discernment in knowing what the person actually needs, and have the strength to stick to "kingdom aims." There is a reason as to why operating surgeons will not let a patient eat food some twelve hours before an operation. Undigested food in the alimentary tract, while nutritional in itself, can prove deadly, even in the simplest of surgical procedures. Likewise, theological debate about non-essential matters of religious tradition only muddy the water and keep lost persons from focusing on their need of a Savior.

Evangelical Christian witnesses should be aware of the importance that Roman Catholics place on undertaking pilgrimages to religious shrines. For example, there are shrines to Mary in many countries in the world. While some are well known and endorsed by the Catholic Church (e.g., Portugal, Fatima; France, Lourdes; Mexico, Guadalupe; etc.), other locations may be nothing more than a private home or open field. Such pilgrimages are usually undertaken to fulfill vows and to accrue merit, either for themselves or for a loved one. Remember that Jesus introduced real worship by elevating the conversation above geographic issues. Do not run the risk of offending your Roman Catholic friend by attacking pious practices. Do stay on message and continue to show the need of worship, which is empowered by the Spirit and founded on a personal relationship with the Father through Jesus Christ. When the believers come to understand the sufficiency of worship Christ gives, they will come to see the obsolescence of many religious practices.

Finally, it should also be kept in mind that often people raise issues of theology specifically to avoid dealing with the work the Holy Spirit may be doing in their lives. The Samaritan woman may well have tried this diversionary tactic on Jesus. Once again, we need to partner with the Spirit of God (Acts 8:29; Rom 8:12-17) and not become a hindrance or roadblock to His work of salvation. This is not to say that there is never a place to discuss religious differences. You will agree, however, that discussing points of theology is more productive when speaking with a person who has been quickened by the Spirit to have the mind of Christ (John 14:17; 1 Cor 2:11-13, 15; 1 Pet 2:1-3). Carrying on a theological discussion with someone dead in trespasses and sin can't hold much promise (2 Cor 2:14).

By focusing on "Relationship"

Jesus responded to the woman's religious issue by elevating the conversation to the ultimate need, felt or otherwise: "true worshipers will worship the Father in *spirit* and in *truth*"(v.23). The religion of the Jews and the Samaritans was narrow and nationalistic (see Acts 1:6). Jesus makes it plain that "Spirit" and "Truth" are worshipful necessities. They are not exclusively under the guardianship of any "provincial" faith group, no matter how venerable. One commentator interprets Jesus' Spirit and Truth pronouncement in this way: "worship will manifest itself *in the sphere of the spirit* [Spirit](Rom 1:9; Eph 6:18), in a man's inner life as opposed to worship in any particular site, . . . and it will be worship of God *as He really is* [Truth], that is, worship with first-hand knowledge as opposed to that mediated through symbolism".[5] It seems clear that from both concepts Jesus is underscoring the need for worship in the "inward sanctuary of the heart" (cf., 1 Kgs 8:27; Isa 66:1; Micah 6:6-8; Mark 14:58; Luke 17:21; Acts 7:48; 17:25), which can only be had by a *personal relationship* with God.[6] Spirit relates to the subjective inner part of the individual, whereas, Truth relates to the unmediated presence of God, the objective object of worship (1 Cor 13:12). Thus, true worshipers are those who have a *spiritual relationship* with Him.

Application: The concept of a personal relationship with God is difficult to communicate to Roman Catholics. Rich in symbolism and steeped in mystery, many of them are awed and overwhelmed by the implied message of Catholic pomp. To them, God is utterly transcendent and can only be apprehended through the mediation of priests and the sacraments. The revelation of God as our heavenly Father, however, can be an effective metaphor for stressing the need of a personal relationship. One's personal testimony can be the best way to communicate the experiential possibility of real communion through Jesus Christ.

Jesus *Communicated* The Message Progressively (4:9,11,19,29)

The various ways in which the Samaritan woman referred to Jesus give us an idea of her increasing understanding and appreciation for this man whom she had just met.

Her initial impression of him was as a *"Jew."*

The woman's initial impressions of Jesus were likely shaped by the accumulation of centuries of hatred, animosity, and suspicion, harbored against the Jewish people. Her acknowledgment of him as a Jew is in juxtaposition to her as a Samaritan. The encounter reveals in a very succinct manner the existence of the ongoing rivalry that kept people from seeing each other with civility and from a common humanity. This is further reinforced by the parenthetical explanation added by the author in verse 9: "For Jews have no dealings with Samaritans." By her attitude, the Samaritan woman reminded Jesus of the great challenge that confronted him in His mission to seek and to save the lost.

Application: There are those who have a very vague or even negative perception of the person of Jesus Christ. This may be true because of a limited understanding of the Gospels, because of the unbiblical religious practices of those around them, or because of harmful relationships with people who call themselves Christians. The question that we must face is, how can we help them to know the real Christ and to get to the point where they desire to have a personal experience of salvation through faith in him?

Her attitude towards him improved by calling Him *"Sir."*

Almost all commentators agree that John has not given us the total text of the conversation. There must have been a considerable exchange that continued between Jesus and the woman. What is clear from the outcome is that during the conversation the iron curtain of hate began to crumble. While the term "sir" can also be translated "Lord"(from kuvrio", *kurios*), it is properly translated as "sir" in its three usages suggesting a growing respect on the part of the woman towards Jesus (vv.11,15,19). Jesus had treated her differently and so she begins to treat him with respect. She was no longer controlled by the negative attitude toward all Jews. The respect that grew toward him allowed the woman to set aside futile rivalries and truly focus on the substance of the problem; how could this gentleman draw living water when he didn't have so much as a bucket to work with?

Application: What will it take for our friends and relatives to have a respectful attitude toward the Christ of Scripture? The Bible recognizes the power of kindness and of treating people with respect (Prov 25:21-22; 2 Tim 2:24-25). Often a good word and a pleasing disposition will go a long way to ease tensions. The Evangelical Christian witness should not let misguided prejudices stop him/her from reaching out in genuine concern. Trust in the power of love. Many can attest that often there will be no greater friend than one we win over by showing love.

Later, she began to see Him as a *"Prophet."*

The woman's recognition of Jesus as a prophet was a further step in the right direction. While the Palestinian Jews venerated the prophets of old (Matt 10:41; 23:29; Heb 1:1), and held prophetic writings as inspired (Acts 13:15), the stature of prophets in Samaritan culture is not as well known. We know for example, that Samaritans did not consider prophetic writings as being inspired. Nevertheless, as this narrative implies, the prophetic gift was recognized. The woman came to understand that Jesus was no mere mild mannered man. Instead, he held special powers divinely bestowed, as exhibited by divulging her whole marital history. At the very least the woman recognized Jesus as God's spokesman or mouthpiece. She began to sense the uncomfortable position of realizing that God had taken notice of her sinful situation.

Application: Paul recognizes the gift of prophesy in several of his letters (Rom 12:6; 1 Cor 12:10, 28; Eph 2:20; 3:5; 4:11). While we often associate prophesy as the ability to look into the future (e.g., John of Patmos, Rev 1:3), prophets always had a contemporary relevance in Israel as well as in the early church (I Cor 14:31). As Paul shows, prophets often brought words of encouragement to the church. This is something that the Christian may be required to do as he works with people who struggle with making a commitment to faith in Jesus Christ.

Exhortation occurs when we stand as God's representative and faithfully pronounce God's non-negotiable standards of right and wrong. An opportunity to "exhort" can easily arise when confronted with the Roman Catholic teaching on sin. Roman Catholics have been taught to classify sin as venial (less serious and pardonable through confession) or mortal (unpardonable). Understanding the biblical concept of sin is essential to recognizing our need of a Savior. The point here is that as heralds of the gospel we may have to exercise our own "prophetic" gifts. When we do so, we must be uncompromisingly faithful to God's word, but we must act with a spirit of humility lest we ourselves fall (Rom 11:20; 1 Cor 10:12; Jas 4:6; Jude 20-23).

Many nominal Christians with a Roman Catholic background have no difficulty thinking of Jesus as a person sent by God. That is an excellent starting point. The problem lies, however, in the fact that they do not have a biblical understanding of the person and work of Jesus Christ. For many, Jesus is either a helpless baby in the arms of Mary or a dead Christ on the cross. While Jesus did go through the stages from the cradle to the cross, the fact is that he neither remained a helpless baby nor a dead Christ. He arose from the dead and is at the right hand of the Father interceding for us. Through meaningful relationships and Bible studies we must commit ourselves to leading these nominal Christians to come to an understanding of the real Jesus of the Bible. Simply knowing that Jesus was a prophet sent from God is not enough to save a person.

Finally she recognized Him as the *"Messiah."*

John notes that the woman herself introduced the subject of the Messiah (v. 25). It is altogether possible that Jesus' sweeping rejection of nationalistic religion gave her reason to wonder if someone speaking with such audacity could be anyone other than the Messiah. He had not only spoken intimately of her personal life (vv.16-19) but had also indicted religion in general and foretold of the installment of genuine worship (vv.20-24).

Like the Jews, Samaritans also had Messianic expectations. Moses' writings, in particular Deuteronomy 18:15-18, was seminal in this regard. Josephus notes that there was also messianic zeal in Samaria during Jesus' time.[7] Samaritans looked ahead to the one who would reveal new truths about God and man.

The woman's comments about Messiah gave Jesus the opportunity to drive the conversation to an immediate climax: "I who speak to you am He." (v.26). With language reminiscent of Isaiah 52:6 (*I am the one who is speaking, "Here I am"*), and undeniable connections to Exodus 3:14 (*And God said to Moses, "I AM WHO I AM"*), Jesus asserts that He is the fulfillment of her hope, and He does it claiming divinity! Although the encounter between Jesus and the woman is "broken up" by the arrival of the disciples and His subsequent discussion with them (vv. 27, 31-38), the woman was surely smitten. In fact, she leaves the well, forgetting her water pot (v. 28). Later, in the village, she recounts to the villagers her remarkable encounter with Jesus and enquires, "This is not the Christ, is it?" There is the impression that even with Jesus' acclamation the woman still harbored some reservations. Although it is not recorded that the woman explicitly confessed Jesus as the Christ, it is evident from the aftermath of the encounter that her testimony caused many in the village to search out Jesus (vv. 30, 39-42). Significantly, John 4:42 implies that, like many in the village, the woman had indeed gone beyond speculation to total acceptance of Jesus as her Savior.

Application: Recognition of Jesus as God's only Savior is crucial to human redemption. A process that takes a person only part of the way to recognizing Him as Savior does not go far enough (cf., Matt 16:13-17; Mark 8:27-29; Luke 9:18-20). Often, people see Jesus as an enlightened religious figure, somewhat like Buddha, Mohammed, or an eastern swami. Roman Catholics, while seeing Jesus as the Messiah, also tend to ascribe "salvific" roles to saints, and the Virgin Mary. Like the woman, many people need to work through their flawed perceptions until they see the uniqueness of Jesus' ministry. Somehow, they need to be instructed carefully until they come to see the singular place that Jesus holds in salvation history (John 14:6; Acts 4:12; 1 Tim 2:5).

Conclusion

Jesus' discussion with His disciples as they returned from the village is instrumental in giving us a handle on how to interpret this story. John shows us that the encounter with the Samaritan woman is to be appreciated for its evangelistic implications. As the disciples returned they were so gripped in the throws of ancient rivalries (v. 27) that they could only focus on Jesus' apparent lapse. However, Jesus used the opportunity to show them the great harvest that awaited them in Samaria, if they had eyes to see beyond their prejudices (vv. 31-38). Jesus' outreach to the woman at the well is a powerful example that challenges us to reach beyond ourselves with confidence knowing that God will reach many with the gospel.

Review

We may need to go out of our way *geographically* and *socially* if we are to meet Roman Catholics and witness to them effectively.

We can create an interest in *spiritual matters* by relating to *felt needs*, which every person experiences.

We must avoid a *spirit of condemnation* when confronted with people's sin and remember that God is able and willing to forgive all who come to Him.

We should acknowledge, honestly, the *positive aspects* of their lives that build esteem and focus on what they can become through the grace and power of Jesus Christ.

We must concentrate on what is *essential to salvation* and avoid discussions that build relational barriers rather than bridges of trust.

We must *communicate patiently* trusting the Holy Spirit to work in the mind of the prospect to create an understanding of the person and gift of Christ.

LEARNING ACTIVITY

Examine Attitudes

Let's play a word association game. Make a mental note of the first thoughts that come to your mind when you hear the following words. Do not try to evaluate these thoughts or second guess me. Just take note of the thoughts that come to your mind immediately when you hear the words: 1) Mormon; 3) Episcopalian 3) Jehovah's Witness; 4) Moonies; 5) Catholics. Take time to do it now, before reading any further.

Now, how many of these thoughts were positive and complimentary? If they were, let me congratulate you. Most of the time when I have played this game in seminars with Evangelicals, the vast majority of their thoughts have been negative and derogatory. If that was the case with you, what are the implications of this for witnessing to people of other religious traditions? Do these preconceived ideas and attitudes help, or do they erect barriers? If they erect barriers, what should you do about it in light of the Bible study of the way in which Jesus related to the Samaritan woman. Now please don't get me wrong. I am not suggesting that we need to agree with these groups in terms of their doctrines or the methods that they use. What I am saying is that they have some positive qualities and values that we can use as bridges of communication. Let me share with you some personal examples:

Mormon

When I think of the word "Mormon," I think of a relative of mine who dedicated her entire life to helping her young daughter who was severely paralyzed with polio. Her daughter is now a successful school teacher. This would not have happened without her mother's love and dedication. Her values regarding her family motivated her to work sacrificially in order to help her physically challenged daughter.

Episcopalian

When I think of the word "Episcopalian," I think of an elderly lady who lived in the city where I was pastoring while I was a college student. Even though she had a severe and painful curvature of the spine, she found the strength to conduct conversational English classes for new immigrants. Her love and commitment were a real inspiration to many of us who benefitted greatly from her sacrificial service.

Catholic

When I think of the word "Catholic," I think of a lady who once lived across the street from us. She was closer to us than our relatives during the prolonged illness and death of our precious 2-year-old daughter. She often volunteered to babysit with our son free of charge when we had to be in the hospital with our daughter. This lady mourned the death of our daughter almost as much as my wife and I. She ministered to us at a very crucial time in our lives.

As you can see, you do not have to agree with people doctrinally or compromise your convictions in order to love them and build witnessing relationships. As we pointed out in the Bible study, Jesus found redeemable fragments even in the lives of some of the most religiously marginalized people.

Throughout His earthly ministry, Jesus met persons with whom He did not agree because of their: (1) lifestyle (the Samaritan woman); (2) theology (Nicodemus); (3) political affiliations (Zacchaeus); or (4) values (rich young ruler). However, it is clear that He *loved* them.

Through His words, and by example, Jesus taught us to:

Love our neighbor as ourselves - (Matt. 22:37-40)

Minister to the needs of those who are different from us (Good Samaritan) - (Luke 10:30-37)

Forgive others - (Matt. 18:21-22)

Love our enemies and pray for those who persecute us - (Matt 5:43-48)

In the past, relationships between many Catholics and Evangelicals have not been cordial. There are two reasons Evangelicals should reexamine their attitudes toward Catholics:

> Christ commanded us to love everyone
> Some Catholics are striving to establish friendships
> with Evangelicals

Listen to what Gerald Williams, a Roman Catholic priest, says:

> In the past, Catholics have not treated other Christians well. We treated them as doubtful Christians with about the same warmth as we show to Communists. We treated their churches as non-churches because we recognized only one church and one unity, the unity with Rome. A sort of peaceful co-existence is all we hoped for.[8]

If there is room for repentance on the Catholic side, there is certainly room for repentance on the Evangelical side. In the past, some have been more interested in proving Catholics wrong than in leading them to a personal, saving knowledge of Christ.

Don'ts

a. Don't criticize the Catholic Church, its doctrines, practices or people. Even if you feel you have a valid point, it is counter productive to criticize for two reasons: (1) It is not in the Spirit of Christ; (2) It will only antagonize people.

b. Don't ridicule any of the practices of the Catholic Church. Some Evangelicals are prone to make fun of their sacramentals (images, statues, crucifixes, etc.) and their religious practices. These things are very dear to Catholics.

c. Don't be negative just because you differ with someone. You can disagree without being disagreeable.

Do's

a. Love your Catholic friends. Find opportunities to show your love in practical ways.

b. Pray with and for your Catholic friends. Many of them have never had the experience of having someone pray for them by name and mention their needs to the Lord. Say: "Lord, I pray for __(name)__. You know that he or she has this need (name the need) and You have promised to hear our prayers. Bless __(name)__; help him or her." You may find it helpful to begin with the Lord's prayer and you will find that quite often they will join you in the prayer.

c. See the best in them. When someone says to you, "I'm a Catholic," be in a position both spiritually and emotionally to say to them, "I'm glad to meet you." Let the love of Christ flow through you. Remember, everyone you meet is a person for whom Christ died.

d. Try to put yourself in their place (see 1 Cor. 9:19-23). Seek to reason, how you would move from a traditional to a biblical position?

We can learn from the advice that some Roman Catholic leaders are giving their people.

97

COMMUNICATING

Williams says:

> "We must live holier lives while we avoid the prejudice and bigotry of the past. Catholics should avoid expressions, judgments and actions which do not represent the condition of our separated brethren with truth and fairness."[9]

Please do not misunderstand this point. We are not suggesting that you compromise your doctrine in any way. You should *speak the truth in love* (see Eph. 4:15). You are obligated to speak the truth. You must do it, however, in a way that conveys God's love. This love leads us to be patient, courteous, and fair as we share the good news of salvation with our Catholic friends.

Degrees of understanding

SAMARITAN WOMAN	PROSPECT
A stranger; "you are a Jew"; alienated (Ezra4;1-5); despised (Neh. 4;1-2)	Jesus is a stranger. I hardly know anything about him.
A respected person, but still not equal to her religious leader (John 4:11) Are you better than our Father?	Jesus is a respected religious person but not necessarily more trust-worthy than the objects of my devotion (Virgin Mary, Saints)
A prophet (John 4:25-26, 29); a religious leader from whom she is willing to learn.	Jesus is a religious *leader* from whom I am willing to learn.
The Messiah (John 4; 25-26, 29); the promised Messiah who has supernatural power (He told me everything)	Jesus is the Christ, the Son of God, whose teachings are devine.
Personal Savior (John 4:39-41). Many believed in him (v. 37). He is the Savior of the world (v. 42)	Jesus is my personal Savior. I have placed my faith and trust in Him.

Use the chart to do the following:

1. Try to determine the level of understanding held by your prospects.
2. Think of how you can get your prospects to progress to the next level.
3. Share this with your prayer partners and spend time praying for one another's prospects.

PRACTICAL INSTRUCTION

Because of the Second Vatican Council (Vatican II), we now have the greatest opportunity ever to share our faith with our Catholic friends. Those who do not understand the implications of Vatican II, take two extreme positions:

"Nothing has *changed*, we must view all Catholics as adversaries."

"Changes within Catholicism are so great that we do not need to share our *faith* with them any longer."

In order to avoid both extremes, let us look at Vatican II and its implications.

Second Vatican Council

What is an Ecumenical Council?

It is a council of all the *bishops* of the Roman Catholic world to consider the state of the Church, to pronounce against heresy, and rule on all matters that pertain to faith, morals, and church discipline.

When did the Second Vatican Council take place?

Pope John XXIII convened the first session of Vatican II which ran from October 11 to December 8, 1962. He died June 3, 1963. Pope Paul VI reconvened the Council for the other three sessions which ran from September 29 to December 4, 1963; September 14 to November 21, 1964, and September 14 to December 8, 1965. The Council met in St. Peter's Basilica.[10]

Who participated in the Council?

A total of 2,860 Fathers participated in Council proceedings. There were also more than 40 observers from Protestant churches.

Why was the Second Vatican Council called?

> "The main business of the Council was to explore and make explicit the dimensions of doctrine and Christian life requiring emphasis for the full development of the Church and the better accomplishment of its mission in the contemporary world."[12]

How many documents did the Second Vatican Council produce?

The Council produced sixteen documents: *Lumen Gentium* (Dogmatic Constitution of the Church), *Dei Verbum* (Constitution on Divine Revelation); *Sacrosanctum Concilium* (Constitution on the Sacred Liturgy); *Gaudium et Spes* (Constitution on the Church in the Modern World); *Christus Dominus* (Pastoral Office in the Church); *ad Gentes* (Decree on the Church's Missionary Activity); *Unitatis Redintegratio* (Decree on Ecumenism); *Orientalium Ecclesiarum* (Decree on Eastern Catholic Churches); *Presbyterorum Ordinis* (Decree on the Ministry and Life of Priests); *Optatam Totius* (Decree on Priestly Formation); *Perfectae Caritatis* (Decree on the Appropriate Renewal of the Religious Life); *Apostolicum Acctuositatem* (Decree on the Apostolate of the Laity); *Inter Mirifica* (Decree on Instruments of Social Communication); *Dignitatis Humanae* (Declaration on Religious Freedom); *Nostra Aetate* (Declaration on the Relationship of the Church to non-Christian Religions); *Gravissium Educationnis* (Declaration on Christian Education); The key documents were the four constitutions, which set the ideological basis for all the others.[13]

What was the ultimate goal of the Second Vatican Council?

The ultimate goal of the Second Vatican Council is stated clearly in the *Documents of Vatican II:*

> The result is that, little by little, as the obstacles to perfect ecclesiastical communion are overcome, all Christians will be gathered in a common celebration in the Eucharist, into the unity of the one and only Church, which Christ bestowed on his Church from the beginning. This unity, we believe, subsists in the Catholic Church as something she can never lose, and we hope that it will continue to increase until the end of time.[14]

This goal, as James McCarthy points out, reveals an ecumenical strategy on the part of the Roman Catholic Church.[15] It is not an ecumenism of equality between the various groups that consider themselves Christians, but one in which the supremacy of the Roman Catholic Church is established when the other groups participate in the celebration of the Eucharist as defined by the Roman Catholic Church.

While it is clear that Evangelical Christians cannot accept this type of Ecumenism, which is not based on sound biblical doctrine, there are a number of changes that have occurred as a result of Vatican II that have opened up new doors of opportunity to share the gospel of salvation with nominal Christians among Roman Catholics. With that in mind, let us examine some of these changes and their implications.

Changes Since The Second Vatican Council

What has not changed?

The dogmas

The dogmas are "official *teachings* proposed with such solemnity that their rejection is tantamount to heresy, which is a denial of some truth of faith deemed by the teaching Church to be essential to that faith."[16]

Some of the principal dogmas that remain unchanged include the Mass, the role of Mary, and the concept of salvation. The *form* of the Mass has changed, but its meaning remains the same. This Mass is still seen as the sacrifice of Jesus. Mary remains a *co-mediatrix*: (mediates along with Christ) of all favors and *co-redemptrix* (redeems along with Christ) of humanity.[17] Other key doctrines relating to salvation, tradition, and the Sacraments have not changed.

The hierarchy ("chain of command")

The *structure* of the church has not changed. The Catholic Church teaches that it "is governed by the successor of Peter and by the bishops in union with that successor."[18] The supreme *authority* of the Pope has not changed. If the doctrines of the authority and infallibility of the Pope were changed, the whole structure of Catholicism would be modified.

What has changed?

Worship

The mass is celebrated in the *language* of the people. The priest faces the congregation. Lay people participate more actively in the mass. Some leaders permit Catholics to participate with Protestants in worship. Gerald Williams encourages Catholics to "join with Protestants for formal religious worship."[19] He explains: "You may act as a witness at a Protestant Church wedding provided the laws of God and the Catholic Church are not violated."[20]

The Second Vatican Council states:"Scripture has gained a new importance in Catholic worship liturgy: lessons from Scripture are in the language of the people, the Psalms, now in the vernacular, are from Scripture; many prayers and songs are scriptural. The homily delivered by the priest or deacon is scriptural. Scriptural study and analysis have gained new importance in the church."[21]

Implications

Catholics are receiving greater exposure to the Scriptures during the mass Catholics are now more likely to attend an Evangelical worship service and less likely to feel out of place.

Attitude

Evangelicals are now considered "separated brethren." The documents of the Second Vatican Council say: "The brethren divided from us also carry out many of the sacred actions of the Christian religion."[22] Catholics are urged to respect and admire the many virtues of Protestants. In his *Contemporary Catholic Catechism*, Williams says:

> "Protestants look to Christ as the source and center of Christian unity; they have love and devotion to sacred Scripture. Though we believe they have not retained the proper reality for the Eucharistic mystery in its fullness, especially because of the absence of the sacrament of orders, nevertheless when they commemorate his death and resurrection in the Lord's Supper, they profess that it signifies life in communion with Christ and look forward to His coming glory. Moreover, Catholics should respect the

Christian family life of Protestants, their sense of justice and true charity toward their neighbor. . .Catholics should unite in prayer and action for the common good of humanity."[23]

Implications

Catholics who obey the teachings of Vatican II are showing an increasing willingness to have fellowship with Evangelicals.

Lay participation

Lay people have been given greater participation in the ministry of the church. The *Contemporary Catholic Catechism* says: "The laymen's apostolate is derived from his Christian vocation and the Church can never be without it. Sacred Scripture clearly shows how spontaneous and fruitful such activity was at the very beginning of the Church. Our own times require of laity no less zeal. In fact, modern conditions demand that their apostolate be throughly broadened and intensified."[24]

Bible reading

Lay people are receiving a greater encouragement to read the Bible. "After the Second Vatican Council (1962-1965), the Catholic Church has placed new emphasis on the importance of Scripture in the Christian life of her members. Private reading of Scripture is urged more strongly than ever before."[25]

We can freely encourage Catholics to read the Bible. The climate is much more conducive for inviting Catholics to join Bible Study Fellowships. While the dogmas and structure of the church have not changed, the changes in worship, fellowship, lay participation, and reading of the Bible must be viewed as open doors for Evangelicals to share their faith with Catholics who have not come to a personal experience of salvation in Jesus Christ.

Conclusion

It is encouraging to learn that since Vatican II, many Catholics are seeking to fellowship with Evangelicals, are reading the Bible more, and are being encouraged to respect the doctrinal positions of Evangelical Christians. This is certainly sufficient reason for Evangelicals to be optimistic about the possibility of helping their Catholic friends to experience personal salvation in Christ. However, Evangelicals must be aware of the fact that there are still obstacles to overcome.[26]

Obstacles Catholics Face In Making a Decision

Persons who have grown up in an Evangelical home do not have the faintest idea of the immense obstacles which prevent Catholics from making a decision to receive Christ in a personal way and to identify with an evangelical congregation. These obstacles revolve around the things they have learned about their tradition, the concepts that they have regarding Evangelicals, and the process that they, in general, follow in trying to make a decision for Christ.

Concepts some Roman Catholics have regarding Evangelicals

When we try to share the message of salvation with Catholic persons it is important that we keep in mind that they already have certain preconceived ideas regarding Evangelicals. Part of this is due to the fact that some of them do not distinguish between Evangelicals and the cults and sects. Many have had the experience of being attacked, criticized and ridiculed by persons of certain sects, and they think that Evangelicals will do the same. Many people of different sects, like enthusiastic, but badly informed Evangelicals, have visited Catholic homes and have accused them of being idolaters, of worshiping images, and making a goddess of Mary. That is why some of them put a sign in their door that says: "This is a Catholic home and we do not accept Protestant propaganda." This is also the reason why some of them listen when Evangelicals visit them and even say that they want to receive Christ, but they do it only out of courtesy and eagerly wait for the moment when the Evangelicals will leave their homes.

In a conference presented by the Catholic priest, Juan Vargas, C.SS.R., he mentioned the following negative concepts that some Catholics have of Evangelicals:[27]

Evangelicals are against family unity

Many Catholics believe that Evangelicals who have been converted from Catholicism are against the family because they have made the decision to receive Christ and join an Evangelical church without considering the feelings of their families. Some families see this type of decision as abandoning "their parents' religion." There are times when a person has to make the decision to follow Christ even if his family is against it. Nevertheless, there are many instances in which Evangelicals pressure prospective believers to "make a personal decision to receive Christ and be baptized" without their having had the opportunity to communicate the message of salvation to their relatives. While it is acknowledged that a decision to receive Christ must be a personal one, it also needs to be pointed out that the unnecessary or premature severing of family ties often contributes to the negative concept that many Catholics have of Evangelicals.

Evangelicals accuse family members of being lost

It is not difficult to understand that, on many occasions new believers have a profound desire to see their relatives come to have a personal experience of salvation in Jesus Christ. At the same time, it is very likely that new believers will adopt the vocabulary of those who have been members of Evangelical churches and, therefore, state that members of their families "are lost." This makes many Catholics angry, thinking that their relatives are judging them, feel superior to them, and do not take into account their religious feelings.

Evangelicals ignore family celebrations and spend a lot of time in church

Because of the dramatic change that believers have experienced, they often do not want to have anything to do with their previous lifestyle. Knowing that the practices that they have abandoned still find expression in the family reunions, they opt to not attend, which gives the impression that they no longer appreciate or respect the celebrations of their family. A new believer in Mexico recounted that he did not attend his father's funeral because it was in a Catholic church. For many years his family did not speak to him. It was very difficult for them to forgive him because "he behaved in such a disrespectful way toward his own father and family." There are also cases in which new believers feel so much joy in having fellowship with their "new family" in the church that they often do not have the time or desire to visit their relatives even on special days. This leads some Catholics to believe that the church is more important for the new converts than their own families.

Evangelicals who want everyone to believe as they do, are aggressive and intolerant in witnessing to their relatives

Often, Catholics have the impression that Evangelicals want to force them to have the same religious experience that they have had. Catholics feel threatened by the attitudes of Evangelicals who give the impression that there is nothing good in the beliefs and in the practices of Catholics. Besides, in their profound desire for their relatives to come to know Christ in a personal way, Evangelicals often pressure them to make a quick decision.

Perhaps some of these impressions are due to the fact that the truth of the gospel makes some Catholics feel uncomfortable. There is also a sense in which, at times, some of these impressions are inevitable. The Bible says clearly that those who have not received Christ as their personal savior are *lost*. Nevertheless, Evangelicals should ask ourselves if some of the impressions that Catholics have of Evangelicals are not due to insensibility on the part of Evangelicals. We don't have to have a negative or aggressive approach in order to share the gospel. New believers should not be advised to sever all ties with their families. The truth is that the new believers should have a more profound love for their families now that they have known the love of Christ in a personal way.

Fears Catholics face in Making a decision

Fear of being rejected by family/friends

In the majority of the cases, the main obstacle that people find in considering the decision to receive Christ as personal savior, to follow Him in baptism and to identifying with an evangelical church is the fear that they are going to be criticized, rejected, and even persecuted by their families and friends. Although they sometimes are convinced that they should make a decision, especially concerning believer's baptism, they often postpone this for fear of the rejection that they will experience. It is very important that we keep in mind that for people who did not grow up in an evangelical home the decision to receive Christ has two dimensions: (1) the spiritual dimension and (2) the social dimension. This requires that we understand their situation, be patient, support them with our prayers, and offer them the fellowship of the church family.

Fear of abandoning traditional religion

There are several reasons why people fear abandoning the Catholic Church. First, for many centuries, the Catholic Church has taught that it is the only true church. The *Contemporary Catechism* affirms: "There is only one true church of Jesus Christ, the Catholic Church. Our Lord gave all the blessings of Christianity to the apostles and their successors, the bishops and priests of the Catholic Church, to be imparted to everyone in all ages."[28] For many centuries, the Catholic Church has taught that outside the Catholic Church there is no salvation. Even though Catholics are being encouraged to fellowship with Evangelicals, they are being reminded that "the Catholic Church is the ordinary means of salvation."[29]

Although many Catholics do not understand the teachings of their church and do not participate in its activities with regularity, there is, in the depths of their hearts, the fear of abandoning the church that they have known since childhood.

Second, many relatives of new believers stress the idea that the Catholic Church "is the religion of our parents." This often makes new believers feel guilty for abandoning the "true church" as well as "abandoning their family" when turn away from the religion that the family has always professed.

Third, some people have the fear of abandoning their devotions to the Virgin Mary and the saints whom they have had in such high esteme in the past. Some have asked: "What if the saint punishes me and causes me to experience a tragedy because I am no longer giving him or her my devotion?" Others also ask: "To whom am I going to turn to when I have problems and needs?"

Fear of losing their cultural identity

For many people, belonging to a cultural group means being Catholic. For a long time, for example, Catholic authors have alleged that the soul of the Latin American is Catholic.[30] Although it is true that many Latin Americans do not attend the Catholic Church, that there is great religious diversity, and that the number of Evangelicals is growing rapidly, it is also true that in many of the official, political, and social celebrations, the presence of the Catholic Church is very prominent. This makes some people ask themselves what social, professional, and political impact their decision to adhere to the evangelical church will have. A Catholic pastoral letter observes:

> For centuries, being Latin American was being Catholic. One would be born and would be baptized, one would live and would die surrounded by people who would make the sign of the cross. Now young people carrying Bibles can be seen crowded together in public buses (Latin American Catholics keep their Bibles in their homes); entire families go to what before were theaters and stores converted into churches across the city, not to celebrate Mass but for "the worship service"; families are divided around their religious differences; and to top it all off, a President has been elected

in Peru with the help of the Evangelicals. Many Catholics
cry out: "What are they doing with our culture?"[31]

Because of their fear of cultural ostracism, we must be patient as we
guide them to a saving experience with Jesus Christ. We must also be careful
to welcome them into our fellowship in order that they might experience a
sense of family in their discipleship group.

Spiritual Obstacles

There may be spiritual reasons for which Catholic persons do not want to
trust in Christ as their Lord and Savior. Like many others, it does not matter
what their religious affiliation is, they may have the spiritual blindness that
the Bible describes in Ephesians 2.

It is obvious that there are doctrinal, historical, and psychological barriers
which must be overcome if we are to lead our Catholic friends to a personal,
saving relationship with Christ. In many instances, it will take more than
quoting Scripture verses during our first witnessing encounter with Catholics.
It will take prayer, the cultivation of personal relationships, a clear presentation
of the gospel, and on-going Bible study.

Conclusion

As we seek to present the biblical concept of salvation to our Roman
Catholic friends, we should be mindful of the fact that some of them will have
serious doubts and misgivings due to the fact that at times their beliefs and
traditions will be challenged by the Scriptures. As we have seen in Chapter
One, many will got through a process in their pilgrimage toward a personal
faith in Christ. In this chapter, there is much that we can learn about the way
in which Jesus dealt with the Samaritan woman. A spirit of love and
understanding as we share the truth of the gospel will go a long way to
overcome social and traditional obstacles.

One final word about the power of prayer in our efforts to share the good
news of salvation. When I was a seminary student, I was called to start a
church in a town about seventy miles away. Our church planting team and I
were very encouraged by the positive response on the part of many people to
the gospel message. Within a few months we were able to start worship services.

One Saturday afternoon I visited the home of a lady I had never met
before. When I started to introduce myself as the pastor of the new Evangelical

church in town, she interrupted me and said in a terse sort of way: "I'm Catholic." I smiled and said, "I am very glad to meet you. I just want you to know that we are praying in our church for your two sons who are with our armed forces in Vietnam." She asked me: "You are praying for my sons in your church?" I told her that one of her neighbors has mentioned their names during our prayer meeting and that we had decided to pray for them on a continuing basis. She then said: "Please come in, I want to know more about your church." We had a very pleasant conversation for a while as I made an effort to answer her questions about what we taught and what we did at church. As I was getting ready to leave, I asked her if it was alright if I prayed for her sons. She agreed. I began by praying the Lord's Prayer and could hear her as she prayed with me. I then prayed for her two sons by name and asked the Lord to protect them and bring them back safely. I also prayed for this lady and asked God to be with her in a very special way because I knew that she was very worried about her sons. I then concluded the prayer "in the name of the Father, of the Son, and of the Holy Spirit." When I opened my eyes, I noticed that she had tears in her eyes. Then she said: "What a beautiful prayer. Would you please write it down so that I can send it to my sons in Vietnam?" I gladly agreed to do so, even though I had to make an effort to remember exactly what I had said in my spontaneous prayer. This prayer, however, overcame her barriers of fear and suspicion. She then became more open to attending our Bible studies and visiting our church services. Through prayer, we were able to minister to her at a very crucial time in her life. Praying *with* and *for* our Catholic friends can help establish bridges of friendship and Christian love.

ENDNOTES

1 Josephus Antiquities of the Jews 20.118; *life* 269.
2 *Antiquities* 13.9.1; *Wars* 1.2.6.
3 Merrill C. Tenney, The Gospel of John, TEBC (Grand Rapids: Zondervan, 1981), 54.
4 Leon Morris, The Gospel According to John, *TNICNT*(Grand Rapids: Wm. B. Eerdmans, 1971), n. 43, 264.
5 G.H.C. Macgregor, The Gospel of John, (New York: Harper & Row, 1928), 105.
6 Ibid., 106.
7 *Antiquities*, 18.4.1
8 Gerald Williams, Contemporary Catholic Catechism(Des Plains, IL: Fare, Inc., 1973), 96.
9 Ibid, 97.
10 Foy A. Felician, editor, 1992 Catholic Almanac, (Huntington: Our Sunday Visitor, Inc., 1992), 123.
11 Walter M. Abbott, *The Documents of Vatican II* , (New York: The American Press, 1966), XVIII.
12 Felician, Catholic Almanac, 123.
13 Felician, Catholic Almanac, 123.
14 Walter M. Abbott, The Documents of Vatican II, (New York: The American Press, 1966), 348
15 James G. McCarthy, The Gospel According to Rome, (Eugene: Harvest House Publishers, 1995), 319.
16 Richard P. McBrien, Catholicism (San Francisco: Harper & Row Publisher, 1981), 28.
17 Abbot, Documents of Vatican II, 91.
18 Abbot, Documents of Vatican II, 25.
19 Williams, The Contemporary Catholic Catechism, 100.
20 Ibid.
21 Ibid., 28.
22 Abbot, Documents of Vatican II, 25.
23 Williams, *The Contemporary Catholic Catechism*, 97-98.
24 Ibid., 129.
25 Private reading of Scripture is urged more strongly than ever before."
26 John Allen Moore, *Catholicism Today and Our Mission Task, Baptist Witness in Catholic Europe,* (Rome: Baptist Publishing House), 116-119.
27 Philip St. Romain, "Catholic Answers to Fundamentalism," presented by Father Juan Vargas, C.S.S.R., (Liquori, Missouri: Redemptionist Pastoral Communications, 1989).
28 Williams, The Contemporary Catholic Catechism, 92-93.
29 Ibid.
30 Pastoral letter from the bishops of Mexico, 1984, cited in Paul G. Schrotenboer, *Roman Catholicism* (Grand Rapids: Baker Book House, 1987), 39-40.
31 Andrés Tapia, 29.

CHAPTER FOUR

ANSWERING SINCERE QUESTIONS ABOUT SALVATION

Introduction: Janie's Enquiry

Some time ago, my wife and I were in the church where we were members and a lady came and sat next to us. We greeted her and told her we were glad to see her. She told us her name was Janie and that she had just moved to our city. Almost immediately I could tell that she was not accustomed to being in an Evangelical church. Janie was having difficulty finding the Scripture passage and knowing how to follow the songs in the hymn book. I pointed out to her how we follow the first line in each segment for the first stanza, etc. She was very appreciative. After the service I asked her if she was visiting us for the first time. "Yes," she said, "I'm Catholic and I hope I did not offend anyone by coming to your church." "Quite the contrary," I responded, "we are truly glad to have you visit with us." I asked her if she would give us her address so that we could visit her. Janie did so gladly. That afternoon when we arrived at her door, Janie was very pleased to see us and she called out to her mother: "Mom, I can't believe it. I visited this church this morning and they have come to visit me already."

When we sat in her living room, Janie said: " I really enjoyed attending your church. Tell me, what are the differences between Catholics and Protestants?" I smiled and said to her: "There are some very important differences between both groups, but would it be okay with you it if we begin to talk about the beliefs we have in common?" She answered: "Yes, I would be very interested in that." I asked her: "Do you believe in God, the creator of heaven and earth?" She answered: "Yes, of course, I learned that in catechism." I told her, "I do too." Then I asked her: "Do you believe in Jesus Christ, the Son of God, born of the Virgin Mary?" She answered me: "Yes, I do." I told her, "I do, too." Then I asked her: "Do you believe that Christ died on the cross for the sins of the world?." She replied: "Yes, I learned that before my confirmation." I told her: "I do, too." Then I asked her: "Do you know that Christ died to forgive you of all of your sins and that if you put your trust in him as your savior you can be sure that he will always be with you and that you will go to heaven with him when you die?" "That," she said, "is what I would like to know more about. I am doing everything I can to do what the Church teaches, but I am not very successful at it." I then proceeded to explain to her how she could invite Jesus into her life. Janie then told me that she

113

would like to have more time to think about this and that she would like for us to continue visiting her. Two weeks later when we arrived, Janie had a big smile on her face and shared with us that she had placed her trust in Jesus as her only savior and that she had the peace and assurance that we had spoken to her about. Janie said that she still had many questions and we assured her that we were going to deal with each one of them in on-going Bible study. She was very excited about being involved in a small Bible study group.

The point we need to make is that we began with the beliefs we had in common, instead of trying to address every doctrinal difference we might have. This kept us from getting distracted. Our purpose was to lead her to place her trust in Christ as her personal savior. Once Janie did this, she was more sensitive to the leading of the Holy Spirit and was truly hungry to know what the Bible taught about the beliefs that she had grown up with. Knowing how to answer sincere questions is a very important part of leading people to Christ, as we will see in the following Bible study.

BIBLE STUDY

How Jesus Dealt With Sincere Questions

Introduction

As we share our faith, there are going to be those who will not fully understand and who will have sincere questions. The reason we emphasize the term *sincere questions* is that we want to make a distinction between people who are genuinely interested in learning more about the Word of God and those who merely want to argue. The Bible teaches us to avoid pointless arguments. It says: "O Timothy, guard what has been entrusted to you, avoiding worldly and empty chatter and the opposing arguments of what is falsely called 'knowledge'— which some have professed and thus gone astray from the faith" 1 Tim. 6:20-21 (NASB). (See also 2 Tim. 2:23)

The Bible teaches us, however, that we must be prepared to answer sincere questions. It says: "But in your hearts set apart Christ as Lord. Always be prepared to give an answer to everyone who asks you to give the reason for the hope that you have. But do this with gentleness and respect" (1 Pet. 3:15-16,). In the Word of God, we find some examples of the way Jesus dealt with sincere questions of inquirers.

How Jesus answered the questions raised by Nicodemus

In the Bible study on Nicodemus, it was obvious that at first he did not fully understand what Jesus was saying. When Jesus mentioned the new birth, Nicodemus asked: "How can a man be born when he is old?" (John 3:4). Jesus responded that He was talking about a *spiritual* and not a *physical* birth. He said: "Flesh gives birth to flesh, but Spirit gives birth to spirit" (v. 6). Jesus helped Nicodemus understand by using the example of the wind: "The wind blows wherever it pleases. You hear its sound, but you cannot tell where it comes from or where it is going."The same thing is true of the *spiritual birth* (v. 8). Nicodemus evidently still did not understand Jesus because he asked: "How can this be?" (v. 9).

Jesus again used a familiar example: the serpent in the desert. Being a teacher of Israel, Nicodemus was well acquainted with the meaning of the incident. Numbers 21 describes how the Israelites spoke against God. The Lord responded by sending serpents that caused the deaths of many Israelites. When Moses plead for the people before God, the Lord instructed Moses to make a bronze serpent and put it up on a pole. Those who trusted God and looked upon the serpent in faith would be healed. Jesus then made the application: "Just as Moses lifted up the snake in the desert, so the Son of Man must be lifted up, that everyone who believes in him may have eternal life" (vv. 14-15).

Jesus took time to answer Nicodemus' questions. He also sought to relate His answer to something that Nicodemus already knew. This is extremely important. Educators tell us the most effective teaching is that which goes from the known to the unknown. In answering questions, it is not enough for us to quote verses of Scripture or the opinion of Bible scholars. We need to relate our answers to what people already know and take them from there to a clearer understanding of Scripture.

How Jesus answered the questions of the Samaritan woman

The Samaritan woman asked Jesus several questions.

(1) Her first question was, "You are a Jew and I am a Samaritan woman. How can you ask me for a drink?" (John 4:9) In other words, "Why are you talking to me?" Jesus answered in John 4:10, "If you knew the gift of God and who it is that asks you for a drink, you would have asked him and he would have given you living water."

(2) Noting that He did not have anything to draw water with, the woman asked, "Are you greater than our father Jacob?" Jesus did not get sidetracked into a discussion related to traditional beliefs. He did not try to put Jacob down or to point out that He was greater than Jacob. He did not spend time questioning the Samaritan woman's claim that Jacob was the father of the Samaritans. Instead, He continued to focus on the living water.

(3) The next question the Samaritan woman asked was, "Where should we worship?" (see v. 19). Again Jesus avoided an argument about the claims of the Samaritans regarding their mountain versus Jerusalem. Instead, He focused on the type of relationship people need to have with the Father—"true worshipers will worship the Father in spirit and truth" (vv. 23-24,). Jesus did not emphasize *religion* but *relationship*.

Application. We learn some valuable lessons about the way we can deal with sincere questions as we examine the way Jesus dealt with the questions put to Him by Nicodemus and the Samaritan woman.

First, Jesus began with what people knew and went from there to what they did not know. Jesus talked to Nicodemus about the serpent in the desert. He talked with the Samaritan woman about water.

Second, Jesus used illustrations from the common life of people. This was true when He spoke about the wind.

Third, Jesus was sincere in His responses. When the Samaritan woman asked, "Why are you talking to me?" (see v. 9), He responded by letting her know His desire was to give her living water.

Fourth, Jesus answered the questions in a way that prevented getting sidetracked or involved in irrelevant matters.

Fifth, Jesus told the truth in love. He did not hold back when He told Nicodemus, "you must be born again," or when He told the Samaritan woman "salvation comes from the Jews." Yet, He did it in a way to avoid ridiculing or putting them down. Instead, He inspired them to continue in their search for truth.

Finally, Jesus did not focus on *religion* but on *relationship*. "The Father is seeking for those who will worship in spirit and in truth" (John 4:23,). Let us keep these principles in mind as we answer the questions of those who are earnestly seeking to know the Lord.

LEARNING ACTIVITY

Activity : Answering Sincere Questions

Quickly read through the questions listed in the Practical Instruction section which follows and take note of any other questions that you might have encountered. Write these down. After studying the following section and learning the principles that are taught there, briefly write some appropriate answers that would address the concern, yet, get you back to the subject of the person's relationship with Jesus Christ.

PRACTICAL INSTRUCTION

The Bible Study for this session emphasizes that Jesus stayed focused on sharing the Good News. He dealt with questions but *was not distracted* from His *primary objective*. In this session, we will discuss some common questions that arise when we seek to lead people to a personal faith in Jesus Christ. Our purpose is not necessarily to give you pat answers that you can memorize and use when questions come up. This will not be an extensive treatment of each question. In the discipleship phase, we will deal with them in more depth. Nor will we attempt to deal here with every possible question that might emerge. Instead, we want to give you an idea of some of the questions that might come up and how you can address them in such a way as to *continue focusing* on the *most important issue*: a personal relationship with Jesus Christ.

I am doing the best I can, isn't that enough?

Reason for asking this question

Many Catholics believe that if they try to live good lives, not commit terrible sins (like murder), attend Mass when they can, and do deeds of kindness, their good deeds will outweigh their bad deeds and somehow they will make it into heaven.

Suggested response

You know, what you are saying is very interesting, but did you know that the Catholic Church does not teach that? It teaches that you have to attend Mass regularly, receive five of the seven sacraments, pay for your sins even after you have confessed them, and if you have not committed a mortal sin, then you may go to purgatory to be purified before entering heaven. On the other hand the Bible teaches that if you repent of your sins, place your trust in Jesus as your personal savior, and allow him to empower you to live a truly Christian life, you will go to heaven to be with him when you die. What would you rather trust, your notions about how to make it to heaven or the promise of Jesus himself? (See Lesson E for more information)

What if I offend my family and friends?

Reason for asking this question

Some Catholics may be genuinely interested in exploring the possibility of receiving Christ as their personal savior and following Him in Christian discipleship, but may be sincerely concerned that this might offend their family and friends. For some, it would be tantamount to repudiating what their family and friends hold very dear.

Suggested response

I know that you love your family, but did you know that becoming a follower of Jesus Christ will help you to love your family and friends even more? The love of Jesus will engender more love in your heart for others. This love will motivate you to model the love of Jesus in your life and to share it with your loved ones so that they too can experience the blessing of receiving Christ. If your family had an incurable disease and you found a cure, wouldn't you want to share it with them? When the jailer in the city of Philippi asked Paul and Silas what he should do, they answered: "Believe on the Lord Jesus Christ and you shall be saved, you and your family" (Acts 16:31). It is important for you to follow Jesus and to trust Him to help you to share this blessing with your family.

Which is the true Church?

Reason for asking this question

Many Catholics believe that salvation is found in and through the Roman Catholic Church.[1] Their principle concern is not academic but existential. They want to find out, "Who or what can I trust for my eternal destiny?"

Suggested response

There are many views about the "true church." All of us agree that the original church was built on the doctrines which Jesus communicated to His apostles (Matt. 28:19-20). The Bible states that the early church "continued daily in the apostle's doctrine" (Acts 2:42). The true church is the one which has continued following the teachings of the apostles concerning Jesus Christ. I would like to invite you to participate in a Bible study with me to find out what the apostles taught (e.g., the Gospel of John, the letter of Saint Paul to the Romans) about salvation and the church.

The Bible says the church is the body of Christ (see Eph. 5:29-30). It is made up of people who believe in Jesus Christ as their Savior and Lord (see Acts 2:41). The ultimate question is not which is the true church, but *are we a part of the true church, the body of Christ?* The Word of God tells us we can be part of the body of Christ by accepting Him as our personal Savior (see John 1:12).[2] (See Lesson L for more information).

Which is our ultimate authority, the Bible or tradition?

Reason for asking this question

Most Catholics believe the Bible and the Traditions of the Catholic Church are of equal importance. The *Documents of Vatican II*, for instance, say: "Sacred tradition and sacred Scripture form one sacred deposit of the Word of God, which is committed to the Church."[3] A verse often cited is: "Therefore, brothers, stand firm. Hold fast to the traditions (teachings)[4] you received from us, either by word or letter"[5] (2 Thessalonians. 2:15). The underlying question is, "On what can we put our trust—the Bible or the Bible and tradition?"

Suggested response

Take into account that the New Testament Scriptures were still being written when the apostle Paul wrote to the Thessalonian church. He wanted to emphasize to the new Christians there that they should continue to be true to what they had been taught *personally* and through *letters*. They were taught what the apostles had received from Christ (see Acts 2:42; 1 Cor. 11:23). These teachings, under the guidance of the Holy Spirit, were put into writing and added to the Old Testament. That which the Holy Spirit inspired the authors of the New Testament to write should be seen as normative. In other words, what was written should not be contradicted by that which was not. Jesus did not present one way of salvation in writing and another passed on by word of mouth.[6] The Word of God says that the Holy Scriptures can make us wise unto salvation (see 2 Tim. 3:15). Verses 16 and 17 say: "All Scripture is God-breathed and is useful for teaching, rebuking, correcting and training in righteousness, so that the man of God may be thoroughly equipped for every good work." We have in the written Scriptures all we need to find salvation in Jesus Christ. Have you found this salvation spoken of in the Scriptures? (See Lesson A for more information).

Isn't the Pope Peter's successor?

Reason for asking this question

Many Catholics ask this to address a more immediate question, "Why shouldn't I trust the hierarchy (structure) of the Catholic Church, with the Pope at its head?"

Suggested response

It is counterproductive at this point to have an extensive debate as to whether Peter was the first Pope or not. It is more helpful to address the question of trust. One way to do this is to say something like this: "Many Catholics believe that when Jesus used the expression "on this rock I will build my church" (Matt. 16:18,), He was referring to Peter.

The reason that Evangelicals believe that the phrase "upon this rock" refers to the confession that Peter made about Christ is that the question to which Peter responded was "Whom do people say that I [Christ] am?" not "Whom do people say that you [Peter] are?" The question, therefore, is "Who is Christ?" "not Who is Peter?" Peter responded: "You are the Christ, the Son of the living God." (Matt. 16:16). It is upon this confession that Jesus builds His church not upon a man whom Jesus rebuked shortly afterwards (see Matthew 16:23) and who denied knowing Jesus just before His death (see Matthew 26:69-75). In other words, the church is built on Jesus Himself. He said: "I will build *my* church." The Bible states very clearly "No one can lay a foundation other than the one that has been laid, namely Jesus Christ" (1 Corinthians 3:11). Jerome in the 4th century and Augustine in the 5th century stated clearly that the Church was founded on Peter's confession (you are the Christ) and not on Peter himself.[7]

The symbolism of the Rock as representing Christ goes all the way back to the Old Testament. For example, Paul's statement, "They all drank of the spiritual Rock that followed them: and that Rock was Christ" (1 Cor. 10:4), points to the incident recorded in Exodus 17. The smitten rock out of which water flowed represented the smitten Christ (see Isaiah 53:4). He is spoken of as the "Rock of my salvation" (see Psalm 19:14, 2 Samuel 22:47; Isaiah 48:21). The New Testament points back to the Old Testament and affirms that Jesus is the Rock of salvation. The church is built upon Jesus Christ who is the Rock.

Look at what the apostle Peter *himself* said. First Peter 2:4-6 says: "Come to him, the living Stone— rejected by men but chosen by God and precious to him—you also, like living stones, are being built into a spiritual house to be a holy priesthood, offering spiritual sacrifices acceptable to God through Jesus Christ. For in Scripture, it says: 'See, I am laying a stone in Zion, a chosen and precious cornerstone, and the one who trusts in him will never be put to shame."[8] Peter says here that Jesus is the *cornerstone* and whoever trusts in Him will not be shaken..The important thing is to put our *trust* in Jesus Christ. Have you come to the place where you have put your trust in Jesus by accepting Him as your personal Savior? (See Appendices H for more information).

What do you think of the Virgin Mary?

Reason for asking this questions

Many Catholics have the impression that Protestants consider Mary *just another* woman. One of the reasons for this is that some Protestants who are careful not to *worship* Mary also fail to give her the place of honor she occupies in *Scripture*. Mary occupies a very special place in the hearts of many Catholics. Part of this is due to their having been taught that Mary is a co-mediatrix (mediates along with Christ).[9] For other Catholics, devotion to Mary has deep *cultural*, as well as *religious* roots. Saying anything disrespectful about Mary is worse than saying something against their own mother. There are several appropriate responses: (1) never *argue* about Mary; (2) never *misrepresent* Scripture—Mary occupies a special place in Scripture; (3) never try to prove she had *other children*. There will be time to deal with this issue. Once they have come to a personal, warm, loving relationship with Jesus, people will be able to put this and other things into a biblical perspective. *Many witnessing efforts have been completely destroyed by witnesses who think it is more important to win an argument than to win the prospect.*

Suggested response

Assure your Catholic friends that you hold Mary in *very high regard*. She had to have been a very special person to be chosen by God to give birth to His Son, Jesus Christ. The Bible says: "The Lord is with you" and "you have found favor with God" (Luke 1:28-30). The Bible also says: "Blessed are you among women, and blessed is the child you will bear!" (Luke 1:42). Furthermore, Mary provides an example of true *Christian discipleship* in her conduct, her obedience, and her faith. It is very important to let your Catholic friends know that you hold Mary in high regard as God's chosen vessel. It is also important to let them know that you follow Mary's *advice*. At the wedding of Cana in Galilee, Mary said to the servants who were concerned that the wine had run out: "Do whatever he tells you" (John 2:5,). And what does Jesus tell us? "I am the way and the truth and the life. No one comes to the Father except through me" (John 14:6,). "Come to me, all you who are weary and burdened, and I will give you rest" (Matt. 11:28).[10] By focusing on John 2:5, John 14:6, and Matthew 11:28, you can avoid an unproductive discussion about Mary and concentrate on Jesus' teachings about *salvation*. (See Appendices B for more information).

What about my religious affiliation?

Reason for asking the question

An impression that some Roman Catholic's have is that we merely want them to join our church. It is important to assure your Catholic friends that you want them to experience salvation in Jesus Christ personally and to continue to grow to be more like Jesus every day.

Suggested response

It is important to stress that your concern is not the persons's *religion* but his or her *relationship* to Jesus Christ. This relationship starts when we receive Christ as our personal savior. It continues as we study the Word of God, have fellowship with other believers, worship together, pray for one another, become involved in ministry to others and share the good news of salvation with others just like we read that the first Christian church did in Jerusalem (Acts 2:40-47). After you invite Christ into your life, you can pray that he will guide you to find this type of Christian group and to become a part of it in order that you might continue to grow spiritually

Are you using a Protestant Bible?

Reason for the question

Some Catholics have the idea that the "Protestant Bible" is very different from theirs. They know they can trust their own Bible but are not sure about other versions.

Suggested response

There are some books in the Roman Catholic Bible that we as Evangelicals do not accept as inspired. In a witnessing situation, however, it is not necessary to enter a lengthy discussion of these books for two reasons:

1. These books are seldom used by the Catholics themselves.

2. These books are not in the New Testament, therefore, we can make a full presentation of the plan of salvation without having to refer to them.

We have several options if there is apprehension about using a "Protestant Bible."

1. We can use a Roman Catholic Bible. The *New American Bible, Saint Joseph Edition* is a modern translation comparable to the *New American Standard Bible*. Some words are different, but the meaning of the passages you use in witnessing is the same.

2. The second option is to use the *Good News New Testament*[11] with the *imprimatur* (seal of approval) of Roman Catholic officials. If questions are raised, point to the imprimatur usually found on the first or second page. Assure your Catholic friend that this version has been approved by the officials of the Catholic Church.

Can a person be saved just by receiving Christ as savior?

Reason for asking the question

Many Catholics believe it is over simplistic to affirm that salvation can be obtained only by believing in Christ. Aside from this, they have been taught that works are needed for salvation.

The Council of Trent stated categorically: "If anyone shall say that justification is nothing else but confidence (fiducia) in divine mercy which remits sins for Christ's sake, or that it is this confidence alone which justifies us - let him be anathema."[12]

Suggested Response

The Bible speaks very clearly about salvation which is received by grace and not obtained by works. Paul states that salvation is "not of works of righteousness which we have done, but according to his mercy he saved us" (Titus 3:5; Acts 5:11; 2 Tim 1:9; Romans 3:24; Eph. 1:7). When people asked "What must I do to be saved?", the answer that was given by the Apostles was: "Believe on the Lord Jesus Christ and you will be saved" (Acts 16:31). (See Lesson E for more information)

Why shouldn't we venerate the saints and holy images?

Reason for asking the question

Many Catholics have devotions to saints and images. We have already stated that informed Catholics make a distinction between veneration and adoration. They also seek to differentiate between "images" (the representations) and "idols" (the objects of worship). Some Roman Catholic writers (e.g., Nevins) explain that "Catholics pray before these images, but are not praying to the image but to what the image represents."[13] The truth of the matter is that many Catholics do make the saints and images the object of their prayers.

Suggested response

The Bible makes it very clear that God commands people to not bow before images (Exodus 20:4; Acts 15:20; 1 John 5:21; 1 Cor. 10:7).

Some Catholics state that God commanded Moses to make a bronze serpent and that this was an indication that He is generally in favor of using images as aids for worship. Those who make this statement fail to see that God did not command the people to bow before the bronze serpent nor to pray to it. Quite the contrary, they were merely to look at it as an indication that they were submitting themselves once again to the authority of God and accept His healing by placing their faith in Him. The Bible states that king Hezekiah "pleased the Lord" when he destroyed the bronze serpent because it had become an object of worship when the people of Israel "were burning incense to it" (2 Kings 18:4).

Conclusion

This study has helped you to deal with some of the most frequently asked questions in a witnessing situation. The doctrinal points in these questions are very important. Our goal has not been to down play their importance. We have suggested a way to prevent getting distracted from the main objective: *to lead persons to a saving knowledge of Jesus Christ.* New believer's are more sensitive to the leading of the Holy Spirit and will be in a better position to understand what the Scriptures say about these and other doctrines. It is not necessary to straighten out people at every point *doctrinally* before they *accept* Jesus Christ. Remember the response of the apostle Paul to the question raised by the Philippian jailer: "What must I do to be saved?" It was: "Believe in the Lord Jesus, and you will be saved . . . (Acts 16:31). Therefore, acknowledge the questions which are raised and find a way to guide the discussion back to the all important question: "What must I do to be saved?"

ENDNOTES

1. See Abbott, *The Documents of Vatican II*, (New York: Guild Press, 1966), 15, 32-33.
2. To explore this question further see Ralph Michaels, *Share the New Life With A Catholic* (Chicago: Moody, 1975).
3. Abbott, *Documents of Vatican II*, 117.
4. Some versions, e.g., NIV use the word "teachings."
5. *The New American Bible*, Saint Joseph Edition, (New York: Catholic Publishing Co., 1970).
6. Michales, *Share the New Life With A Catholic*, 20.
7. Bartholomew F. Brewer, *The Primacy of Peter*, audiotape, *Mission to Catholics*, P. O. Box, 19280, San Diego, CA: 92119.
8. Quoted from *The New American Bible*, Saint Joseph Edition, (New York: Catholic Publishing Co., 1970).
9. Abbot, *Documents of Vatican II*, 91-92.
10. For an excellent discussion of this see Dr. Jose Borrás' *"Lo Que Creen Los Evangélicos Sobre Maria,"* (What Evangelicals Believe About Mary) audio taped presentation, *Abundant Life Crusades*, 4910 Branscomb, Corpus Christi, Texas, 78411.
11. *The Good News New Testament* is printed by the American Bible Society.
12. See Schrotenboer, *Roman Catholicism*, 63.
13. Albert J Nevins, *Answering A Fundamentalist* (Huntington: Our Sunday Visitor, 1990), 105.

PART THREE

DISCIPLING NEW BELIEVERS

CHAPTER FIVE

ENCOURAGING THE NEW BELIEVER'S PILGRIMAGE

Introduction: Pablo's Pilgrimage

When my wife and I were serving as missionaries in Central America, Pablo, a young man whom I had never met before, came to visit me in my office. He said: "Father, a friend asked me to talk with you because I am in desperate need of help. My mother died giving birth to me. The first words I remember my father saying to me were: 'You killed your mother, I hate you.' I grew up with a horrible sense of guilt for killing my mother whom I had never seen. As a youngster I was sent to a Catholic orphanage. Despite the fact that we all got religious instruction and the nuns were good to us, I was not happy there either. I had too much anger and guilt that I didn't know how to get rid of. As soon as I was able to, I ran away and started living on my own. I have committed every imaginable sin. Do you think that God could ever forgive me?" I said to him: "Pablo, the Bible says that the blood of Jesus Christ cleanses us from all sin." He answered, "But you don't know how many sins I have committed." I said: "I don't, but Jesus does and he promises that if you pray and confess your sins to him he will forgive you." He said: "But I don't know how to pray." I told him "Just tell Jesus that you are sorry for your sins and invite Him into your heart." As Pablo prayed, he sobbed and his body shook as he was asking God for forgiveness and invited Jesus to come into his life. I then prayed for Pablo, thanking God for having forgiven him and for having saved him. When we got up from our knees, there was a radiant smile on his face, which was still bathed in tears. He exclaimed: "I don't know what happened, but I feel like a new person."

Knowing that this was a brand new experience for Pablo and that he still had a lot to learn, I invited him to join our new believer's class. From the very beginning, Pablo had many questions. He would say: "what you are saying is probably true, but that's not what I have learned in the Catholic Church." I would then reply: "Well, let's look at the Bible and see what it says and pray that the Holy Spirit will guide us." Each time he would agree to search the Scriptures. At times, I would even give him "home work" so that he would spend more time studying the assigned passages of Scripture. There were times when he would say: "I find this so difficult to understand. It is not what I grew up believing." I sought to provide Scripture portions from Scripture for him to study and pray over. After several months, Pablo shared with group that he had never had any doubts about his conversion to Christ. His life had changed miraculously that day he invited Christ into his life. He added that he went through a period, however, in which he had to sort out what he was studying in the Bible in light of his traditional beliefs. As he continued to grow in his faith in Christ, Pablo went on to be an outstanding national youth leader and assisted in starting a church in a poverty stricken neighborhood. The fact that he had a miraculous conversion experience did not mean that he understood every biblical doctrine over night. It took a long time for him to find answers to his questions and to proceed toward a firm commitment to discipleship.

BIBLE STUDY

Saul of Tarsus: A Case Study in Nurturing New Believers

Introduction

Paul's influence on the development of Early Christianity is hard to overstate. His place in the annals of early church formation reinforces the tremendous *tour de force* of his person and accomplishments.[1] His life and work stand as a testament to what God can do with a person who is solidly grounded in Christ.[2] There is plenty in the life of this apostle to inspire us all. We are left breathless when we read the biblical account of his dramatic conversion and his far-reaching ministry.[3] His body of work compels us to look into his life in an effort to find the answer that explains the man. What was the quality of his spiritual formation that prepared him to do the seemingly impossible? While we seldom give much attention to his pre-conversion background, not to mention what happened in his life between conversion and ministry, it is probably during these times that God equipped him to do this great work. Let's examine some of the details surrounding the pilgrimage of this remarkable servant of God with a view to equipping believers to disciple new converts.

Paul Was a Very Devout Person

Paul's Ethnic Background

Paul (originally Saul)[4] referred to himself as a "Hebrew of Hebrews" (Phil 3:5; cf., 2 Cor 11:22). As F.F. Bruce shows, not only were both of his parents Jewish, it is likely that though he was born in Tarsus in Cilicia, he was reared with a strict Jewish upbringing, where Aramaic was the language spoken in his home.[5] Paul could trace his roots to and through the tribe of Benjamin, which was practically incorporated into the southern tribe of Judah after the fall of the Northern tribes to the Syrians in 722 BC. This alone says something about the superciliousness of his family pedigree. To be able to show a continual line of succession within the Benjamin line suggests he came from a family that took its genealogical purity seriously. Paul emphasizes the point that his "Jewishness" was untainted by foreign bloodlines.

Application: The impeccability of Paul's ethnic background is important. He cannot be accused of being a Hellenist Jew or a Jew with Hellenistic leanings. Israel would have to wrestle not only with the fact of the Gospel, but also with the fact that one of its best and brightest native sons had articulated it!

Paul's Religious Training

Paul also mentions he was a Pharisee who had been trained by Gamaliel, one of the leading Jewish scholars of his day in Jerusalem (Phil 3:5; cf., Acts 22:3). There, Paul had learned the Rabbinical approach to interpreting the Law. This is an indispensable aspect of his pre-conversion training. It is Paul whom God chose to show how the *Law* and *Grace* dichotomy is reconciled "in Christ," thus making salvation through faith in Jesus possible.

Application: Interestingly, Paul confessed that as a Pharisee his observance of the law had been "blameless" (Phil 3:6). Later, he would come to understand that it was the law, good and pure as it was, which kept all people condemned because it was impossible to ever keep fully (Gal 3:10-13, 21-22; Rom 4:15; 5:20).[6]

Paul's Zealous Dedication

In addition to having the qualifications mentioned above, Paul was zealous for his tradition. We get a sense of his zeal by his agreeing to the stoning death of Stephen (Acts 8:1). Luke, however, shows that Paul's zealotry was not quenched by the death of one follower of Jesus. Paul gave ample expression to his fervor, giving himself wholeheartedly to the task of routing followers of "the Way" from Israel and surrounding lands (Acts 8:3; 9:1-2).

Application: When Paul came to faith in Christ his zeal was employed in the service of spreading the gospel to Jews and Gentiles alike. There is an important lesson here. Many people come to faith in Jesus from a life of ungodly and unhealthy excesses. When a person is saved God can use their natural zeal and fervor if it is for promoting things that glorify Him (1 Cor 15:10).

Paul Had an Encounter With Jesus

Stephen as a Contributing Factor?

The question of Stephen's influence on Paul has been asked. Is the stoning of the first Christian martyr something Paul soon forgot as he continued to persecute the church? Luke's brief summary of Paul's continuing action suggests many followers of Jesus suffered as a result of his activity (Acts 22:5, 19; I Cor 15:9). Ananias knew of Paul's reputation and had no interest in making his acquaintance (Acts 9:13-14). Luke also points out that apart from Paul's program, Herod also killed James and, seeing the favorable reaction by the crowds intended to give Peter the same fate (Acts 12:1-5). There is every reason to believe that increasing numbers of believers were paying with their lives for trusting in Christ.

Still, Stephen was probably Paul's first introduction to followers of Jesus, and what an introduction it was. He probably heard Stephen's message recorded in Acts 7:1-53, incidentally, the longest speech recorded in Acts! When we compare Stephen's implication that necessary ties to the land of Israel and its temple were superfluous to faith in Jesus (see vv.44-50), Paul's principle of outreach to the Gentiles is amazingly logical and consistent. Paul does not mimic Stephen. Instead, Paul brings to full expression the implication of Stephen's speech for missiology, the very thing God would commission him to accomplish (Acts 9:15). Thus, one commentator concludes, "We might say, then, that Stephen was the precursor of the apostle to the Gentiles."[7] Surely, the way that Stephen died praying for those who were putting him to death undoubtedly shook the young Pharisee (Acts 22:20). However, Stephen's contribution to Paul's missionary and evangelistic formation must not be overlooked either.

Application: It is impossible to measure the magnitude of the impact for good or bad that a Christian mentor can have on a young convert. It behooves mature Christians, to make sure that our investment in people's lives is of quality as well as quantity. This means that we ourselves are walking in fellowship with the Lord to ensure our integrity and a wholesome and lasting impact for the Kingdom in the new convert.

The "Conversion" of Paul

Paul's "Damascus Road" experience (Acts 9:3-9) was truly the defining moment of his life. Previously, he had been a zealous persecutor of the church. From that moment on, he sought to glorify Christ. How did this event change Paul? As it turns out there is some disagreement as to the nature of Paul's experience. For some scholars, Paul's experience is not unlike that of the prophets in the Old Testament. The many points of resemblance between the apostle's experience and that of the prophets suggest he underwent not so much a "conversion" but rather a "commissioning" experience.[8] Paul did not "convert" according to the typical western pattern of rejecting one faith while accepting another. Such scholars insist that he was essentially given a new missionary orientation. Other scholars insist that the total reorientation of his faith from one based on works righteousness to one of trust in the finished work of Christ is nothing short of a radical conversion.[9]

Both positions make a strong argument and make it plain that the truth lies somewhere in the middle. We should acknowledge that Paul was not simply converted to Christianity and away from Judaism. Rather, it's as if Paul came to understand that the Judaism of his day was the end product of a deliberate decision on Israel's part to veer away from simple faith (Rom 10:1-3; cf., 2 Tim 3:5). Paul was able to see where Judaism had gone wrong and he sought to bring Israel back in line by imploring Jews to recognize Jesus as their Messiah. His conversion was not a total rejection of Judaism and an embrace of Christianity. No, the gospel Paul preaches recovers legitimate Judaism, exhibited in the faith of the patriarchs, specifically Abraham (Rom 4; Gal 3:6-20). Paul saw faith in Jesus as a faith that was in continuity with the faith espoused in the Hebrew Scriptures (Rom 9:3-6). While there is no doubt his encounter with Jesus shattered his previous convictions, the event did not leave him a "shattered man," looking introspectively into the failure of his past life. Quite the contrary, while his pre-conversion work had focused on the provincial needs of Israel, he now had a global mission and a life long purpose. He came to understand the missionary element that God had always desired from His people (Rom 10:1-15).

Application: Christianity is often presented as a faith that is so unique that its roots in the Old Testament are rarely understood. There is a need, however, to show that Christianity is the fulfillment of the Old Testament. God's salvation history runs as a seamless cut of cloth through both canons. Not only Catholics, but also all Evangelicals need to understand that God did not start something totally new with Christianity because His initiative through Israel failed at its inception. Paul came to understand that all people of faith, from the patriarchs forward, had their eye of faith fixed on Jesus, the Messiah of Jew and Gentile alike (Rom 10:12; Heb 11:1-12:3). Setting the gospel in the context of "Salvation History" may help the new convert see the temporality of the Roman Catholic Church rather than seeing it as the only "Arch" for salvation.

Paul Began His Discipleship

His Earliest Instruction by Ananias

Jesus confronted Paul personally and made provision for his immediate instruction in the faith: "Now get up and go into the city, and you will be told what you must do" (Acts 9:6). Acts 9:10-18 gives an account of a believer in Damascus named Ananias. Though he had every reason to be hesitant at the thought of approaching this persecutor of believers, Ananias had a greater reverence and holy fear of God. Ananias had been chosen to open the door of Christian fellowship to this newest convert. The account of Ananias' outreach to Paul reveals how God used him to make some indispensable elements available to Paul at the start of his new life.

First, Ananias was instrumental in helping Paul be incorporated into the Christian body (Acts 9:17-19). He ministered to Paul's emotional needs by embracing him and calling him "Brother Saul." He also ministered to Paul's physical needs when he said "the Lord has sent me that you may receive your sight" and when he fed him. Ananias also ministered to Paul's spiritual needs by laying hands on him and baptizing him. This was a necessary work that gave Paul the opportunity to be restored to health, to be encouraged, and to formally identify himself with Jesus and his followers.

Ananias then introduced him to the family of faith in Damascus and made available the ordinary but necessary fellowship for his initial growth (9:19). Significantly, according to Luke, while Paul was directed by Christ to enter Damascus and wait for further direction (9:6), the first indication of Paul's ministry was actually given to Ananias (9:15-16). Paul always claimed that his commission came by direct revelation with no human mediation (Gal 1:12). It is likely that Ananias, while he knew something of the role Paul had been chosen to play, kept the knowledge to himself, knowing that God would reveal the same to his chosen instrument.

Paul never forgot the service that Ananias rendered to him. Years later, standing before a crowd in Jerusalem, the apostle to the gentiles recounted the service Ananias gave to him (Acts 22:12-16). While Paul undoubtedly met and worked alongside many powerful and dedicated believers across the years of his ministry, Ananias is the only person that Paul mentions when speaking of his first days as a follower of Jesus. Undoubtedly, the Bible only begins to hint at the profound influence of this godly man.

Application: How often is it the case that Christian mentors are the people God uses to bring clarity to the direction God may be leading a young convert.

Paul Spent Time Soul Searching

From the brief account in Acts 9, some may get the impression that Paul began preaching immediately after his visit with Ananias. Acts 9:20-22 goes on to describe Paul's preaching ministry in the synagogues of Damascus, wherein he asserted that Jesus was the Son of God. What is clear from this account is that the initial encounter with the risen Lord provided Paul with a basic understanding of the new life in Christ. Like a newborn horse that begins to stand on its legs almost immediately, there were instinctive aspects of the gospel that Paul could begin to communicate almost immediately upon conversion. Paul did not need extensive theological training to confess (witness to) what he now believed about Jesus as God's Son and to share what God had done in his life. But, this is not all there was to his training, not by far.

Many biblical scholars actually believe that there is a gap in Luke's account of Paul's initial years as a believer.[10] By their reckoning, Paul's visit to Arabia and then return to Damascus (Gal 1:17) fits chronologically between Acts 9: 19 and 20. While Luke records that Paul began to proclaim the Lord Jesus, he omits that it actually began to happen some three years later. Thus, Paul's sojourn in Arabia should be "inserted" in between the events of verses 19 and 20. Such a reconstruction is plausible. Remember that Acts does not give us an exhaustive history of Paul's life. For example, many of the apostle's "trials and tribulations" mentioned in second Corinthians (11:23-33) cannot be fitted into his life as given in Acts.

It is interesting to speculate about what Paul did during his three years in Arabia. Most scholars believe that he may have copied the earlier examples of Moses and Elijah in seeking the face of God, perhaps near Mount Horeb (Exodus 3:1-3; 1 Kings 19:8-18). F.F. Bruce notes, "It took time for him to think through all that was involved in this reorganization." [11] Paul never states clearly that he spent time praying, meditating, or studying the Scriptures to come to grips with the gospel in light of his previous convictions. However, knowing what we know about the total consecration of Paul to the gospel, we can be sure that his time in Arabia was used by God to further prepare him for his mission to the world.[12]

Application: Paul's necessary sojourn in Arabia tells us that here is no substitute for time spent alone with God. As enjoyable as it is to spend time with fellow believers in fellowship and corporate worship (Psalm 84:1-4; 122; 133) there is a kind of spiritual work that can only happen when the person seeks solitude to commune with the Lord (Matt 26:36-46). Our fast-paced lifestyle does not promote seeming idleness. There are no convenient rest stops provided for along the busy highway of our life to stop and make time to pray and to reflect and to meet with God. But, if there is anything that will do more to build a strong foundation in the new believer, it is this practice. Thus, just as Jesus' disciples learned the value and power of prayer by seeing the Master (Luke 11), so must we lead new converts by example. Remember that praying is a big part of Roman Catholic piety, but often it is rote and repetitious. New believers need to see that prayer can be vital and expressive.

Lessons on Discipleship From Paul

A. A person can be very *religious* and yet be very *wrong*. Paul had the finest of Jewish pedigrees and theological credentials, yet he was fighting against Jesus.

B. It often *takes time* for the seed of the Word of God to germinate. We can be sure that Stephen's testimony as a righteous follower of Jesus left a powerful impression on Paul. Both his words and the way in which he died left the seed of the gospel in his life.

C. The fact that a person has had a personal experience with Jesus does not mean that he or she *understands* all of the Christian doctrines *immediately*. Despite the dramatic conversion of Paul, he had to spend time thinking about the implications of that miraculous encounter with the Lord. Think of the shock he received! What about those interpretations he had learned about the Messiah? What about the religious tradition he had inherited from his devout parents? What would be the reaction of his close friends and colleagues when they heard Paul had become a follower of that despised Nazarene? It is extremely important for Evangelical Christians to realize the pilgrimage to saving faith for people from other traditions *can be challenging in many ways*. We must allow time for new Christians to sort things out until they come to understand all of the implications of discipleship.

D. The human touch is ***indispensable*** in the discipleship process. The ministry of Ananias and was crucial in Paul's first steps as a new follower of Jesus. It must have been refreshing for Paul to hear Ananias' words as he laid hands on him, "Brother Paul, the Lord—Jesus . . . has sent me " (Acts 9:17). Time we spend leading people in Bible study and discipling them is time which has vital implications for this life and for eternity. May God help us to be this type of discipler.

Conclusion

Concerning the apostle Paul's Damascus Road experience, F.F. Bruce says, "No single event, apart from the Christ-event itself, has proved so determinant for the course of Christian history as the conversion and commissioning of Paul."[13] It is certainly amazing to stop and see just how God reached down to touch Paul with His grace and give him new life in Christ. As marvelous as Paul's experience must have been, however, we should never underestimate the power inherent in our own experience with the risen Lord. The salvation of every person is a miraculous event, and one filled with great promise. Only God knows what can be accomplished for the sake of His kingdom when new believers, or not so new ones, begin to live out the full implications of the life of Christ in them. Paul's experience should not be seen as something so utterly remote that we find no point of contact for our own experience. The apostle's life is an encouragement and assurance that God continues to call and to equip His servants to be a blessing in the world today.

LEARNING ACTIVITIES

Activity 1: Evaluate Your Own Discipleship

Divide the group into twos. Ask each person to take five minutes to share with the other person his or her experience in discipleship as a new Christian. Who discipled them? What were the strong points of the discipleship effort? What were the weak points?

Activity 2: Design Discipleship Strategies

Ask each person to take five minutes to share with the other person what he or she would do in discipling a new believer with a Roman Catholic background. What are some topics (issues, doctrines) that they would discuss?

What are some things about an Evangelical church that they would want to explain? What efforts would they make to fellowship with these new converts?

Conclusion of Learning Activities:

Reconvene the group and ask for volunteers to share some insights from the small groups. List these insights and suggestions on a chalkboard. Ask the group to take notes for future use in discipling new converts.

PRACTICAL INSTRUCTION

The material in this section can be used in two ways:

1. To continue to cultivate those who have not made a decision to receive Christ.

2. To help those who have received Christ to grow in understanding their salvation.

Bible Study Methods

There are several approaches to Bible study that can be helpful in accomplishing these objectives:

Chapter by chapter

This is a study of selected Bible books (chapter by chapter). Study, in this order, the Gospel of John; the Letter to the Romans; the Letter to the Galatians; the Epistle to the Hebrews. This approach can be very helpful to people who have a limited knowledge of the Bible. This study can help them to gradually understand more about the Word of God. As they study, they can also learn more about the biblical teaching regarding salvation.

In the chapter by chapter method, the following outline may be helpful:

a. Who are the key people in this chapter?
b. What does the chapter teach about Christ?
c. What does it teach about salvation?
d. Is there something in this chapter that speaks to my life today?

Transformed lives

This is a study of persons whose lives were changed by Jesus. One of the greatest benefits of this approach is that it exemplifies the personal experience of salvation with Jesus Christ. These persons did not just know something about Jesus or hold Him in high regard. They received Him as their personal Savior. This is one of the emphases missing in many Roman Catholic churches. Many Catholics emphasize belief in specific doctrines and the observance of the sacraments. They often do not focus on a personal and vital relationship with Jesus Christ as Savior and Lord. This approach to Bible study can help people to understand the importance of the new birth in Christ.

Use the following characters to study the lives of people who changed through a relationship with Jesus.[14]

Nicodemus	John 3:1-21
Samaritan Woman	John 4:1-42
Zacchaeus	Luke 19:1-10
The Man Born Blind	John 9
The Ethiopian	Acts 8:26-40
Paul	Acts 9:1-22
Cornelius	Acts 10:1-48
Lydia	Acts 16:11-15; 40
The Jailer	Acts 16:23-34
Others	

Method: Assign one character for each Bible study and ask the participants to answer the following questions:

a. What was the character's life like **before knowing** about Jesus?
b. How did he or she come to have a **personal faith** in Christ?
c. How was his or her **life** changed?
d. What can I **learn** from his or her experience?

A study of topics relating to salvation

When time is limited or when the persons in the group already have some knowledge about the Bible, study the following topics relating to salvation:

a. Romans

1. Need for being in right relationship with God—(Rom. 1:18; 3:20).
2. Method and provision for being in right relationship with God—(Rom. 3:21-31)
3. Example of a person who was in right relationship with God—(Rom. 4:1-25)
4. Result of being in right relationship with God—(Rom. 5:1-11)
5. The life of those who are in right relationship with God—(Rom. 6:1-4)
6. The liberation of those who are in right relationship with God—(Rom. 6:15-23)
7. Fellowship with Christ—(Rom. 7:1-6)
8. Life in the Spirit—(Rom. 8:1-17)
9. How a believer in Christ faces suffering—(Rom. 8:10-30)
10. The eternal security of those who are in right relationship with God—(Rom. 8:31-39)

b. Galatians

1. The gift of grace—(Gal. 3:1-9)
2. The curse of the Law—(Gal. 3:10-14)
3. The covenant that cannot be changed—(Gal. 3:15-18)
4. The effects of sin—(Gal. 3:19-22)
5. The coming of faith—(Gal. 3:23-29)

c. Ephesians

1. Life without Christ—(Eph. 2:1-3)
2. The work of Christ—(Eph. 2:4-10)
3. Before Christ came—(Eph. 2:11-12)
4. The end of barriers—(Eph. 2:13-18)
5. Fellowship with God—(Eph. 2:19-22)

d. Hebrews

1. Introduction: Christ the complete revelation of God (1:1-3)[15]
2. Christ's superiority over the angels (1:4 - 2:18)
3. Christ's superiority over Moses and Joshua (3:1 - 4:13)
4. The superiority of Christ's priesthood (4:14 - 7:28)

5.   The superiority of Christ's covenant (8:1 - 9:22)
6.   The superiority of Christ's sacrifice (9:23 - 10:39)
7.   The primacy of faith (11:1 - 12:29)
8.   Pleasing God (13:1-19)
9.   Closing prayer (13:20 - 21)
10.   Final words (13:22 - 25)

Method: Use the following questions for the topics listed above:

What does this portion of Scripture teach about salvation?

Which is the most meaningful verse to me?

How does this teaching lesson affect my life?

Caution: Do not assign all of these chapters, character studies, or topics at one time. Assign them one at a time with the corresponding questions. Then allow enough time for discussion.

Suggestion: Get acquainted with these chapters, character studies, and topics yourself. They will be a blessing to you and help you provide guidance for your friend.

Follow-up Suggestions

Observe the following suggestions after you have led your Catholic friend to a personal relationship with Christ.

Continue to **involve** your friend in Bible study.

Continue to **pray** with and for your friend. He or she will need a lot of support from you and other Evangelical friends.

Be **patient**. Don't expect your friend to change an entire belief system overnight. It may take months or years before a complete transition is possible.

Refrain from **pressuring** your friend about not depending on relics or saints. It is only as he or she becomes totally full of Christ that dependence on anyone or anything else is no longer necessary.

Use a **discipleship** plan. The *Survival Kit for New Christians* is an excellent resource. (See Lesson N for more information).

ENDNOTES

1   Periodically, New Testament scholars ask whether Jesus or the Apostle Paul was the actual founder of Christianity. In some sectors of academia, Paul is seen as the one who took the simple message of Jesus and directed it into the theological and ecclesiastical system it ultimately became. Evangelical and conservative Christian scholars reject such a position. They see Jesus as "the only cornerstone" of the Christian faith. See David Wenham, Paul: *Follower of Jesus or Founder of Christianity?*, (Grand Rapids: Wm. B. Eerdmans, 1995).

2   Our primary source for Paul is the *New Testament.* Of the 27 books, thirteen letters are written by him. Furthermore, Luke dedicates more than half of *The Acts of the Apostles* to Saul/Paul (Chas 8:1-3; 9:1-31; 13-28). The Apostle Peter recognizes and defers to Paul's expertise (2 Pet 3:14-16). For a good overview of Paul the person, his background, life and mission see *Christian History* 47 Vol, xiv, No.3 (Aug 1995), dedicated mostly to Paul.

3   Paul may have traveled as many as 17,250 miles, by conservative estimates, in the unfolding of his known missionary journeys. See *"On the Road with Paul,"* by E.M. Yamauchi, *Christian History*, 18.

4   Even though the book of Acts initially utilizes Paul's Hebrew name, for the sake of uniformity we will refer to him as "Paul" in this chapter.

5   F.F. Bruce, *Paul Apostle of the Heart Set Free,* Grand Rapids: Wm. B. Eerdmans, 1977), 41-52.

6   See Joseph A. Fitzmyer, "Paul and the Law," *Readings in Pauline Theology: A Companion to Paul,* M.J. Taylor, ed. (Staten Island, NY.: Alba House, 1975), 76-77.

7   M. E. Boisnard, "Stephen," *The Anchor Bible.*

8   For this position, see Krister Stendahl, *Paul among Jews and Gentiles and other Essays,* (Philadelphia: Fortress, 1976).

9   For this position, see Alan A. Segal, *Paul the Convert,* (New Haven: Yale University Press, 1990).

10 Bruce, *The Apostle of the Heart Set Free,* 80-82. For a good overview of the problems related to Paul's life chronology see "Paul, The CH Timeline," by Janet Meyer Everts, *Christian History,* 30-31.

11 Bruce, *The Apostle of the Heart Set Free,* 80.

12 John the Baptist (Luke 1:80) and Jesus (Luke 2:40, 52; 3:1-4:15) underwent times of preparation before their "vocational" ministries began in earnest.

13 Bruce, *The Apostle of the Heart Set Free,* 75.

14 G. Campbell Morgan's book *The Great Physician* (London: Marshall, Morgan & Scott) has some excellent material which can be used in these Bible studies. Also helpful are William Barclay's commentaries *Bible Study Series* (Philadelphia: Westminster Press). A Bible Dictionary can also be helpful in providing background material.

15 This outline is in the "Letter to the Hebrews," *Today's English Bible* (New York: American Bible Society, 1976), 212.

CHAPTER SIX

ENABLING THE NEW BELIEVER'S SPIRITUAL DEVELOPMENT

Introduction: Pam's Discipleship

At the end of a workshop on how to share our faith with our Roman Catholic friends, a young lady named Pam came to talk to me. She got teary eyed when she told me that she really appreciated the fact that I had told the seminar participants that they needed to love Roman Catholics. I replied that I truly felt that it was very important for us to build genuine bridges of friendship with Catholics. She said: "The reason I appreciated what you said is that I'm Catholic. My parents went to church from time to time, but they made sure I went to religious instruction during school once a week. For a long time, however, I had many questions about God and heaven which no one seemed to be able to answer. I did talk to a priest and told him that intellectually I believed that God existed, but that spiritually there was nothing that assured me of his existence. He told me to pray to God and ask Him to help me believe in Him" She explained that, at first, she thought it was kind of weird, but one day she prayed: "God, If your really exist - really, really, then I want to believe in you with all my heart so that no matter what, I will *know* you exist." She continued: " My life changed. Suddenly desires I used to have (i.e. to get drunk) were gone. I began to experience love as I never knew it before. I also felt a strong desire to read the Bible. I then asked Jesus to forgive me of my sins and to guide my life. I know that he is with me all the time and that if I die, I will go with him." She then asked me: "Do you think I'm saved?" I replied: "Why are you asking me. Do you have any doubts?" She answered: "I have some Evangelical friends who have told me that I cannot be saved because I have never seen a tract in my life and no one has read to me the 'Roman Road to Salvation,' and aside from that I haven't left the Catholic Church." Then she added: "I haven't made a decision about my involvement in the Catholic Church because I still have a lot of questions and further more I think that I can share my experience with my Catholic friends if I stay in the Church." And then she asked me again: "Do you think I'm saved?" I replied: "Pam, that is something that you alone can know for sure. If you have truly invited Jesus into your life, you will have the assurance in your spirit that you belong to him. With regard to your church affiliation, you should ask the Lord to guide you to a congregation where you can continue to grow in your Christian experience. She then asked: "Well, what do you think the Lord wants me to do?" I replied, "Ask Him and He will let you know."

Pam returned to the town where she lived and promised that she would stay in touch with me.

The very next week, Pam wrote me and asked me if I thought she should be baptized. She said that she felt a strong desire to be baptized, even though she had been baptized as a baby. When she asked the priest, he said that this should only be done once. I gave her some portions of Scripture to study and to pray about. She then told me that she had talked to Sister Grace and she thought it was wonderful that Pam had invited Jesus into her life, but that this would only make the sacrament of baptism, that she had received as a baby, more meaningful to her as time went on. Pam wrote me again and asked what I thought about the advice this nun whom she admired so much had given her. I responded by giving Pam additional portions of Scripture related to the meaning of believer's baptism. She then asked the priest what the true meaning of communion (the Eucharist) was. Her main questions were: "Why does Christ have to be present in the wine and the bread when he is already present in my heart? Why do we worship the Host (the bread) physically when we can worship Christ with our spirit?" The priest told her that these were the teaching of the Church and that she had to accept them. He then asked her to promise him that she would receive the sacrament of the Eucharist the following Sunday. She told me that she did it just for the priest, but that she did not feel comfortable with it. She admired him very much because of his selfless life and didn't want to hurt him. She then decided to ask Sister Grace. Her opinion was that the Eucharist would have even greater significance for Pam now that Jesus was dwelling in her heart. She wanted to know what my views were on this. I responded by giving her additional Scripture passages and asked her to study these prayerfully. After several weeks, Pam wrote and said that she did not see how she could take part in a ritual that continues to offer Christ as a sacrifice. She also said that she continued to have a strong desire to be baptized.

This kind of correspondence went on for about nine months as Pam would ask about other doctrines and practices of the Catholic Church. Then, a number of months went by without hearing from Pam. I continued to pray for her but wanted to be sure not to pressure her, as her Evangelical friends had done in the past. She had a difficult time not only sorting out her doctrinal beliefs, but attempting to adjust to the "Evangelical culture." The terms that Evangelicals used (e.g., "born again, saved, redemption, sanctification, witnessing") were not only difficult to understand but made her feel excluded. She said: "I felt like an immigrant going into a country that spoke a different language." What was even more difficult was the "attitudes and prejudices" she found on the part of some Evangelicals. When they found out that she was attending the Catholic Church from time to time, they would say, "Well, we thought you had accepted Christ, why are you still involved in those pagan practices?" What was even more hurtful was when she would visit other Evangelical churches and would hear people criticize and ridicule Catholics in their informal conversations, in their Sunday School classes or even from the pulpit. She would ask herself: "Are these people really reflecting the spirit of Christ?"

Almost a year later, I went to lead a workshop in an Evangelical church in the town where Pam lived. After some introductory remarks, the pastor told the group that the adults would stay with me in the auditorium, that the children would go with another worker, and that the young people would go with Pam. I was anxious for the meeting to be over so that I could speak with Pam. After the meeting, she apologized for not keeping me updated, but said she had a lot to share. She said: "I am now a member of this Evangelical church and I love it. I have found wonderful Christian fellowship, am growing a lot, and am very involved in our youth ministry." She added: "There were two important factors in my making this decision. One was the love that the pastor of the Evangelical church and his wife have shown to me. They always tell me they appreciate me, are always willing to help (even helped me look for my lost dog), are always willing to pray for those I am concerned about, and are always willing to listen to me when I want to talk." She went on to say: "The second thing was that you and the pastor of this church never pressured me to leave the Catholic church and join this one. I was having a very difficult time with my family, especially my grandmother who said that she 'felt leery around me because I don't go to the Catholic Church anymore.' I also felt deeply hurt that many in the Evangelical church were doubting my relationship with the Lord. You and the pastor, however, always kept encouraging me. One of the things that helped me the most was that you never gave me your opinions; you simply kept referring me to the Word of God. Gradually that began to have an effect on me. Somehow, the Word of God kept impressing on my heart what I should do to follow Jesus more closely. Now, I don't have any doubts about my salvation or about the way I should serve the Lord." She concluded by saying: "If more Evangelicals would focus on the Word of God instead of their opinions and would be patient, allowing the Holy Spirit to work in the hearts of those who are searching for the truth, we would see more people turn to Christ and follow him in churches where they can grow spiritually." This type of discipleship is needed in our day.

THE DIMENSIONS OF DISCIPLESHIP

Introduction

Immediately after a child is born, the doctors place him/her in the arms of his/her mother. Why do they do this? They do this because they have learned the very important concept of establishing a vital bond between the baby and the mother. Veterinarians learned this concept before obstetricians. Veterinarians noticed that if they placed the egg of a duckling under a chicken with the other eggs, when the duckling hatched, the first thing it would see would be the chicken, which instantaneously became the duckling's "mother." From that moment on the duckling would follow the chicken, which in turn would care for the duckling, along with her chicks. Psychologists have confirmed that the bond that is established between children and their parents is important for the children's development for the rest of their lives. What would happen if a couple brought their new- born baby home from the hospital, put him/her on a crib and leave to go on vacation saying: "It took a lot of effort for us to bring you into this world. We are going on vacation, and we hope you will do alright" Upon returning home two weeks later and finding the baby dead, they would say: "It is evident that you were not sincere about wanting to be a part of our family." Could it be that we act in a similar manner toward those who have just been born spiritually?

If we would stop to think, we would acknowledge that the bond that are established between new believers and more mature Christians is of utmost importance. The spiritual, social, and doctrinal bond that is developed helps new believers as they go through the conversion process that we described earlier (Discovery, Deliberation, Decision, Dissonance, Discipleship).

Social Bonding

For new believers, relationships with their biological family and their spiritual family are very important.

The Spiritual Family

Because many new believers with a Catholic background encounter negative attitudes, criticism, and pressure from their *biological* families when they make a decision to receive Christ, it is very important that they find love, encouragement, and fellowship within their *spiritual* family.

One of the best ways to achieve social bonding is to assign a person or a family to relate closely to the new believer. The discipling person or family should encourage the new believer in the following ways: 1) Be in constant communication (especially during the first days after the person's conversion; 2) Listen attentively to the new believer's problems, victories, and questions; 3) Be available to meet with the new believer; 4) Include the new believer in the social activities of the church; 5) Introduce the new believer to other church members who might some common interests; 6) Support the new believer in times of crisis.

The Biological Family

There are times in which new believers are faced with such hostile attitudes on the part of their families that they are forced to sever social ties. In these types of circumstances new believers must adhere to Christ's admonition to leave ones father and mother in order to follow him. There are other instances, however, when families are not in agreement with the decision that their loved one has made but they do not sever their social ties with them. In these instances, it is important to instruct new believers to keep the door open so that they will be able to witness to their family members.

In his book, *Bring Your Loved Ones To Christ,* Don Wilkerson makes the following suggestions for new believers to witness to family members:[1]

1. Avoid giving the impression that "I have found it, but you are still lost." Even though it is true that without a personal relationship with Christ, people are lost, an attitude of pride, superiority, or impatience will offend and alienate them.

2. Distinguish between renouncing their past lives and rejecting their family. It is true that the new believer should not participate in sinful practices (e.g., drunkenness) This does not mean that the new believer can totally ignore family responsibilities and family celebrations (e.g, weddings, anniversaries)..

3. Avoid a spirit of condemnation toward their families. Telling them that they are lost, their actions are sinful, and their religious practices are wrong, will cause them to become defensive and unwilling to hear.

4. Avoid pressuring their families to make a decision for Christ. Many new believers feel such joy from having received Christ that

they do not understand why their relatives don't want to have the same experience immediately.

5. Anticipate that their loved ones are going to test them just to see how genuine their new found faith is. New believers have announced to their family members that they have had a life changing experience with Christ. Family members often will look for attitudes and actions to prove that new believers have not attained the spiritual level that they claim to have reached. The new believer should expect this type of testing and should pray for strength and patience from the Lord in order that he might be faithful and give witness of his new life in Christ.

6. Be honest about the errors he commits. Upon committing errors (e.g., losing one's temper, becoming angry), the new believer should admit that he has made mistakes and should let his family know that he is still learning and growing in his spiritual life.

7. Depend on the leadership of the Holy Spirit. The Holy Spirit knows which is the most appropriate moment for the new believer's family to respond to the message of the gospel. For some it has taken years. The new believer will need to continue to pray and to be patient.

8. Learn to share the good news of salvation. New believers have a marvelous enthusiasm. This enthusiasm should be used and we should not wait until "they get over it." At the same time, many new believers have the tendency of criticizing, attacking, and debating. This, at times, is motivated by the feeling "the Catholic Church kept me in darkness for such a long time that I have to tell people about it." The sad part about it is that this approach is counter productive because it alienates people instead of drawing them to Christ. New believers need to learn to cultivate friendships, to share their testimony in positive ways, and to share the message of salvation with patience and love.

In his book, *The Gospel According To Rome,* James McCarthy makes some additional suggestions that can be very helpful in leading people to a personal faith in Christ:[2]

1. Pray for them. The Bible tells us that the gospel "... is veiled to those who are perishing" (2 Corinthians 4:3,4).

2. Develop friendships. "Since Catholicism tends to run along family and ethnic lines, many Catholics do not have even one non-Catholic Christian friend. Ask God to increase your love for Catholics. Then look for ways to nurture friendships with them."

3. Stimulate thought. "Many Catholics are more dutiful than devout. They don't ask much of the Church and the Church doesn't ask much from them... Take the initiative. Get your Catholic friend to think about his spiritual condition."

4. Promote Bible Study. "The average Catholic is trusting the Church to care for his soul and to tell him what to believe about God and salvation. In coming to Christ, such a person must learn to think for himself, to take personal responsibility for his soul, and to base his faith upon God's Word. This requires a major shift in his thinking."

5. Address the real problem. "The real problem is not the Catholic Church: it is his sin. So don't let Roman Catholicism become the focus of your discussion. Help your friend to see what God says about sin in the Bible. Explain the way of salvation. Go directly to the Scriptures "

6. Encourage a clean break. " The Lord commissioned us to make disciples, to baptize them, and to throughly instruct them in the Christian faith (Matthew 28:19,20). The work of evangelism, therefore, is not complete until your Catholic friend is saved, baptized, and incorporated into a sound, Bible-teaching church."

Spiritual Bonding

Receiving Christ as personal savior is not exclusively a cognitive experience. There is also a spiritual dimension. In other words, receiving Christ does not involve simply accepting certain biblical concepts related to salvation (even though this is an indispensable part). It also involves a spiritual decision to trust ones life to Christ.

Bonding With God

One of the first things that a new believer needs to learn is how to be in touch with God through prayer and a devotional life.

1. How to pray

Many nominal Christians among Roman Catholics know how to recite memorized prayer but they do not know how to pray in a spontaneous, direct manner. It is important to teach them how to communicate their praises, gratitude, petitions, and confession to God in prayer.

2. How to have a devotional life

Many nominal Christians with a Catholic background have devotions to some saint or to the Virgin Mary. Their devotions involve such tangible things as lighting a candle, praying the Rosary, making a pilgrimage, going to early Mass every morning, or building an altar in their home.

At times when new believers attend an Evangelical church they get the impression that they should not be concerned with having personal devotions any more.

While it is true that their past devotions to the saints did not contribute to their salvation, it is also true that a proper devotional life will help them to grow spiritually. For that reason, it is very important that new believers learn how to feed themselves spiritually through Bible study, meditation, prayer, and worship.

Bonding With The Family Of God (The Congregation)

As we have stated, it is very important that new believers bond socially with someone in the church who can help them to grow spiritually. At the same time, it is important that new believers relate to the spiritual life of the church. This includes worship services, fellowship, training activities, and participating in the ministries of the church. Because many new believers do not have a biblical concept regarding the body life of the church, they need to learn about the importance and function of each activity and how these contribute to their spiritual development.

Doctrinal Bonding

The doctrines of the Word of God are like a genetic code that needs to become a part of the life of the new believer from the moment of spiritual birth. If the code is communicated correctly, the new believer will grow, mature, and produce the fruit of the Spirit that God expects. In the discipleship process, we need to focus on the biblical doctrines that are essential for the growth of the new believer.

ENDNOTES

[1]   Some of these suggestions are taken from, Don Wilkerson, *Bring Your Loved Ones To Christ* (Old Tappan, New Jersey: Fleming H. Revell Company, 1979), 69-85.

[2]   These suggestions are from James G. McCarthy's, *The Gospel According to Rome*, (Eugene: Harvest House Publishers, 1995), 315-20. For a more extensive discussion read his "Epilogue: The Junction," 311-20.

CHAPTER SEVEN

ADDRESSING KEY DOCTRINAL ISSUES

Introduction: Martha's Decision

Martha lived in Mexico with her family. An uncle of hers was a Bishop in the Roman Catholic Church and one of her cousins was a priest. The pride of having close relatives who had prominent roles in the Church motivated Martha's family, especially her mother, to be very active in their local parish. Martha received most of her education in Catholic schools operated by nuns. From time to time, she would go on missions to other parts of the country with her uncle whom she admired very much. She also had a great deal of appreciation for her parents who had taught her important moral principles. During Lent, Martha's mother went to Mass every morning. Martha's father attended Mass sporadically, but was there with his entire family during important events (e.g., baptisms, weddings, funerals). Martha went to Mass with her mother often, but, there was a spiritual void in her life that she could not fully understand.

One day, Martha met Ricardo in her place of employment. She noticed almost immediately that there was something different about him. For one thing, he was South American and there were some cultural variations. The main difference, however, stemmed from the fact that he seemed to have a real sense of purpose in his life and that he treated his fellow workers with dignity and respect. It didn't take long before Martha and Ricardo sensed an attraction for each other. On their first date, Martha could not resist her curiosity any longer and she asked him why he was different. He smiled and told her that he was different because of a very strong influence on his life. He explained that he had received Jesus Christ as his savior and that his life had changed completely from that moment on. She responded by asking, "How can this be, I believe in the Virgin of Guadalupe and, like you, I believe in baby Jesus. Why don't I have the joy and peace that you seem to have?" Ricardo explained further that it was a matter of her placing her complete trust in Jesus as her personal savior and that this would result in her experiencing the presence of Christ in her daily life and having an assurance that she would go to heaven with Christ when she died. At that point, Martha became somewhat confused and nervous and suggested that perhaps it would be better not to continue the discussion until later. He agreed.

When she was alone, Martha kept asking herself, "How can this be possible?" "The priest has told us to continue to go to church, to receive the sacraments, and to keep doing good deeds of kindness so that God will take this into account when we die." But Ricardo says that this sense of peace about life and about eternity comes as a result of receiving Christ." In a subsequent date, Ricardo asked Martha if she would go to church with him. Her first thoughts were "No way, my family would be furious if they knew I attended a Protestant church." She told him that she would think about it. As time went on, however, Martha began to feel a desire to go to church with Ricardo just to see what it would be like. When she visited the church, Martha was a bit uncomfortable because many things were quite different. She was impressed with the friendliness of the people, but, wondered if she was doing the right thing by being there. Her apprehensions, however, began to diminish when the minister began to preach and she felt that everything he was saying was going straight to her heart. When the minister asked people to go to the front if they wanted to invite Jesus into their lives, she felt like going, but, she still had many apprehensions. Later, when they were by themselves, Martha told Ricardo that the sermon had really touched her heart, but that she had many questions and doubts. Ricardo asked her if she would be willing to meet with his pastor to see if he could help her with her questions. One of the things that impressed Martha the most was that the pastor told her: "Do not listen to what I say or what the priest says. Read the Bible and go by what it says."

After a year of courtship, Martha and Ricardo decided to get married. When she told her parents, they said that they held Ricardo in high regard but that they were deeply disappointed that he was not a Catholic. She told them: "Don't worry, I will make sure that he becomes a Catholic." Theirs was a ceremony in which the Catholic priest as well as the Evangelical minister officiated. However, the ceremony did not solve their problems. Martha was experiencing constant pressure from her family, even though she and her husband were alternating their attendance between both churches. The pressure got to be so great that Martha and Ricardo decided to move to the United States. When they arrived, Ricardo quickly found an Evangelical church and would attend twice on Sundays and on Wednesday nights. Martha began to feel a sense of jealousy. She would attend the Catholic church on Sunday mornings and would not accompany him to any of the services in his church. She was experiencing a lot of turmoil. She would say to him: "I left my family and my country to follow you, but I am not going to leave my religion for you. I will not let you take my religion and my tradition from me." Ricardo was not forcing her to go to church with him. His being so active in his church, however, bothered her quite a bit. She was so upset that she decided to go to Mexico to speak with her uncle, the Bishop. She had many questions and doubts. "Did I make the biggest mistake of my life by attending the Evangelical church and listening to that minister? What if what he said is wrong and the Church rejects me? Will I be lost forever? What about my family? Have they been wrong all this time?"

When Martha arrived in Mexico, her parents were waiting for her and gladly took her to visit her uncle. She told him that she had been reading the Bible and that she had many questions. Her uncle told her that instead of answering her questions he would invite a Doctor of Theology to converse with her. When the Doctor came in, Martha told him that she had many questions about the veneration of the Virgin Mary, about purgatory, and about invoking the saints in light of the fact that none of this is found in the Bible. His answers simply did not satisfy her. She asked, "Why do I have to pray to the saints to intercede for me when the Bible says that God loves us and is willing to hear our prayers?" He answered, "It is because God is angry at us and we need to pray to the saints so that they will mediate for us." She answered: "That is not the God I have found in the Bible." At that instant she excused herself and walked out of the room.

Deeply disappointed, she returned to America to be with her husband. Despite her disappointment with the priest's answers, she was still not willing to invite Jesus into her life. One Wednesday night she noticed that her husband did not attend church. She asked him why, and he said that it just seemed that every time he attended church the tension between them increased. She got angry and walked out of the house. As she kept walking she felt strangely drawn to the Evangelical church her husband attended. As she walked in and sat on the last pew, the song that was being sung pierced her heart. After the sermon, the minister invited anyone who wanted to receive Jesus to come forward so that he could pray with them. With tears in her eyes she did so and told the minister that she wanted to give her life to Christ. She then experienced a deep peace that she had not felt before. When she got home she told her husband that she had received Jesus Christ as her personal savior. They embraced and began to cry. She then told him: "I want to follow Jesus the rest of my life." Looking back on this experience she stated, "For me this was a process. For an entire year I was convinced that I needed to receive Christ, but the influence of my family and my tradition were too strong. I truly have peace in my heart now. This does not mean that I have not had any problems and difficulties, but, it does mean that I know that I am not alone. Jesus is with me always." As time has passed, Martha has become more patient and sympathetic with her family, for she realizes that she went through a process that led her to a personal experience of salvation in Jesus.

DISCIPLESHIP LESSONS

In this section we will deal with some of the essential doctrines with which the new believer needs to become thoroughly acquainted in order that he might grow in his relationship with the Lord and his Church.

This section can be used in several ways:

1. It can help the witness answer questions about the doctrines held by Catholics. The group that has studied this book can meet to pray for one another as they witness to their Catholic friends, to share the progress of their witnessing efforts, and to study some of the key issues in Roman Catholicism. One of the "key issues" (listed in this section) could be studied at each session.

2. It can help those who have already received Christ but have questions about church doctrine. A discipleship program can be used with the following "key issues" to help new believers grow in their faith and knowledge of Jesus Christ.

3. It can help deal with questions that may come up as you are sharing doctrinal concerns. Deal only with the questions that come up, not with the entire list. It is always better to guide new believers in Bible study so they will *discover for themselves* what the Word of God says about these crucial issues.

LESSON A

THE SUPREME AUTHORITY: THE BIBLE OR TRADITION?

Introduction

Catholics are receiving greater incentive to read the Bible. Since the Second Vatican Council (1962-1965), the Catholic Church has put great emphasis on the importance of the Scriptures in the Christian life of its members. The private reading of the Scriptures is being stimulated more strongly than ever before. The Scriptures have acquired a new importance in Catholic worship (liturgy). Scripture lessons are in the common language (vernacular). the Psalms in the common language of the people are from the Scriptures. Many prayers and hymns are scriptural. The homily or sermon preached by the priest or the deacon is scriptural.

Catholics are now being more influenced by the Scriptures during Mass and in their private devotions. This helps us to encourage Catholics to read their Bibles. This also creates a more propitious atmosphere to invite Catholics to participate with Evangelicals in fellowship Bible studies. When doing this, however, some questions of great importance will arise that we should be prepared to answer.

What Version of the Bible Should Be Used to Evangelize?

There are times when Catholics have reservations about using a "Protestant" Bible in an Evangelical dialogue or in a Bible study. In these cases there are two options: (**1**) use a Catholic Bible or (**2**) use a translation that has the approval of the Catholic Church.

Use a Catholic Bible

A Catholic Bible can be used effectively in evangelistic endeavors. In the session which deals with the subject of salvation, we have included an extensive list of texts from the Catholic Bible which can be used in witnessing. When doing this, it is important to keep several things in mind. First, use only references from the New Testament. This avoids questions arising about the additional books that have been included in the Old Testament of the Catholic Bible. The truth is that the majority of nominal Christians among Catholics know little about the additional books in their Bible. In an evangelistic dialogue, therefore, it is beneficial not to enter into a discussion about these books, but simply to concentrate on the passages of the New Testament that speak about salvation. Second, it is important that attention not be given to the additional notes that the Catholic Bible has in the margin. If a question arises about this, it is useful to explain that those are notes of the editors and do not form part of the revelation from God. If one focuses on the key passages of the New Testament, one can present the plan of salvation in a clear and simple way.

Use A Mutually Acceptable Version

The American Bible Society has published versions of the New Testament that have the imprimatur (seal of approval; from Latin, "let it be purified") of the Catholic bishops. The English version, *Good News For Modern Man,* has the imprimatur of the Archbishop of Hartford. The Spanish Version, *Dios Llega al Hombre* has the Latin American Episcopal Council's imprimatur. This seal of approval is found on one of the pages near the front cover. The Latin American imprimatur says: "We share the desire that the Word of the Lord fall on 'the good soil' of the hearts willing to hear it and that it give the fruit of 'a good harvest.'" Antonio Guarracino the Secretary General of Latin American Episcopal Council, Bogota signed it. It is dated September 5, 1980. The English version is approved by the Archbishop of Hartford. As we have said, this version can allay the fears of Catholic persons with regard to the Bible that ought to be used in evangelistic dialogues or in discipleship sessions.

How Do the Catholic and Evangelical Bibles Differ?

Both in evangelistic dialogues and in discipleship sessions, it is likely that questions will arise about the additional books that are found in the Catholic Bible. There are seven deuterocanonical books (also called apocryphal books) that the Catholic Church has included in the Old Testament. These books cover the period between the Old Testament and the New Testament and, for some, have a certain historic value. The main question is: Are these deuterocanonical books divinely inspired like the other were? Adolfo Roberto gives six reasons why Evangelicals should not consider them as divinely inspired Scripture:

1. These books are not found in the Hebrew cannon of the Old Testament.

2. The insertion of these books into the Greek version of the Old Testament (the Septuagint) was inappropriate and accidental. This was done in Egypt, but the Jews of Palestine never accepted these books.

3. Not even one reference in the New Testament is made to them. Jesus never cited a single passage from these books.

4. These books did not receive the approval of the Roman Catholic Church for many years. It was not until the Council of Trent in 1546 that these books were declared canonical.

5. Some of the authors of the apocryphal books recognized their lack of inspiration (see I Maccabees 4:46; 9:27; II Maccabees 2:23; 6:17).

6. These books contain passages that go against the revelation of the Bible. Tobias 4:10, for example, says: "Inasmuch as alms giving frees from all sin and from eternal death, it will not let the soul fall into the darkness of hell."[1]

The Catholic Church considers these books as if they were divinely inspired and bases its doctrine of purgatory primarily on one of them. For these reasons mentioned here, Evangelicals do not place these books on the same level with those which have been seen as inspired through the ages.

Which Is the Source of Authority: the Bible or Tradition?

One of the most crucial questions Catholics ask has to do with the source of authority for the church. Tradition is "that body of knowledge which is transmitted orally from one generation to another." Evangelicals assembled at the Lausanne Congress produced a covenant which states:

> We affirm the divine inspiration, the veracity, and the authority of the Scriptures of both the Old Testament and the New Testament as the only Word of God written without error in all that it affirms, and the only infallible rule of

faith and practice. We also affirm the power of the Word of God to fulfill its purpose of salvation. The message of the Bible is directed toward all humanity. Therefore, the revelation of God in Christ in the Scriptures is immutable. Through the Scriptures, the Holy Spirit still speaks today. He illumines the minds of the people of God in every culture to receive the truth through their own eyes and in this way reveals to the entire church the multiform wisdom of God[2].

The participants in this congress affirmed the Evangelical concept of *sola scriptura*, which declares that the Bible is the only rule of faith and practice for the Christian and for the church. This means that the only authority for the Christian and for the church is the Bible. Only on it should the doctrines and practices of the church be based.

In contrast to this, the Catholic Church teaches that there are two sources of revelation. The Documents of Vatican II teach that: "Sacred tradition and sacred Scripture form one sacred deposit of the Word of God, which is committed to the Church."[3] The documents of the Second Vatican Council affirm:

There exists a close connection and communication between sacred tradition and the Holy Scriptures. Therefore, both flowing from the same source on a certain way join and tend toward the same end. The sacred Scriptures are the Word of God to the degree that they were written under the inspiration of the divine Spirit. Sacred tradition gives to the successors of the apostles the Word of God, which was entrusted to the apostles by Christ the Lord and by the Holy Spirit. Therefore, guided by the Spirit of truth, these successors can in their preaching preserve this word of God, explain it and make it known more extensively. As a result, it is not only from the sacred Scriptures that the Church receives its certainty of all that which has been revealed. Therefore, both sacred tradition and the sacred Scriptures are accepted and venerated with the same devotion and reverence. Sacred tradition and the sacred Scriptures form a sacred deposit of the Word of God, which is entrusted to the Church.[4]

The teachings of the Catholic Church make it very clear that tradition holds the same authority as the Scriptures in matters of faith and practice.

When the Catholic Church speaks about tradition, it does not have in mind only the source of knowledge that was transmitted verbally until the Bible was written, but also the continuous tradition which the church establishes across time. A note from the documents of the Second Vatican Council explains:

> This formula does not exclude the opinion that all revelation in one form or another, perhaps obscurely, is contained in the Scriptures. But this perhaps may not give sufficient certainty, and in fact the Church always understands and interprets the Scriptures in light of its continuous tradition.[5]

Pope Pius XII based his judgement on this concept of the continuous tradition of the church when he proclaimed the dogma of the Assumption of Mary. Although he did not have any biblical base for this doctrine, and even when tradition was lacking any documental evidence before 300 A.D., the Pope declared that this doctrine was found in revelation. This revelation is that the church not only is the **guardian** of all that which was given to the apostles, but **exhibitor** of the faith in every age until the end of time. The Catholic Catechism explains:

> Together with the sources of revelation (Scripture and tradition), God has given to his Church a living magisterium to clarify and explain what is contained only obscurely and by implication in the deposit of faith. The degree of obscurity does not matter. Given this faculty by its founder whose Spirit of truth dwells with it all the time, the Church can infallibly discern what pertains to revelation, no matter how hidden its content is.[6]

Some Roman Catholic writers affirm that there are different types of traditions: (1) false traditions (Matt. 15:6); (2) human traditions (Colossians 2:8); and (3) true traditions (2 Thessalonians 2:15).[7] The first two types of traditions are very clear. It needs to be pointed out, however, that the third one (2 Thessalonians. 2:15) refers to the doctrine which the Thessalonians had received from Paul which he in turn had received from Christ. Paul was very careful to guard the message from human distortions (see Galatians 1:8).

Catholics use two biblical texts to support their argument that tradition and Scripture have the same authority: John 21:25 and 2 Thessalonians 2:15.

John 21:25 states: "Jesus did many other things as well. If every one of them were written down, I suppose that even the whole world would not have room for the books that would be written." This is undeniably true, however, two statements of explanation need to be made. First, if the Holy Spirit inspired both the oral communications and the writings, they would not contradict each other. The second statement of explanation is that Scripture that *is* *essential* for salvation is included in the Protestant canon.[8] John makes this point when he states: "Jesus did many other miraculous signs in the presence of his disciples, which are not recorded in this book. But these are written that you may believe that Jesus is the Christ, the Son of God, and that by believing you may have life in his name" (John 20:30-31). In the second passage, the reference is quite clear. Second Thessalonians 2:15 talks about the *doctrine* which the Thessalonians had received from Paul. This is the doctrine spelled out in the content of the epistle.

Roman Catholic authors also make a distinction between Tradition (capital "T" which they define as "the body of teachings of Christ and his apostles which are not explicitly contained in the Bible")[9] and tradition (lower case "t", which they define as "things and actions which may have been long customary and accepted by the People of God").[10] They affirm categorically that "nothing in Tradition can contradict the Bible."[11] A study of Scripture, however, reveals that nowhere in the Bible is the door left open for such "Traditions" as Purgatory (A.D. 593); the Immaculate Conception of Mary (A.D. 1854); the Infallibility of the Pope (A.D. 1870) and the Assumption of Mary (A.D. 1950).

Some Roman Catholic authors explain this as "the development of doctrine." Nevins, for instance, states:

> "Some critics object that these ideas (e.g., the primacy of the pope) were not present in the Apostolic Church. Of course they weren't, except in embryo. The church is a living organism, and, like all living organisms is subject to growth and development. The simple apostolic liturgy of the blessing of the bread and the blessing of the cup has developed into today's liturgy of the Eucharist. Essentially both liturgies are the same but accidentally they are different."[12]

The sad truth is that not only has the Lord's supper changed from a remembrance to the re-offering of the sacrificing of Christ but numerous other doctrines which have absolutely no Biblical foundation have been added by the Roman Catholic church under the banner of "Tradition." We agree with

Schrotenboer when he states: "It is not the Church that gives birth to the Word, but the Word that gives birth to the Church (1 Peter 1:23; James 1:18). We have but one Master whose infallible teaching is contained once for all in the Scriptures. Listening to and obeying the Word, we hear the message of the one and only Lord."[13] Traditions (whether with a upper case "T" or a lower case "t") which are given equal status with the Bible undermine Scripture and mislead the people.

In light of these declarations, it remains very clear that the Catholic Church does not consider the Bible as the sole source of authority but places tradition on the same level with the Scriptures. Moreover, this tradition is not only what was entrusted to the apostles by Jesus Christ, but also a continuous tradition that the Catholic Church establishes as time marches on.

Who Should Interpret the Bible?

Since the Second Vatican Council, Catholics have been encouraged to read the Bible more. This is good, because the Word of God is being read more in worship services and in private devotions. However, it is important to explain that even though the Church encourages its members to read the Bible, it reserves for itself the right to interpret it. The documents of the Second Vatican Council declare:

> The task of authentically interpreting the Word of God, whether it be written or communicated verbally, has been entrusted exclusively to the magisterium (the teaching office) of the church, whose authority is executed in the name of Jesus Christ.[14]

Let us note that the Catholic Church clearly teaches that only the magisterium (i.e., the Pope and the bishops collectively) has the right to interpret the Bible and tradition to formulate the doctrines that people ought to believe. John Calvin (1509-1564) energetically opposed the idea that the Church could judge the Scriptures to determine what should be believed. He declared:

> Paul testified that the church "is built on the foundation of the apostles and the prophets" (Ephesians 2:20). If the doctrine of the apostles and the prophets is the foundation of the Church, the doctrine had to have its certainty before the Church began to exist. . . Nothing can be more absurd than the fictitious idea that the power to judge the Scriptures

is in the Church, and that the certainty of the Scriptures depends on the approval of the church. When the Church receives the Scriptures and gives them its seal of authority, it does not make authentic what otherwise would be doubtful or controversial, but it recognizes it as the truth of God; following its duty, it shows its reverence by obeying it.[15]

What reformer John Calvin maintained was that the church is a servant of the Scriptures and not the other way around.

What Does the Bible Teach?

The Bible Teaches That In It Is Found Everything Essential for Salvation

John says that Christ did many things that were not written, however in the following verse John affirms: "But these have been written so that you may believe that Jesus is the Son of God, and so that by believing, you may have eternal life in his name" (John 20:31). What was written was what is necessary for people to know Christ as their Savior. What was not written might have been very interesting, but not essential for salvation. It is true that Christ said many things which are not written, but it is inconceivable to think that Christ would present one form of salvation in the Scriptures and another form outside of them[16].

Paul says to Timothy: "and from childhood you have known the sacred Scriptures, which can make you wise for salvation by faith that is in Christ Jesus. All Scripture is inspired by God and useful for teaching, for refuting error, for correcting, for instructing in righteousness, so that man of God may be perfect, fully prepared for every good work." (II Timothy 3:15-17).

It remains very clear that the Scriptures contain all that is necessary to attain salvation and to live the Christian life.

In the Bible, the Word "Tradition" Is Used to Refer to the Doctrines That the Apostles Received

Paul admonishes the Thessalonians to be firm and to retain the doctrine (or tradition) that they had learned "either by word, or by letter" (II Thessalonians 2:15). This is the doctrine expressed in the letter. In I Corinthians 11:1, Paul explains that what he taught was what "he received from the Lord."

168

Luke affirms that the new believers "continued to persevere in the doctrine of the apostles" (Acts 2:42). The doctrine of the apostles was what Christ has commanded them to teach (Matthew 28:20).

The Bible Speaks Against The Traditions of Men

Christ condemned the Pharisees who "teach as doctrines the commandments of people" (Matthew 15:1-9).

Christ accused the Pharisees of "invalidating the Word of God with their tradition" (Mark 7:13).

Paul admonishes the Colossians when he says to them: "Watch out that no one deceives you by means of philosophy and empty subtleties according to the traditions of people in accordance with the rudiments of the world and not according to Christ" (Colossians 2:8).

Scripture speaks very clearly against the traditions of men that contradict what is found in the Bible.

The Bible Teaches That God Made Provision For The Interpretation Of The Holy Scriptures

Christ is the head of the Church not the Pope (John 13:13; Colosians 1:18)[17]

The Holy Spirit is the authoritative teacher of the Church, not the Magisterium (John 14:26; 16:13; 1 John 2:27).

Scripture is the only infallible interpreter of Scripture (Acts 17:11)

Scripture is the Word of God (John 10:35; 2 Timothy 3:16; 2 Peter 1:20,21).

Scripture is to be interpreted in the original sense intended by the Holy Spirit (2 Peter 3:14-16).

Every Christian, aided by the Holy Spirit, has the ability and the right to interpret Scripture (Acts 17:11; 1 Corinthians 2:12-16).

169

Scripture is the Church's only rule of faith (Mark 7:7-13; 2
Timothy 3:16,17).

Scripture warns against adding to what has already been revealed
by God (Revelations 22:18-19).

Conclusion:

It should gladden us greatly that Catholics are being encouraged to read
the Bible more frequently, both in the Mass and in private devotions. Let us
remember that faith comes by hearing and hearing by the Word of God (Romans
10:17). This new emphasis on the Bible represents for Evangelicals new
opportunities to invite their Catholic friends to participate together in Bible
studies. When doing this, it is important to use a version that is acceptable for
both groups. In the process of evangelization, it is important that one
concentrate on what is essential for salvation. Nevertheless, the witness should
be prepared to answer questions about the Bible. In the process of discipleship,
it is essential that one studies what the Bible teaches with regard to the authority
of the church and the interpretation of the Scriptures..

LESSON B

VENERATION OF MARY AND OF THE SAINTS

Introduction

As one witnesses to Catholics, there is not a more delicate subject than that of Mary. This is due to various reasons. First, in their sincere desire to avoid the adoration of Mary, Evangelicals at times have gone to the extreme of not giving Mary the place that she occupies in the Gospels. That is to say, many Evangelicals give the impression that Mary was a common and ordinary woman. The impression that many Catholics have of Evangelicals is that they lack respect for Mary and that some even hate her. Second, this is a very delicate subject because many Catholics believe that if someone speaks badly of Mary, it is worse than if they insulted their mother. In other words, many Catholics have such profound emotional, religious, and social ties with Mary that they will feel offended by anything that is said about her in a disrespectful way and will immediately close their ears and hearts. For many Catholics, there is a cultural connection with the Virgin Mary. Some Catholic leaders allege that the Virgin Mary is tied with the cultural identity itself of Latin Americans. One example is the close connection between the Virgin of Guadalupe and the cultural identity of many Mexicans.[18] To be Mexican is to be devoted to the patron saint, the Virgin of Guadalupe. One of the things that offends some Catholics the most is that Evangelicals try to prove to them with the Bible that Mary had other children besides Jesus. Due to the fact that the subject of Mary is so delicate, it is important that Evangelicals understand what the Catholic Church teaches and that they know how to deal with this subject in such a way that it facilitates the presentation of the message of salvation and discipleship without creating unnecessary obstacles.

Official Doctrine of the Catholic Church Concerning Mary

The development of the devotion of Mary has deep roots in the history of the Catholic Church. Certain rites and festivals dedicated to Mary were practiced in the Mediterranean world and in Europe. The Council of Ephesus (431 A.D.), while trying to emphasize the true humanity of Jesus Christ, used the word "theotokos" (God bearer), indicating that Mary was the one who gave birth to the Son of God. It needs to be pointed out that the Council of Ephesus did not use the term *"mater Theou"* (mother of God), but, *"theotokos"* which referred to the act of giving birth.[19] In actuality the term *"Christotokos"* (Christ bearer) would have been more accurate. With time, however, there were those who used this term to declare Mary the "Mother of God," which encouraged people to established devotional practices related toMary.

By the time of the Reformation (1517-1648), there already was a great concern that the image of Mary was overshadowing the centrality of Christ. The Council of Trent (1545-1563) in it declarations against the Reformation declared the sinlessness and perpetual virginity of Mary. These came to be official doctrines of the Catholic Church in the declarations of the Popes in the following years.

The Catholic Church Teaches the Perpetual Virginity of Mary

Catholic dogma holds that Mary retained her virginity throughout all her existence. In the Latarene Council in 649 A.D. under Pope Martin I, Canon 3 of that council declared that after the birth of Jesus, the virginity of Mary remained indissoluble.[20] The Council of Trent confirmed this declaration in 1555 under the constitution of Pope Paul IV entitled Cum quorundam. The Pope warned the Socinian religious order not to teach that "the very blessed virgin Mary is not really the mother of God and did not remain in the integrity of virginity; that is, before birth, and perpetually after birth."[21] In this declaration are based the classic theological terms; *ante partum* ("before birth"), *in partu,* *(*"in birth"*),* and *et post partum* ("and after birth").[22]

This dogma of the perpetual virginity of Mary is based on the rest of the dogmas such as the Immaculate Conception and the Assumption of Mary because these presuppose that Mary's body was not corrupted by sin.

The Catholic Church Teaches the Immaculate Conception of Mary

In 1854, in the document entitled Ineffabilis Deus[23], Pope Pius IX declared the immaculate conception of Mary. He declared that "the very blessed Virgin Mary, in the first instance of her conception, by grace and singular privilege bestowed by Almighty God and by virtue of the merits of Jesus Christ, the Savior of the human race, [was] preserved immune from every stain of original sin."[24] This declaration affirms that the immunity that Mary received was a special favor from God, that it was through the merits of Christ that Mary was exempt from the original sin which the rest of humanity bears, and that this immunity happened at the moment of her conception. Moreover, the Catholic Church teaches that

Mary was not only born without sin but remained without sin throughout her life. The Pope did not claim that the Scriptures reveal this doctrine explicitly but that there are certain texts (such as Genesis 3:15) that give the implication that Mary was conceived without sin. They explain that the "seed of woman" is Jesus and the "the woman" is Mary. This declaration of the Pope accepts the interpretation that Mary, by her intimate relationship with Christ, had enmity toward the malignant spirit, triumphed against it completely, and crushed it with her immaculate foot.[25]

Let us note that the doctrine of the Immaculate Conception was not proclaimed until 1854. The Catholic Catechism admits: "Without claiming that the Scriptures reveal these doctrines explicitly, he [the Pope] shows that the most common interpretation of the revelation of the texts by the ancients Fathers and contemporary theologians sees in these texts an explicit teaching that Mary was conceived without sin.[26] It is clear that this is a matter of interpretation of people and not a matter of a revelation from God.

The Catholic Church Teaches the Assumption of Mary to Heaven

The Roman Catholic church teaches the doctrine of the assumption of Mary. The *Documents of Vatican II* state:

> Finally, preserved from all guilt of original sin, the Immaculate Virgin was taken up body and soul into heavenly glory upon the completion of her earthly sojourn. She was exalted by the Lord as Queen of all, in order that she might be more thoroughly conformed to her Son, Lord of lords (cf. Apoc. 19:16) and conqueror of sin and death.[27]

One tradition holds that the apostles were summoned when Mary became ill. All of the apostles but Thomas got there before she died. However, as he was transported there on a cloud, Thomas saw the body of Mary ascending into heaven. Upon arrival he told the other apostles what he had seen. They then went to the grave and found it empty[28]. The interesting thing about this (and other similar traditions) is there is no mention of them in Scripture. Even John does not mention this event though Mary was entrusted to him and he lived after her death. John later cites the words of Jesus without adding an explanation as he did in other occasions (e.g. John 4:9; 21:20-23): "No one has gone up to heaven except the One who came down from there—the Son of Man [who is in heaven]." Mary's assumption (taken up bodily) into heaven would have been alluded to by John with a note of explanation[29]. There is *no biblical basis* for the assumption of Mary.[30]

Immediately after Pope Pius IX defined the dogma of the Immaculate Conception of Mary, Catholics throughout the world began to send petitions asking that the Church define the bodily assumption of Mary and establish this as an official dogma. In May of 1946, Pope Pius XII sent a questionnaire to all the bishops of the Catholic world asking them if they believed "that the bodily assumption of the Blessed Virgin Mary should be proposed and defined as faith, and that if they together with their clergy and faithful desired it."[31] Within a few months the answers received were almost unanimous. The Pope concluded that he ought to make this proclamation in view of the fact that he had the consent of the persons "whom the Holy Spirit has placed to govern the Church of God."

In November of 1950, Pope Pius XII made the following declaration: "By the authority of our Lord Jesus Christ, of the Holy Apostles Peter and Paul, and by our own authority, we pronounce, declare and define as divinely inspired dogma: The Immaculate Mother of God, Mary always the Virgin, having concluded the course of her earthly life, was taken, body and soul to heavenly glory."[32]

Almost a hundred years after the immaculate conception of Mary was proclaimed, the doctrine of the assumption of Mary was proclaimed by Pope Pius XII. This was due in great part to the fact that the definition of the doctrine of the assumption of Mary. The Catholic Catechism explains: "It is estimated that from 1870 to 1940, more than four hundred bishops, eighty thousand priests and member of religious orders, and more than eight million laity formally had signed petitions asking for this definition."[33] We have to ask if these Christian doctrines ought to be defined based on what is revealed clearly in the Bible or if they ought to be the result of a popular vote. Toward the end of the twentieth century, an effort was also made to gather signatures so that, before the end of the twentieth century, the Pope may declare Mary officially "Co-redeemer with Christ, Mediatrix of All Grace and Defender of the People of God."[34] Between 1993 and 1997, the Pope received 4,340,429 signatures from 157 countries - an average of 100,000 per month - supporting this proposed dogma. Among the persons who back this petition are around 500 bishops and 43 cardinals.[35] Pope John Paul II has done much to promote the devotion to Mary. In a speech in April 1997, he declared:

> Having created humanity "male and female," the Lord also wants to place the New Eve next to the New Adam in redemption. . . Mary, the New Eve, therefore, comes to be an icon of the Church. . We, therefore, can turn to the Blessed Virgin confidently imploring her help with assurance in the unique part entrusted to her by God, the part of coworker in redemption.[36]

It is interesting to note that throughout time, the Catholic Church has tried to develop a theology for Mary which parallels what the Bible teaches about Jesus Christ: 1) Jesus was born without sin - "the immaculate conception of Mary," 2) Jesus died on the cross to redeem us - "Mary suffered with Him and for that reason is Co-redeemer," 3) Jesus ascended into heaven - "Mary experienced the Assumption," 4) Christ is at the right hand of the Father as our mediator - "Mary is Co-mediatrix.[37] In spite of the fact that the Catholic Church officially teaches that Mary should not be adored (only venerated) and that her mediation is subordinate to that of Christ, the sad reality is that many of the persons through out the world (e.g., Latin America) do not make these distinctions. The truth is that what the Catholic Church has added to the biblical teachings regarding Mary has become object of adoration among Catholics. As a consequence, many of them know little about how to have a personal experience of salvation in Christ.

The Catholic Church Teaches That Mary Is Co-Mediatrix

The Roman Catholic church teaches that Mary is co-mediatrix with Christ. There are several implications: First, it means that Mary is a go-between for us. The argument which some Catholics use is that if we need the help of someone, the most logical person to persuade him is his mother. While this may be impeccable human logic, it is not accurate theology. The Bible teaches explicitly that Jesus is the sole mediator by virtue of His death for the sins of humanity. I Timothy 2:5-6 states, "There is one God and *one* Mediator between God and men, the man Christ Jesus." The Scriptures also affirm that Jesus Christ is at the right hand of God (see Rom. 8:34). I John 2:1 states this even more clearly, "My dear children, I write this to you so that you will not sin. But if anybody does sin, we have one who speaks to the Father in our defense— Jesus Christ, the Righteous One." Mary is not mentioned anywhere in Scripture as carrying out the functions of mediator or intercessor in addition to Christ. Nowhere in Scripture is Mary described as the right hand of the Father. (See also Eph. 2:18; Heb. 4:15-16.).

The Second Vatican Council (1962-65) affirmed several doctrines about Mary. Even though the bishops who participated in this Council emphasized that the maternal duty of Mary "does not take away anything from nor adds anything to the dignity and the efficacy of Christ, the only Mediator,"[38] at the same time they affirmed that Mary plays a part as Intercessor. They explained that Mary, "on arriving at heaven, did not put aside her saving role, but, by means of her multiform acts of intercession, she continues winning for us gifts of eternal salvation."[39]

The Catholic Catechism asserts: "She deserves the title 'Mediatrix' because she cooperated in a unique way with Christ in his redeeming labors on the earth, and because in heaven she continues to intercede for those who still work for their salvation as pilgrims in the Church Militant or for those souls suffering in purgatory."[40]

The Catholic Church Teaches Devotion To Mary

The Second Vatican Council declared that it recommended enthusiastically the worship of Mary (especially liturgical worship) and that devotion to Mary ought to continue being proclaimed within the limits of sound and orthodox doctrine of the Church. The council declared: "That the entire body of the faithful participate in persevering prayer to the Mother of God and Mother of human beings; that they implore that she, exalted in heaven with all the saints and angels, who helped begin the Church with her prayers, now intercede with her Son in the fellowship of all the saints[41]. The Council added that since the Council of Ephesus, the worship of the People of God toward Mary had grown in veneration and love, in invocation and imitation, in agreement with its own prophetic words: "for behold, from henceforth all generations shall call me blessed" (Luke 1:48).[42]

The implication of this Roman Catholic doctrine is that people are strongly encouraged to render homage to Mary and pray to her as mediatrix.

Popular Religiosity with Regard to Mary

The official proclamations of the church have contributed to popular religiosity regarding Mary. In many cases, dogmas have been pronounced simply to recognize officially the religious practices that already exists among the Catholic people. An example of this has to do with the supposed apparitions of the Virgin Mary in different countries.

The Catholic Church has officially recognized seven apparitions.[43] These are: (1) In 1531 the Virgin of Guadalupe is alleged to have appeared to Juan Diego (an Indian) four times and instructed him to tell the bishop that they were to build a sanctuary in Tepeyac (the place where Indians worshiped the goddess Tonanzin); (2) In 1830 in Paris, Catherine Labourne, a nun, claims she saw Mary, who asked that they make a medal in her honor and that they promote devotion toward her; (3) In 1858, in Lourdes, France, Mary is alleged to have appeared 18 times and referred to herself as "The Immaculate Conception"; (4) In 1846, in La Salette, France, Mary allegedly appeared mourning to two peon children. The message that she entrusted to them, about the need to do penance, was entrusted to Pope Pius IX in 1851. After this, the devotion to "Our Lady of La Salette" was championed by the Catholic Church and in 1870 a basilica was constructed in her honor; (5) In 1917, in Fatima, Portugal, three shepherd children from 8 to 14 years of age, said they saw Mary six times. She referred to herself as "the Immaculate Heart"; (6) Between 1932 and 1933, in Beauraing, Belgium, in the garden of a convent, Mary is said to have appeared 33 times to five children (between the ages of 9 and 15). She appeared to them as the "Virgin of the Heart of Gold"; (7) In 1933, in Banneux, Belgium, Mariette Beco (12 years of age) claimed she saw Mary eight times, and she referred to herself as the "Virgin of the Poor" and promised to intercede for the poor, the sick, and those who suffer.[44]

Besides these, there are many other alleged appearances such as the Virgin of Cooper in Cuba and Medjudorje in Yugoslavia. In the majority of the cases, the Virgin Mary supposedly appeared to children, to simple persons (such as Juan Diego of Mexico) or to persons in danger (like the fishermen in Cuba).

As a result of this, thousands of people go to sanctuaries that have been built to receive those who arrive and prostrate themselves before Mary's image to ask for miracles, to fulfill promises, or to express gratitude for answered petitions. The majority of the time that persons go on their knees, spend a moment before the statue of Mary, light a candle, and then return to their homes without reading any portion of the Word of God, without listening to a biblical message, and without having someone counsel with regarding their problem or need and pray for them. There have been times in which the Pope has visited these shrines to Mary and has given his approval of the worship that is rendered there. For example, after the attempted assassination against him in 1981, Pope John Paul II visited the sanctuary of Fatima and prostrated himself at the feet of her statue, thanking her for having saved his life. Both the official proclamations of the Catholic Church and the example of its highest leaders have promoted popular religiosity related to Mary.

The Catholic Church officially teaches that the mediating work of Mary is subordinate to the work of Christ. That is to say that the work of Mary cooperates with Christ but does not take His place. The Catholic Church also teaches that devotion to Mary ought to be proclaimed within the limits of sound and orthodox doctrine of the church. Moreover, the Catholic Church makes a distinction between the different ways in which devotion is expressed. The Catholic Catechism explains:

Being that God is the Supreme Being and the Absolute Lord of the universe, worship in its highest degree belongs to Him. The technical name for the praise of God is worship or latrial worship (from the ancient Greek term *"lateria,"* which meant service rendered to the gods). The less elevated form of veneration given to the angels and the saints that Catholicism recognizes has the theological name of *"dulia"* (from the Greek term *"douleia"*, which means respect shown to the master by his slave). The Blessed Virgin is honored with *"hyperdoulia,"* i.e., a more elevated form of worship that is essentially the same veneration afforded to other creatures among the saints but in essence different from the worship given only to God.[45]

Informed Catholics make a distinction between the Greek words *latria, dulia*, and *hyperdulia*[46] Officially, therefore, Catholics do not worship Mary, "only God is adored."[47] However, in practice many Catholics do not make this distinction and do worship her as they would God or Christ. In many countries, more emphasis is placed on Mary than on Christ.

A Biblical Response To The Veneration of Mary

Despite the warnings of the Catholic Church that the devotion to Mary should be practiced within the limits of sound and orthodox doctrine of the Church, that the mediation of Mary is subordinate to that of Christ, and that the worship of Mary is different from the worship of God, the overwhelming evidence is that the majority of Catholics do not understand or observe these differences. The sad reality is that, in the many regions in the world, like Latin America, the worship of Mary takes the place of the worship of Christ. Adolfo Robelto expresses this profound concern when he says:

Daily, among Roman Catholics, more prayers are prayed to Mary than to Jesus Christ. During the year, the holidays that are celebrated in honor of Mary are more than those that are celebrated in honor of Jesus Christ. In many cities more temples are dedicated to Mary than those which are dedicated to Jesus Christ. It is not an exaggeration to say that the Catholic faith revolves around Mary in a greater proportion. Highly elevated titles are given to her; entire monastic orders are consecrated to her; many extraordinary apparitions are attributed to her, and an infinity of miracles. They burn candles to her statues and carry them in public processions.[48]

One of the concerns of Evangelicals is that, in the supposed apparitions of Mary, she asks that sanctuaries be built for her, that medals be made in her honor, that they refer to her with titles that she assigns herself (e.g., "the Immaculate Conception" etc.), and that devotion to her be established. In none of these cases is there mention of Jesus Christ as the Savior of the world. How different this is from what Mary did during Jesus' ministry! In the supposed apparitions, Mary seems to focus on herself. As a result of this, many Catholics know more about Mary than about Jesus Christ. Many of them see Jesus as a helpless child in the arms of Mary or as a dead Christ on the cross, but not as the resurrected Savior who dwells in the hearts of believers and guides them in their daily lives. It is for that reason that they go on pilgrimages (sometimes on their knees) to Mary's altars and spend so much time asking her to pray for them now and at the hour of their death. Clearly, this is not the picture of Mary that we find in the Gospels.

In view of this tradition, so rooted in the minds and hearts of many Catholics, the crucial question is, "How can we lead them to know Christ as their personal Savior and to come to hold a biblical concept regarding Mary?" To achieve this, it is important that we make a distinction between the process of evangelization and that of discipleship.

The Process of Evangelization

When I was a child, one of things that fascinated me the most in the circus was seeing people go from one swing to the other with such ease. At first I was very worried that they would die if they fell from that height, but after a while I realized one thing. They did not let go of one swing until they had taken hold of the other. I am afraid that, in many cases, in our desire to evangelize people, we concentrate our efforts on getting them to let go of the doctrinal swing that they are holding without their having taken hold of Jesus Christ. In other words, we spank their hands and say "let go, let go," but they hold on more tenaciously because they have not gotten a hold of Christ yet. When they feel criticized and attacked, they focus on holding on to their beliefs more strongly instead of being receptive to the gospel.

In view of this, there are certain things that we should not do. We should not enter into a heated discussion about Mary. We should not give the impression that we do not respect Mary. Above all, we should not try to prove to them that Mary had more children. These people are not prepared to hear this at this point. Many Evangelicals and persons of some sects (like Jehovah's Witnesses) have attacked them so much that Catholics feel threatened when they are criticized for their devotion to Mary.

179

In contrast to this, there are several things that indeed we should do. In the first place, if they ask us what we believe with regard to Mary, we ought to say what the Bible says. Mary was a very special person, because God chose her to be the mother of His Son, Jesus Christ. In Mary we find an inspiring example of obedience, submission, faith, perseverance, sacrifice, and love. The truth is that we all should follow the advice that she gave at the wedding of Cana in Galilee when she said: "Do all that he should say to you" (John 2:5). Above all, we should concentrate on Christ when witnessing to our Catholic friends. I do not know of anyone who has been saved because it had been proven to him that Mary had more children, but I do know of many who have been saved on hearing the message of salvation. Let us concentrate on Christ in the process of evangelization.

The Process of Discipleship

Once we have led the person to a personal experience with Jesus Christ, we can lead them in discipleship. In the course of discipleship, we can involve them in Bible studies which make clear the part that Mary played as the mother of our Savior.[49] The Roman Catholic teachings about Mary need to be examined in the light of Scripture. Catholics teach that: (a) she was conceived without sin (this is the doctrine of the immaculate conception of Mary)[50]; (b) she always remained a virgin (she had no other children aside from Jesus)[51]; (c) she was taken up into heaven body and soul[52]; (d) Mary is a co-mediatrix (she is a go-between, and people can pray to her)[53].

Catholics base the doctrine of the *immaculate conception* of Mary on the phrase translated "full of grace" in some versions (Luke 1:28). The argument goes that if she was full of grace she could not have sinned. Actually the rendition of this phrase in the more modern Roman Catholic editions is more accurate: "you are highly favored."[54] The phrase "full of grace," was used of other persons (e.g., the apostles, Acts 4:33), yet that does not mean they were sinless[55]. Furthermore, study Luke 1:47 and see the term Mary uses to refer to God. Does this reflect her need of God's grace? Yes.

The Roman Catholic church teaches that Mary was a *perpetual virgin*. As Evangelicals we believe there is biblical support for the doctrine that Mary was a virgin *before* the birth of Jesus. This is known as the *ante partum* (before birth) virginity of Mary. The New Testament, however, does speak about Mary having other children. Mark 3:32 says, "The crowd seated around him said, your Mother and your brothers and sisters are outside asking for you." Some Catholics explain that these were actually Jesus' cousins.

Jose Borrás, a former Roman Catholic priest, explains that the New Testament uses different words for cousins and for brothers[56]. Luke 1:36 says, "Even Elizabeth your relative is going to have a child." The Greek uses different words for "relative" *(suggenis* see Luke 1:36); for "cousin" *(anepsios* see Col. 4:10); and for "brother" *(adelfos).* This word is used in Matthew 4:18 which speaks of Simon Peter and his *adelfos* Andrew. This is precisely the word used in Mark 3:32 "Your mother and your *adelfoi* (plural) are here." This same word is used in Mark 6:3 in which the names of Jesus' brothers are given (James, Joseph, Judas, and Simon). See also Matthew 12:46; 13:55-56; Luke 8:19-21; Acts 1:14; and Galatians 1:19. These passages are quite clear that Mary had other children. It must be emphasized that the belief that Mary had other children is not essential to salvation (see Acts 16:31; Rom. 5:11)[57]. It is not wise to dwell on this when witnessing to people with a Roman Catholic background. However, in the discipleship process, it is a good idea to help them study these passages from Scripture.

The passages that speak about the infancy of Jesus (Matthew 1 and 2; Luke 1 and 2) present an inspiring picture of Mary, who was prepared to do the will of God even though she would run the risk of being criticized and misunderstood.

There are passages that speak about Mary as a mother and wife (Matthew 1 and 2 and Luke 1 and 2). Matthew 1:24,25 says that Joseph received Mary as his wife and that he did not know her (that is, he did not have marital relations with her) until she gave birth to her firstborn. Both the word "firstborn" and the passages that mention the brothers and sisters of Jesus (Matthew 12:46; 13:55-56; Mark 3:31-35, 6:3,4; Luke 8:19-21; Acts 1:14), make it very clear that Mary had more children.

Then, there are passages in which Jesus makes Mary's part clear (Mark 3:31-35; Matthew 12:46-50; Luke 8:19-21; 11:27,28). In these passages Jesus makes it very clear that the spiritual relationship is more important than the physical relationship. Who are the brothers and sisters of Christ? Those who do His will. Also in these passages (as well as in Luke 2:48 and John 2:4) Jesus was not lacking respect for Mary, but was making it clear that His instructions came from the Heavenly Father and not from her.

In discipleship Bible studies, these and other passages can be studied at length so that new believers may understand what the Word of God teaches with regard to Mary. This can lead them to hold Mary in high esteem but at the same time to know that they should depend only on Jesus Christ as their mediator and intercessor. The following key passages of Scripture require additional study. Due to the fact that such important doctrines hinge on a proper understanding of these passages, attention is given to them in this segment.

Biblical Support for the Bodily Assumption of Mary?

The bodily assumption of Mary was first articulated *ex cathedra* by Pope Pious XII in 1950 when it was pronounced, "Just as the glorious resurrection of Christ was an essential part, and final evidence of the victory, so the Blessed Virgin's common struggle with her son was to be concluded with the 'glorification' of her virginal body."[58] In support of this progressive deification of Mary Catholic theologians often turn to some or all of the following biblical texts.

Gen. 3:15: In the Catholic *Douay-Rheims Version* this text reads as follows:

> I will put enmities between thee and the woman, and
> thy seed and her seed: ***she*** shall crush thy head, and thou
> shall lie in wait for ***her*** heel." (emphasis mine)

The Douay-Rheims Bible follows the Latin *Vulgate* and suggests that the woman, who Catholics interpret as Mary, is involved in the defeat of Satan. Thus, Catholics go on to propose that because Mary also had a share in Jesus' battle against Satan, she also partook in his victory over death. Thus, in Catholic dogma this verse is an implicit statement about Mary's assumption to heaven.

Psalm 132:8: Some church Fathers refer to this Psalm to state that "the Ark of Thy strength" was a type of the incorruptible body of Mary. Thus, both The Lord (Jesus) and the "Ark of Thy strength" (Mary) arise to their resting place (assumed bodily to heaven).

Matt. 27:52-53: This passage is used to suggest that since many saints arose from the grave after Jesus' resurrection it follows that the Mother of the Lord must have been called to perfection also (bodily assumption implied).

Luke 1:28: Catholic doctrine teaches that since she was "full of grace" Mary could not have been corrupted by original sin and consequently simply died and been buried. Mary died and was buried, but remained preserved from the corrupting consequences of sin. Again, Pope Pious affirms, "The body was preserved unimpaired in virginal integrity."

Revelation 12:1-6: Roman Catholics argue that the woman here is a reference to the "transfigured mother of Christ." They teach this text implies the assumption of Mary on the basis of her son being "caught up to God and His throne."

Thus, while it is generally believed that Mary suffered a "temporal" death her body did not see corruption, but she was taken soul and body directly to heaven where today she reigns as Queen of Heaven in her own right. But, does the Bible support the bodily assumption of Mary? Concerning the biblical passages that are often cited we make the following observations:

Gen 3:15: It is generally recognized today that Jerome in writing the *Vulgate* mistranslated the masculine pronouns *ipse* as feminine thus, *ipsa*. In the Hebrew text and Greek Septuagint the pronouns are masculine thus, the reading should be "***he*** shall bruise thy head" and later "thou shall bruise ***his*** heel." Also, even Catholic scholars acknowledge that in its context this passage is a clear reference to Eve as the woman from whom would one day be born one who would crush the serpent's head. Thus, there is nothing in the text to suggest the sinlessness or bodily assumption of the Mary—it's all about Eve's eventual offspring, her seed, Jesus.

Psalm 132:8: Here Catholics simply create an analogy with no merit whatsoever. There is no support in the Bible to sustain that the "ark" is a type of Mary. But there is clear teaching that only Christ would not see corruption (Acts 2:30-31) and that all humans (including Mary) suffer death and decay (Rom. 3:23; 1Cor. 15:42, 53).

Matt. 27:52-53: First, it is dangerous to use this problematic text as support for any doctrine—there is little scholarly consensus on the nature and or significance of the events in question. One thing is clear, however, Mary's assumption in no way follows from the fact that some dead saints were raised from the grave after the resurrection. In fact, the text only says that they appeared to many in Jerusalem, not that those who were raised were taken to heaven. If, however, we grant the Catholic version of this text, are we to assume that all those who were raised also had the same incorruptible nature during their length of time in the grave, something the Catholic church ascribes solely to Mary?

Luke 1:28: Again, the reading "full of grace" comes from the Latin *Vulgate*, which most scholars recognize as an incorrect reading. The Greek should be rendered, "Hail, *favored one!*" or "Hail, *woman richly blessed!*" Furthermore, while Catholic theologians insist that this ascription is a timeless characterization of Mary, as one who from birth to death was full of grace (Mary was perfect intensively and extensively), contextually the participle *keacharitomene* simply means she was favored in the specific instance of being chosen to give birth to the Messiah (cf. 1:30). It is worth noting that this participle *keacharitomene* rendered "full of grace" by Catholic theology is also used of Christian saints in general (Eph. 1:6). Thus, if this term means all that they say it means for Mary (namely that she was intensively filled with all grace and extensively filled throughout her life so as to exclude any possibility of original sin) then, it must mean the same for all believers in Christ. Obviously, such a reading would be heretical by a broad margin!

Revelation 12:1-6: The woman in this text is the nation of Israel (the people of God), not the Virgin Mary. That this is the correct interpretation is clearly evident by comparing this text with Genesis 37:9, which provides the Old Testament background. There, the sun and moon are interpreted by Jacob (or Israel) as symbolizing himself and Rachel his wife (v.10a). The eleven stars are Joseph's eleven brothers thus, symbolizing "Israel" as a people (v. 10b). There are several compelling reasons for not concluding that Mary is the woman mentioned in this passage.

First, as Svendsen points out, "from a purely literary standpoint, it is significant that the dragon is identified by John as Satan, the woman remains unidentified."[59]

Second, "the description of Revelation 12 does not fit the Gospel portrayal of the events surrounding the birth of Jesus. The birth, the snatching up, and the woman fleeing are all situated in heaven." [60] Note that the woman in Revelation 12 flees to the wilderness where God sustains her for 1260 days (v.6). There is nothing in Mary's life as revealed in Scripture that resembles this aspect.

Third, we should note that only the son is caught up to God and his throne (v.5). The woman is not similarly taken up.

Fourth, it is worth noting that while the "woman" of Revelation 12 "cried out being in labor and in pain,." Such a thing directly contradicts what Roman Catholicism teaches about Mary. It is said that because of her sinlessness "Mary gave birth in miraculous fashion without opening of the womb and

184

injury to the hymen, and consequently also without pain."[61] The Roman Catholic Church, therefore, cannot have it both ways. On the one hand it adheres to the dogma that Mary retained her virginity *in partu*, while on the other hand it teaches that Mary is the woman in Revelations 12 which the texts describes as experiencing "birth pangs."

Fifth, it should be additionally noted as Svendsen asserts, that "no church writer for the first several centuries saw any reference to Mary in this passage at all. It is not until the fifth century (in Quodvultdeus) and the sixth century (in Oecumenius) that we find positive evidence for seeing , respectively, Mary as a second reference unintended by the author of the Revelation and Mary as the primary referent in the interpretation of the text." [62]

Finally, this material should be seen as a future prophecy related to Israel. The nation of Israel metaphorically is the "woman" who gave birth to the Messiah. The imagery is a reference to the sufferings of Israel (Isaiah 26:16-18) and the deliverance of Israel (Isaiah 27:1-12).

In conclusion it should be noted that Catholic theologians by and large seem to be aware of the tenuous nature of many of their biblical interpretations. Often they fall back to some perceived safety zone by saying that the assumption of Mary is "probable" or "possible" based on something implied by the text. But such an approach is pure folly for theirs is more an exercise in eisegesis (reading something into a text) than exegesis (drawing out the meaning of the text). Though it stands as a piece of papal declaration the doctrine of the bodily assumption of Mary is nowhere taught in the Bible.

Biblical Support for the Intercessory Role of Mary?

Evangelicals generally use John 2:1-5 to demonstrate that Mary did not play an intercessory role during her earthly existence but merely pointed people to Jesus. Some Roman Catholic theologians, however, use this passage to try to prove that Mary did in fact play an intercessory role during her earthly existence and that this role continued when she went to heaven. Several things are clear from the reading of the passage. Mary as well as Jesus and his disciples had been invited to a wedding at Cana of Galilee (vv. 1,2). Quiet likely the family who invited them was close to Mary for she was privy to the information that the wine had run out. Mary then conveyed this information to Jesus: "they have no more wine" (v.3). What is the most accurate interpretation of this passage? Was Mary merely communicating her anxiety about this potentially embarrassing situation to Jesus? Did she do so in the hope that Jesus might find a way to help this couple? Did she do so with the expectation that he would perform a miracle and save the day for this family? [63]

The last option, as Svendsen states, is not in accordance with the passage because John makes it clear that this is "the *first* part of his miraculous signs." [64] Mary could not have been expecting something from Jesus which he had not done previously. While it is difficult to ascertain precisely what Mary had in mind when she uttered these words to Jesus, it is clear that Jesus viewed this as a form of request. He responded by saying : "Woman, what have I to do with you.?" This reply, as Svendsen points out, implies that she was overstepping her bounds.[65] This view is supported by a number of distinguished Catholic writers. Svendsen explains:[66]

> Yet as even McHugh admits, both Augustine and Chrysostom believed that Jesus was reprimanding his mother in this passage.[67] This understanding of Jesus' words as a reprimand is not uncommon in the patristric writings; it shows up in Iranaeus, who understands Jesus' tone toward Mary to be harsh in this passage: " When Mary pressed on toward the admirable sign of the wine and wanted prematurely to participate in the anticipated cup, the Lord said, repelling her untimely haste: 'Woman, what have I to do with you?"[68] It may also be found in Theodoret, who, commenting on our passage, writes: "At one time [Jesus] gives her honor as his mother as to her that gave him birth; at another time he rebukes her as her Lord."[69] Our passage is also commented on by Gregory the Great, who, in a treatise on the distinction between Christ's deity and humanity, paraphrases Jesus' words in John 2:4: "In this miracle, which ability comes not from your nature, I do not acknowledge you."[70]

The fact that these words of Jesus need to be seen as a reprimand is borne out by the rendering of the passage in Greek *(ti emoi kai soi, gunai)* "what to me and to you, woman." It is clear that in this passage, Jesus in using this expression and calling her "woman" instead of " mother" is distancing himself from his human family and stressing that his orders come from his heavenly Father.

What was Mary's response to Jesus' reprimand? She told the men: "Do whatever he tells you" (v.5). She did not tell Jesus what to do, nor did she tell the men that she would get Jesus to do what she felt needed to be done. Instead, she pointed the men to Jesus and instructed them that they follow his will, not hers. In other words, what ever he decides to do, it will be according to his will. As Carson states: "In short, in 2:3 Mary approaches Jesus as his mother, and is reproached; and in 2:5, she responds as a believer, and her faith is honored,"[71] This places Mary at the level of a follower of Jesus who continued to learn progressively as time went on about the divine nature and mission of Jesus. The fact that Jesus performed a miracle does not place her in a role of an intercessor any more than it would his brothers (John 7:3-5,10) and others (John 4:46-54) who made requests of him. This is consistent with John's portrayal of Jesus' ministry as Svendsen points out:

> All agree that John's gospel presents a high Christology. It would not be inconsonant for John to show right from the beginning that biological ties had no claim on Jesus. The fact that John refers to Mary as "the mother of Jesus" in this episode, whereas Jesus refers to her as "woman" speaks more for the necessity for John to identify just what relationship is being severed than it does of an ontological status for Mary.[72]

In this passage Mary is portrayed as a growing disciple who was still struggling to understand the ministry of Jesus. The clear meaning of the passage is not that we should go to Mary to seek to attain divine favor. Quite the contrary, it teaches that we should follow Mary's instructions: "What ever He says to you, do it" (v. 5). As McCarthy points out, "these are Mary's last recorded words in the Scriptures. They stand as excellent advice for anyone seeking to please God."[73]

Conclusion:

In summary, there is no New Testament basis for the doctrines of the perpetual virginity (that she had no other children), the immaculate conception (that she was born free of original sin), the role of co-mediatrix (that she mediates alongside of Christ) or the assumption (that she was taken up bodily into heaven) of Mary. Evangelicals do not have to believe these Roman Catholic doctrines to have a high concept of Mary. We can always emphasize her holy conduct, her obedience, her faith, and her willingness to point people to Jesus. As Borrás states:

> Mary deserves our appreciation and love as well as our most sincere recognition that she was a pious woman,

187

humble and full of faith, and that she was chosen by God to carry in her womb the redeemer of the world. Therefore, as was said by the angel when he announced to her the privilege which God had given her, she will always be called blessed by all generations. The best way to honor Mary is to obey what she told the people at Cana, "do whatever he [Jesus] tells you" (John 2:5)[74].

If the Catholic Church would limit itself to only that which the Bible says about Mary, Evangelicals would not have any concerns regarding this doctrine. The sad reality, however, is that the Catholic Church has added numerous doctrines which do not find any biblical foundation to these clear and simple accounts about Mary's important role as the earthly mother of Jesus. Some Catholics accuse Evangelicals of not honoring Mary. The truth of the matter is that Mary is truly honored when she is remembered and emulated in accordance with her role in Scripture. It is not an exaggeration to say that she would be appalled if she knew that some people give her the place that belongs only to her son Jesus Christ.

LESSON C

CATHOLIC TEACHING ABOUT THE SACRAMENTS

Introduction

The Catholic Church defines a sacrament as: "a sign instituted by Christ to give grace."[75] The Church views the sacraments as "the actions of Christ and his Church (itself a type of sacrament) which signify grace, cause it in the act of signifying it, and confer it to the person appropriately prepared to receive it. The Church teaches that the sacraments perpetuate the activity of Christ, making it present and efficacious. The sacraments infallibly convey the fruit of that activity - that is to say, grace - to persons receptive with faith."[76] The Catholic Church also teaches that the Sacraments are necessary for salvation[77]. The seven sacraments are viewed as the "primary means by which God bestows sanctifying and actual grace upon the faithful."[78] Each sacrament is not viewed by the Church as a mere symbolic expression of grace, but as a channel of God's grace. It is through the sacraments that God confers grace. John O'Brien affirms:

> [Christ] likewise established the sacraments which serve as so many channels through which the grace and blessings of Redemption reach the soul of each individual recipient... Christ by his suffering and death gained a vast reservoir. It is necessary that some means be devised to tap the reservoir and carry its riches to our souls. The sacraments are the means: channels of divine grace to the souls of men.[79]

Baptism

According to Catholic theology, baptism removes original sin, justifies the person, and makes the person a member of the Roman Catholic Church.

> "Baptism is the Sacrament of rebirth through which Jesus gives us the divine life of sanctifying grace and joins us to his mystical body."[80] "Baptism is the Sacrament which gives our souls the new life of grace by which we become children of God. Baptism removes original and present sin, if there is any, and all the punishment that it brings with it."[81]

The Catholic Church teaches that baptism washes away all sins, brings rebirth to life by grace, and makes the infant a member of the church. It is expected that the parents baptize the child as soon as possible. In baptism, the priest puts water on the forehead of the child and says: "I baptize you in the name of the Father, and of the Son, and of the Holy Spirit, Amen."

If the person cannot be baptized, the Catholic Church also accepts as valid the baptism of the blood of the martyrs and the baptism of desire, which indicates that the person had the intention of being baptized. In case of emergency, people who are not Catholics are allowed to baptize infants if they use the formula already mentioned above.[82] Baptism is considered absolutely necessary for salvation. The council of Trent decreed: "If anyone says that baptism is optional, that it is not necessary for salvation, let him be anathema."[83] (For additional information see lesson I).

Confirmation

The Catholic Church teaches that "Confirmation is the Sacrament through which Jesus confers on us the Holy Spirit, making us full-fledged and responsible members of the Mystical Body. We also receive the graces of the Holy Spirit especially those that enable us to profess, explain and spread the faith."[84] "Confirmation is the Sacrament by which the Holy Spirit comes to us in a special way to make us profess our faith as strong and perfect Christians and soldiers of Christ."[85] The bishop usually administers this sacrament by anointing the forehead of the person with oil, placing his hands on the person's head, and saying, "receive the seal of the Holy Spirit, the Gift of the Father." [86] The church teaches that through this sacrament a person receives the gifts and the strength of the Holy Spirit to live a life with Christian maturity. According to the Church, this sacrament completes the initiation of the person, having begun in baptism, gives character to the soul, and should be received only once. Children have to receive instruction (or rather, catechism) before receiving the sacrament of confirmation. Catholics are usually confirmed at the age of twelve after receiving the prescribed instruction on the doctrines of the Church.

The Eucharist

"The Holy Eucharist is a sacrament and a sacrifice. In the Holy Eucharist, inside the appearance of bread and wine, the Lord Jesus Christ is contained, offered, and received."[87]

The Catholic Church teaches that the priest transforms the bread and wine in such a way that they come to be literally the body and blood of Christ. As a result, the bread and the wine ought to be worshiped as the person of Christ himself is worshiped.

This internal change of the bread and wine (because externally they remain the same) is known as "transubstantiation" and forms the foundation for the Mass. That is to say, the priest transforms the bread and wine into the body of Christ so that He can be offered as a real sacrifice, an offering for the sins of the living and the dead.[88]

Evangelicals see the bread and wine as symbols of the body and blood of Christ, while Catholics believe that these literally become the body and blood of Christ.

Penance (Confession)

Catholic theology affirms that "Penance is the sacrament by which Jesus through the absolution of the priest, forgives sins committed after baptism."[89] "The Sacrament of Penance is the means by which sins committed after baptism are forgiven and the person is reconciled with God and with the Church."[90] People are told to confess to the priest sins that they have committed after baptism. The Catholic Church teaches that individual and complete total confession and absolution are the only customary means for the forgiveness of serious sins and for reconciliation with God and the Church. After hearing the confession, the priest declares: "By the ministry of the Church, God grant you pardon and peace. And I absolve you of your sins in the name of the Father, and the Son, and the Holy Spirit, Amen."[91] This sacrament is based on the doctrine that the priest, in view of his ordination, has the power to forgive sins. Generally, Penance is first received at the age of eight, prior to the First Communion. Subsequently, Catholics are expected to confess their sins to a priest who in turn proposes a penance and declares absolution.

Extreme Unction (or Anointing of the Sick)

This sacrament was previously known as Extreme Unction. "The Sacrament of the Sick is the sacrament in which Jesus through the anointing and prayers of the priest, gives health and strength to the person who is now seriously ill."[92] "The Sacrament of Extreme Unction gives health and strength to the soul and sometimes to the body when we are in danger of death."[93] Catholics base this sacrament on James 5:13-15. This sacrament is administered to persons who are in danger of losing their lives. While anointing the person with consecrated oil and offering prayers, the priest confers comforting grace to the person through this sacrament: the remission of venial sins and the declaration of not guilty for unconfessed mortal sins, which on occasion results in the amelioration of his state of health.[94] When persons are at the point of death, however, this sacrament is given along with Penance and the Eucharist. These are then called the "last rites." This sacrament can be administered more than one time.

These first five sacraments are considered essential for salvation. The remaining two impart grace but are not essential for salvation.

Marriage

The sacrament of marriage is the marriage ceremony of the Catholic church. "The wedding ceremony is seen as an agreement that joins them not only as a couple but with Christ and with the Church. While participating in that agreement, they should show to everyone the presence of the Savior in the world and the genuine nature of the church."[95] According to the Church, this sacrament "gives the graces needed to live a Christian married life."[96] "The Savior and the husband of the Church comes to the lives of married Christians through the sacrament of marriage. He dwells with them afterwards. Just as He loved the Church and gave himself for her, the husband and wife love one another with perpetual fidelity and mutual submission."[97] "Because marriage is seen as a sacrament by the Catholic Church, it hopes that those who enter into this agreement will raise their children within that faith and observe all the rules of the church." "The Catholic Church claims to have jurisdiction over all members in matters which have to do with marriage, which is a sacrament."

Holy Orders (Ordination)

The Catholic teaches that "Holy Orders are the sacrament in which spiritual power and grace are given to constitute and empower the ministry ordained to consecrate the Eucharist, forgive sins, carry out other pastoral and ecclesiastical functions, and form the community of the people of God. Holy orders impart character to the soul and should be received only once."[98]

The church, through the ages, has ordained persons for a great variety of ministries. These have included Subdeacons (to help with the Mass), Acolytes (to serve the Mass), Lectors (to read biblical passages and other passages in the liturgy), Porters (to assure that improper persons will not enter the churches), and Exorcists (to cast out demons). Many of these functions have been assigned to priests and lay persons without having to ordain persons for this. Nowadays, there are three basic types of ordination practiced by the Catholic Church.

1. Bishops

The fulfillment of the priesthood belongs to those who have been ordained as bishops. Bishops in a hierarchical union with the Pope and other bishops are considered the apostles and pastors of the church. They have individual responsibility for the care of local churches and carry out, together with their colleagues, labors which have to do with the universal Church. In their ordination or consecration, the sanctifier places his hands on the head of the candidate and prays the prayer prescribed for this ceremony.

2. Priests

A priest is a minister ordained with the power to celebrate the Mass, administer the sacraments, teach the Word of God, impart blessings, and carry out pastoral functions that are assigned to him by his ecclesiastical superior. Priests are ordained by ordained bishops, who place their hands on the head of the priests and follow the ceremony prescribed for this occasion. This ceremony includes the presentation of the implements for the sacrifice, such as the chalice and the plate that contains the Host, with prayers prescribed for this ceremony.

3. Deacons

There are two types of deacons that are ordained: those who receive ordination and remain within it permanently and those who receive ordination while they are advancing toward the priesthood. The position of the deacons is considered inferior to that of the priests in the Catholic hierarchy. They are not ordained for the priesthood but for the ministry of service. Deacons can be authorized by their superiors to administrate the sacraments and minister to people in need. They also help in the ministries of charity and administration.

A New Sacrament?

The Second Vatican Council (1962-1965) declared that the church is "a type of sacrament." The documents explain: "By virtue of its relationship with Christ, the Church, is a type of sacrament of the unity with all of humanity; that is to say, it is a sign and an instrument of such a union and unity."[99]

This doctrine supports the idea that salvation is found through the Church. The Catholic Catechism explains that:

> God established the church as the universal sacrament of salvations sent with a mission to all the world as the light of the world and the salt of the earth. For that reason, it is necessary to maintain these two truths together; that is to say, the possibility of salvation in Christ for all humanity, and the necessity of the church for salvation.

The doctrine of the Church as a sacrament is not biblical. Acts 2:41 states that the early Christians were added to the church because they had been saved. They were not saved because they were added to the church, as if this in and of itself were the sacrament (the channel) through which they received saving grace.

Conclusion:

The Catholic Church teaches that there are seven sacraments and that five of them are essential for salvation (Baptism, Confirmation, the Holy Eucharist, Penance, and Extreme Unction). The sad truth is that even after participating in all these sacraments, a person does not have the assurance of his salvation, because if he has committed a sin after having gone to confession and dies, he will have to go to purgatory and remain there until he is purged of his sins. The message of salvation, therefore, is truly "good news" for people who have not had a personal experience with Christ. Biblical salvation does not depend on a series of sacraments, but on receiving Christ as personal savior and Lord (John 1:12; 3:16). This last passage, for instance, does not say: "that whosoever is baptized, confirmed, does penance, participates in the Eucharist, and receives the last rites should not perish but have ever lasting life." What it does say is that "whosoever believes in Him, should not perish but have ever lasting life."

LESSON D

THE ELEMENTS OF CATHOLIC WORSHIP

Introduction

Generally, when Evangelicals think about Catholic worship, they only think of the Mass. The truth is that, for Catholics, the liturgy (worship) includes four elements: (1) the Eucharist Sacrifice (the Mass); (2) the Seven Sacraments; (3) the Liturgy of the Hours; and (4) the Sacramentals. It is clear, then, that the Catholic Church has a very broad concept of the liturgy which entails much more than the Mass. Because we want to concentrate a large part of this session to the Mass, we will leave this discussion for last.

Before we begin to talk about the individual elements of the liturgy, it is important that we define what the Catholic Church means when it uses the word "liturgy." The Catholic catechism defines the sacred liturgy as:

> The official public worship of God by the Mystical Body of Christ. By this worship, we proclaim the reconciliation of humanity and God. We are sanctified, or made holy, by means of these sacred actions and symbols. The liturgy, therefore, is the most significant form through which the faithful can express their lives and manifest to others the mystery of Christ and the true nature of the true church.[100]

The Catholic Almanac adds:

> The liturgy is considered as an exercise of the priestly office of Jesus Christ. In the liturgy, the sanctification of the person is manifested by means of the perceptible signs to the senses and effected in a way that is appropriate to each one of these signs; in the liturgy, full public worship is exercised for the Mystical Body of Christ; that is to say, for the Head and its members.[101]

> In the Catholic Church, the liturgy, therefore, is the public adoration of God through which the church, by means of sacred actions and symbols, proclaims the mystery of Christ and is sanctified. The liturgy is expressed in several forms.

The Seven Sacraments

The Catholic Church defines a sacrament as "a sacred sign constituted by Christ to give grace."[102] The Catechism adds: "The sacraments do not only make us conscious of divine life; they produce life in us. . .The sacrament of baptism does not only represent divine life but produces it."[103] The seven sacraments of the Catholic Church are: Baptism, Confirmation, Penance, the Eucharist, Extreme Unction, Ordination, and Marriage.[104] The Catholic Church teaches that, when participating in the sacraments, the person is participating in a liturgical activity that constitutes adoration and edification.

The Sacramentals

The Catholic Catechism defines sacramentals as "blessings or blessed objects that the church gives us to inspire our devotion and gain for us certain spiritual and temporal values."[105] The sacramentals differ from the sacraments in several ways. First, the Catholic Church teaches that the sacraments were instituted by Christ while the sacramentals were instituted by the Church. "The sacraments were instituted to impart grace; the sacramentals to impart a blessing or some special protection. The sacramentals have the effect of ' remitting venial sins, of repressing evil spirits, of granting grace through prayer, and of giving health to the body and material blessings."[106]

Principal Sacramentals

Some of the principal sacramentals are: (1) the crucifix; (2) the sign of the cross; (3) holy water; (4) statutes; (5) paintings (of Jesus, Mary, Joseph, and the saints); (6) medallions; (7) the Rosary; (8) scapulars; (9) the unction in baptism; (10) prayers used in Extreme Unction; (11) marital blessing; and (12) the Way of the Cross. Catholics may participate in these as the need and opportunity present themselves.

Specific Sacramentals

Some of the sacramentals are given only during certain days of the year. These include: (1) candles blessed and distributed on February 2nd; (2) the blessing of the throats on February 3rd; (3) Ashes placed on the foreheads of persons on Ash Wednesday; (4) the sacred palms distributed on Palm Sunday; and (5) the blessing of the fields on August 15th.

General Sacramentals

General sacramentals can be given at any time. These include the blessing of a home or of a mother during her pregnancy and the blessing of the child after birth.[107]

The Rosary

The Rosary consists of a chain of beads used to count the number of times that certain prayers have been offered. The name "rosary" comes from the word "rose" and reminds people of a garland of roses. Roses are also viewed as prayers offered to Mary. The rosary consists of five groups of ten beads each. These groups are called "decades" (ten). Each group is separated from the rest by beads bigger than those of the decades. There is an introductory chain of beads which begins the Rosary. This includes the crucifix, a separate bead, a group of three beads, and then a bead by itself.

When praying the Rosary, the Catholic recites the Apostle's Creed while holding the crucifix in his or her fingers. At each of the isolated beads, the person prays the Lord's Prayer. At each of the 50 beads that are in groups of ten, the person prays the "Hail Mary." This prayer is also known as the "Angelical Salutation." The prayer that is used is: "Hail Mary, full of grace. The Lord is with you. Blessed are you among women, and blessed is the fruit of your womb, Jesus. Hail Mary, mother of God pray for us sinners now at the hour of our death. Amen."[108]

After praying ten Hail Marys at each group of little beads, the person comes to a big bead. There is a total of five of these beads. On coming to each one of these beads, the person should meditate on one of the "Mysteries of the Life of Jesus and Mary." There are three series of mysteries: (1) Joyous Mysteries, (2) Painful Mysteries, and (3) Glorious Mysteries. There are five mysteries in each series. Under the Joyous Mysteries are: The Announcement of the birth of Jesus; The Visitation of Mary to Elizabeth; The Nativity; The Presentation, and The Finding of Jesus in the Temple. Under the Painful Mysteries are: The Agony of Jesus in the Garden of Gethsemane; The Flagellation (Jesus being whipped in Pilate's prison); The Crown of Thorns; The Bearing of the Cross; and The Crucifixion. Among the Glorious Mysteries are: The Resurrection of Christ; His Ascension to heaven; The Coming of the Holy Spirit on Pentecost; The Assumption of the body of Mary to heaven after her death; and The Coronation of Mary as the Queen of Heaven.[109]

The use of the Rosary includes praying and meditating on the mysteries. The majority of the prayers are directed to Mary. The Catholic Church Catechism explains: "As can be seen by the number of Hail Marys that are said, the Rosary is principally a prayer to the Blessed Mother of God. In this prayer we ask that she use her influence with her Son to obtain for us all the good things for our present needs and especially in the hour of our death. . .This is a prayer for times of crisis. She has proven and will prove again her power for our day."[110]

The Way of the Cross

In many Catholic Churches there are fourteen pictures representing important events in Christ's walk toward the cross in front of which members should meditate and pray. This type of prayer is known as "The Way of the Cross." Each one of these pictures tells the story of the last week (especially the last twenty-four hours) in the life of Jesus: (1) Jesus being whipped; (2) The cross placed upon Jesus' shoulders; (3) Jesus falling under the weight of the cross; (4) Mary gazing at Jesus; (5) Simon of Cryene carrying the cross of Jesus; (6) Veronica cleaning the face of Jesus; (7) Jesus falling again despite Simon's help; (8) Jesus stopping to console women; (9) Jesus falling again while having Calvary in view; (10) The soldiers removing Jesus' clothes; (11) Jesus nailed to the cross; (12) Jesus suffering on the cross until death; (13) Joseph of Arimathea and Nicodemus lowering the body of Jesus from the cross; and (14) Jesus placed in the tomb[111]. In addition to seeing these moving pictures in certain churches, there are persons who go to Jerusalem or to other countries (like Cordoba, Spain) to walk through the stations of the cross. In accordance with the Catechism, this experience helps people to meditate on the events related to the death of Jesus, and as a result of this, to receive spiritual benefits and divine help.[112]

The Sacramentals are seen as external practices (actions, words, or objects) that help people stimulate their inner feelings of prayer and meditation. The Catholic Catechism warns members: "We should avoid superstition in the use of medallions and other blessed objects, remembering that they, like other sacramentals, do not produce any effect automatically, but as a result of the prayers of the church and the devotion that they inspire in us."[113]

The Liturgy of Hours

The Liturgy of Hours (Divine Office) is the public prayer of the Church to sanctify the day by praising God. Its daily recitation, or celebration, is a sacred duty of ordained men and of religious men and women in accordance with their rule of life. "In the Liturgy of Hours, the Church exercises the priestly office of its head and constantly offers to God the sacrifice of praise."[114] The revised Liturgy of Hours consists of prayers by day or night. The liturgy includes selected readings and helps for meditation. The Catholic Catechism teaches that this liturgy is a reminder of the heavenly worship offered constantly before the throne of God and of the Lamb.[115]

The Eucharist Sacrifice (The Mass)

The Catholic Church considers the Mass as the holiest act of worship without exception. The catechism explains: "In the Last Supper, our Lord surrounded the moment of sacrifice with ceremonies, the supper itself, the washing of feet, the sermon and the hymn.[116]" The Mass today, in the Latin rite, is divided into two parts, the Liturgy of the Word and the Liturgy of the Eucharist.

The Liturgy of the Word

The Liturgy of the Word consists of the rite on entry, the reading of the Scriptures, a homily from the Word of God, and the prayer of the faithful. Although there is a geographical and cultural variety with regard to the style of the liturgy (music, instruments, etc.), the Liturgy of the Word follows the following structure.

1. The people talk to God

   a) The Rite of Entry

The most common form is that a hymn is sung while the celebrant (the priest) enters. The first word is directed to God by confessing sins and asking for his forgiveness.

   b) The Gloria

Here the second word is expressed, one of adoration. This is directed to the three persons of the Trinity.

c)   The Opening Prayer

In this, the third and fourth words are found. They consist of a word of thanks for favors received and a word of petition for favors in the future.

2.   God talks to the people

a)   The First Reading

This, generally, is a reading from the Old Testament. The people are expected to listen to the revelation of God for his people as the passage is reasd.

b)   Psalm of Response

This is a prayer of reflection related to the theme of the lesson. This prayer is made in an alternating form by the reader and the congregation.

c)   The Second Reading

The second reading is taken from the New Testament.

d)   The Acclamation of the Gospel

This is a hallelujah given as an introduction to the reading of the Gospel for that day.

e)   The Homily

This is the message from the Scriptures (based on the readings) given by the priest applying the message to the present day.

f)   The Creed

This is considered an answer to the words of God as an expression of faith on behalf of the members of the church. "When reciting the creed, the members of the church come together with Christians of all ages to express the basic doctrines of the Christian faith."[117]

g)   The Prayer of the Faithful

These are some series of petitions for the needs of the Church, the civil government, and all of humanity.

The Liturgy of the Eucharist

The Liturgy of the Eucharist is composed of two principal parts: "The people give to God" and "God gives to the people."The first consists of "The Preparation of the Gifts." The second part includes The Lord's Prayer, The Rite of Peace, The Communion, and The Conclusion.

1.   The people give to God

a)   The Preparation of the Gifts

This begins with a few members who represent the entire congregation by bringing the gifts of bread, wine, and water to the priest, who is celebrating the Mass. Other gifts such as the collection, charity gifts, and symbolic offerings may be included.

b)   The Eucharistic Prayer

The most important part of the Mass is introduced by a song of thanksgiving, called the preface. The Catholic Church teaches that "During the Eucharist Prayer, Jesus offers the sacrifice of his body and his blood to God. Once more he renews his offering made on the cross. The consecration occurs in the center of the Eucharistic Prayer. In that moment, Jesus, through the priest, converts the bread and wine into his body and blood. The priest then invites the congregation to proclaim its faith in the new Eucharist presence of Jesus on the altar."[118]

2.   God gives to the people

a)   The Lord's Prayer

The worship service of communion begins with the prayer that Jesus taught. The congregation asks for the bread which is Jesus, forgiveness from those whom it has offended, and asks for God's forgiveness.

b)   The Rite of Peace

Killgallon explains that "before approaching the altar to receive Jesus in the communion, persons should be in peace with their families and their

201

neighbors."[119] When doing this, the local customs are observed while giving the sign of peace, symbolizing peace with all humanity.

c)   The Communion

Killgallon states that "the priest gives the persons the true bread of life. Through this sacred meal we join intimately with Jesus and with all who participate in this holy banquet."[120]

d)   The Conclusion

After a short prayer of thanks, the priest gives his blessing and the people are sent to live the message of the Word and of the Eucharist.

Those who participate in the Mass are: (1) The Celebrant (or Celebrants), who preside over the assembly; (2) The Deacon, who helps the Celebrant and reads the Gospel; (3) The Commentator, who explains to the congregation the different parts of the Mass; (4) The Choir (or group), which helps the congregation with the hymns; (5) The People, who pray and sing in accordance with the part which corresponds to them; (6) The Servers, who help the priest at the altar.

The priest wears clothing of different colors in agreement with the liturgical calendar. On ordinary Sundays, the priest wears green vestments. During the seasons of Advent and Lent, the priest wears purple vestments. During Christmas and the Resurrection, the priest wears white vestments, and on Pentecost, red vestments.

Conclusion:

As we can see, the Catholic concept of worship (liturgy) covers the whole life of the members of the church. Through the sacraments, the liturgy of hours, the sacramentals, and the Eucharist (Mass), Catholics have actions, words, and symbols to express their faith in every circumstance in life. We should also note that all of these liturgical elements are interwoven in such a way that Catholics are given the opportunity to worship whether it be in front of an altar in their home, in front of an image in a sacred place, or in the Mass itself. Although we know that there are many persons who do not understand what their church teaches with regard to the liturgy, there are several things that we ought to keep in mind. First, it is important that we know what the liturgy means so that we can understand the spiritual needs of our Catholic friends and family members. Second, it is of very important that we treat with respect the practices and implements (sacramentals) which Catholics use, knowing that these are very sacred to them. Third, it is important that we understand that many people have profound social and emotional connections with the sacramentals (for example, the crucifix) which go beyond the religious understanding that they may have. Methods that focus only on convincing people intellectually are not effective. It requires time and the establishment of a close relationship to deal with these social and emotional connections. Finally, it is very important that we give attention to ritual, social, and devotional voids that at times exist in persons who accept Christ and join an Evangelical church. They no longer have rites and ceremonies related to the most important experiences of life (for example, birth or the anniversary of a death of a loved one). What can we do to fill these voids in a throughly biblical and culturally appropriate way? We will address this need in chapter 8.

LESSON E

JUSTIFICATION

Is justification received by faith alone or are works essential for our salvation?

In its sessions (1545-1563), the Council of Trent made several declarations against the doctrine of justification by faith:

> If someone should say that justifying faith is nothing other than confidence (fiducia) in divine mercy, which remits sins by the merits of Christ, or that it is this confidence only which justifies - let him be an anathema. If someone should say that received faith is not preserved and also increased before God by good works, but that these works are merely fruits and signs of justification obtained, but not the cause of its increase - let him be an anathema.[121]

These and other declarations of the Council of Trent were made by the Catholic Church to refute the central doctrine of the Reformation: "justification by faith alone." Let us note the implications of these declarations. The first one is that salvation cannot be reached by simply and only placing our confidence in Christ as our savior. The second implication is that justification is increased and preserved by good works. The third implication is that good works are not fruits and signs of justification received. The Catholic Church utilizes the concept of justification being received and being increased by good works as a basis for its doctrine of good works, which includes the participation of persons in the sacraments, works of charity, and other devotional practices.

Evangelicals base the doctrine of justification by faith alone on such passages as Romans 3:28; Ephesians 2:8-9, and Galatians 2:16. This last passage says: "know that a man is not justified by observing the law, but by faith in Jesus Christ. So we, too, have put our faith in Christ Jesus, that we may be justified by faith, and not by observing the law, because by observing the law no one will be justified."

James White explains:

> Justification is by faith because it is in harmony with grace. Grace — the free and unmerited favor of God —

cannot be earned, purchased or merited. By nature it is free. Faith has no merit in and of itself. It performs no meritorious work so as to *gain grace or favor.* It trusts in the Giver of grace and is the only basis by which God declares a sinner, in light of the work of Christ, "righteous."[122]

In leading people to a saving knowledge of Christ and in discipling them, it is very important that we understand the biblical doctrine of justification. We are saved by grace through faith in Christ alone. Our good works are the result not the cause of our justification. The study of the following portions of Scripture will shed further light on this truth.

James 2:14-26:
Salvation by Faith and Meritorious Works?

According to Roman Catholic doctrine, James 2:14-26 teaches that meritorious works along with faith are essential to the salvation of the person. To do so the church points to the usage of "justify" and "works" to commend Abraham (2:21), Rahab (2:25) and, therefore, all believers (2:24). Thus, the Roman Catholic Church insists that lifelong works of merit are an integral part of justification. And what are these works? As it turns out, the person is turned directly to the sacramental system created by the church. But is this what James teaches?

First, any honest reading of the second chapter of James makes it clear that the author is really talking about the need to demonstrate one's faith, rather than describe a way to achieve it.[123] James is simply saying that faith without works is an oxymoron. Like Matthew 11:19, where wisdom, it is said, *is justified by her children,* likewise here the works of the righteous justify, that is, verify that the believer's justification is for real. Douglas Moo recognizes this fundamental thrust. He notes: "It is absolutely vital to understand that the main point of this argument, expressed three times (in vv. 17, 20, and 26), is not that works must be *added* to faith, but that genuine faith *includes* works."[124] (emphasis his) To support this position we must look at several issues.

Second, note that in James 2:14 in part reads, "What use is it, my brethren, if a man *says* he has faith, but he has no works?" (emphasis mine) James is referring to people who ostensibly are people of "faith" in tension, holding them accountable to the verification of works. As Luther realized, people are justified by faith alone, but not by a faith that is alone.

Finally, although both James and Paul use the terms "works" and "faith" they use them in different ways. While Paul excludes the possibility that any work generated to fulfill the legal requirements of the law so as to justify can be of any salvific value (Rom. 3:20; Gal.2: 16), James, for his part, teaches that true faith will always be accompanied by works generated by the perfect law of liberty (1:25; 2:12). Though both use the term "works" they mean things that are diametrically opposed to each other—legalistic works for Paul, charitable deeds born of love for James. Thus, James is in complete agreement with Paul who elsewhere acknowledges that while salvation is not by works, that no one may boast (Eph. 2:9), the righteous are saved unto good works, for the production of deeds of charity (2:10). Accordingly, for Paul genuine faith is solely the work of God and without human intervention while for James pseudo faith is self-serving and results in no practical benefits in the world.

LESSON   F

CONFESSION

The Roman Catholic church teaches that Christ gave the apostles the power to forgive sins.[125] Keeping the sacrament of confession means Catholics are urged to confess their sins to the priest.[126] The question we need to address is: to whom should we confess, according to the Bible?

In Luke 24:47, Jesus reminded His disciples that "repentance and forgiveness of sins will be preached in his name to all nations." In Acts 8:22, the apostle Peter rebukes Simon the Sorcerer and tells him, "Repent of this wickedness and pray to the Lord. Perhaps he will forgive you for having such a thought in your heart." Notice that Peter does not ask Simon to confess to *him* nor does he make an attempt to absolve or forgive Simon. Instead, Peter asks Simon to pray to the Lord. In Acts 10:43, Peter explains to Cornelius that everyone who believes in Jesus receives forgiveness in his name. Peter does not ask Cornelius to confess to him. In Acts 13:38, Paul reminds his audience that through Jesus the forgiveness of sin is preached to them. The Bible teaches that confession should be made to the Lord. In 1 John 1:9, we read: "If we confess our sins, he is faithful and just and will forgive us our sins and purify us from all unrighteousness" (Study also Ps. 32:5; 51:4; 2 Sam. 12:13; Dan. 9:9).

While we find in the Bible such concepts as reciprocal confession (James 5:16) "Confess your sins one to another") and public confession prior to baptism (see Matt. 3:6), there is no teaching in Scripture that instructs people to confess to a priest.

What about the "keys to the kingdom?" Catholics teach that the "keys to the kingdom" mentioned by Jesus represented the apostle's right to forgive sins. However, as we examine the Scriptures, we can answer the following questions raised by Brewer.[127]

What were the keys to the kingdom? As we study the following passages we can see clearly that the keys were the message of salvation. In 1 John 1:5, we see that John was careful to communicate "the message we have heard from him." It is the response to this message which results in salvation and not the activity or pronouncement of a servant of Christ. John explains: "If we confess our sins He is faithful and just and will forgive us our sins and purify us from all unrighteousness" (1 John 1:9). There is no hint here that John sees

207

himself as the dispenser of God's forgiveness other than through the proclamation of the message of salvation. The same is true for Peter. In Acts 8:22, he does not offer to forgive Simon (the sorcerer) but instead urges him to "pray to the Lord. Perhaps he will forgive you for having such a thought in your heart." In Matthew 28:19-20, we see once again that the keys to the kingdom were the message of the gospel which the apostles were commissioned to proclaim in all the world.

Were the keys given to Peter alone? In the following passages we see that "the keys to the kingdom" (the message of salvation) were not given to Peter alone. In Matthew 28:18-20 and John 20:22-23, we see that the Great Commission was given to all of the apostles (except Judas) by Jesus after his ascension. It can be stated, therefore, that the other apostles also had "the keys to the kingdom" because they had the message of salvation to proclaim.

What about intermediaries—Can we go directly to Christ? As we have stated previously, the Roman Catholic Church emphasizes the role of the Church, Mary, and others as intermediaries (or go-betweens). The study of Scripture, however, leads us to the conviction that we go directly to Christ with our prayers, praise, and petitions. In John 10:9 Jesus states: "I am the gate; whoever enters through me will be saved." In John 14:6 Jesus declares: "I am the way and the truth and the life; no one comes to the Father except through me." Jesus does not speak of any mediators through which people may come to him. The apostles understood this clearly. Before the high priest, who was seen as a mediator by many Jews, Peter declared: "Salvation is found in no one else; for there is no other name under heaven given to men, by which we must be saved," (Acts 4:12). Paul emphasizes this when he writes to Timothy: "For there is one God, and one mediator between God and men, the man Jesus" (I Timothy 2:5). Hebrews 7:25 clearly stresses the role of Jesus as our only and sufficient mediator: "Therefore he is able to save completely those who come to God through him, because he always lives to intercede for them."

LESSON   G

PURGATORY

Although the Catholic Church teaches that Jesus Christ died on the cross to save humanity, it has added the doctrine of purgatory to the biblical doctrine of salvation.

In 1274, the Second Council of Lyons made the following formal declaration of the doctrine of purgatory:

> If those who have truly repented die in charity before they have done sufficient penance for their sins of omission and commission, their souls are cleansed after death in purgatorial or in cleansing punishments. The suffrages of the faithful on the earth can be of great help in relieving these punishments, as, for instance, the Sacrifice of the Mass, prayers, almsgiving, and other religious deeds which, in the manner of the Church, the faithful are accustomed to offer on behalf of others of the faithful.[128]

Roman Catholic theology teaches that purgatory is an intermediate realm between death and the final judgment and that the soul of the faithful who die in venial sin go to purgatory to be purged of sin. There is divergence of opinion as to the type of suffering and the place where this occurs. However, the concept of purgatory is an official doctrine of the Roman Catholic Church. Purgatory did not become an official doctrine until the Council of Florence in 1439. The subsequent Council of Trent "defined the existence of purgatory, insisted that the souls detained there are helped by acts of intercession of the faithful, and especially the sacrifice of the Mass."[129]

Catholic theologian, Friar Avery Dulles, admits that "purgatory is not specifically taught in the Bible." He mentions two quotes. One of them is 2 Maccabees 12:45, which refers to the action of Judas Maccabees in sending an offering to Jerusalem to make a sacrifice for his soldiers who had died in idolatry.[130] This passage describes the event during the Maccabean wars in which "amulets sacred to the idols of Jamnia" (v. 40) were found in the clothing of Jewish soldiers who had died in battle. Judas Maccabees considered this a desecration. He collected money from his soldiers and sent an offering to Jerusalem as an expiatory sacrifice to be offered for the soldiers' sins.

Three additional New Testament passages which some Catholics use to support the doctrine of purgatory are: Matthew 5:26; Matthew 12:32; and 1 Corinthians 3:15. As can be seen, the first passage speaks about an earthly situation with an earthly judge; the second passage speaks about the sin against the Holy Spirit which is not forgiven in this life nor in the next. This passage contradicts the concept of purgatory which claims that a person can be forgiven after death. The third passage uses the analogy of fire "as if by fire," to explain how the *works* Christians do will be tested (not the *persons* themselves but the work they do).

The Catholic Church utilizes this passage to teach that people who die in a state of grace, but with unconfessed sin, will have to go to purgatory where they will be cleansed and made ready to go to heaven. This cleansing can be accomplished through the celebrations of special Masses by the priest and prayers offered by loved ones on behalf of the deceased.

Several observations need to be made regarding this passage. First, Maccabees is describing a *Jewish* practice not a *Christian* practice.[131] Second, this passage is talking about the belief in the *resurrection*, not the belief in *purgatory*. Third, this passage, according to Roman Catholic theology would need to refer to *mortal* sin (idolatry). According to Catholic theology only persons with unconfessed venial will go to purgatory. Those with mortal sins will go to hell, not purgatory.[132]

The Bible teaches that persons go to heaven or to hell after dying. Such passages are: Luke 23:43; II Corinthians 5:8-9, Luke 16, Matthew 25:31-46, I John 5:13. This is another of the doctrines that the Catholic Church has added that does not find any Scriptural basis. The danger of this doctrine is that it can give a false hope to persons who have not received Christ as their savior, that, when they die, their families will pray for them so that they will go to heaven. One of the saddest things about this doctrine is that it undermines the assurance of salvation. People can live a devoted life, fulfill all the requirements of the church, and even then not have the joy nor the assurance of their salvation.

An examination of these passages leads one to agree with Roman Catholic theologian Richard McBrien: "There is, for all practical purposes, no biblical basis for the doctrine of purgatory."[133]

The following passages speak about the completeness of Christ's forgiveness and the assurance of salvation: Luke 23:43; 2 Corinthians 5:8-9; Matthew 25:31-46, 1 John 5:13; 1 John 1:7.

210

LESSON H

HEAD OF THE CHURCH

In 1870, the First Vatican Council declared the primacy of the Pope as the successor of Peter and the head of the church. The Catholic Almanac explains that:

> The primacy of the pope is a real and supreme power. It is not simply, a prerogative of honor - that is to say of being recognized as first among equals. Nor does primacy imply that the pope is simply the official who presides over the collective body of bishops. The pope is the head of the church. The Second Vatican Council elaborated this doctrine. This entire teaching is based on Scripture, tradition, and experience through the centuries of the church.[134]

The *Documents of Vatican II* states:

> In order that the episcopate itself might be one and undivided, He [Christ] placed blessed Peter over the other apostles, and instituted him a permanent and visible source and foundation of unity of faith and fellowship. All this teaching about the institution, the perpetuity, the force and reason for the sacred primacy of the Roman Pontiff and of his infallible teaching authority, this sacred Synod again proposes to be firmly believed by all the faithful.[135]

The principal Scripture portion that the Roman Catholic Church uses to bolster its contention that Jesus built the Church upon Peter is Matthew 16:18 "And I tell you that you are Peter and upon this rock I will build my church and the gates of hell will not overcome it." The argument the Catholic Church presents is that the "rock" refers to Peter. However, the Greek language, in which the New Testament was written, makes a distinction between Peter and the rock. The word for Peter is *"pétros"* and the word for rock is *"pétra."* The word *"pétros"* is in the masculine gender and means a detached stone. The word *"pétra"* is in the feminine gender and means a bolder or bedrock. Peter is always referred to in the second person (you), while the "rock" is referred to in the near demonstrative third person (this). Christ is pointing Peter to something other than himself as the foundation of the Church. It is important to point out that the verse does not say: "You are *"pétros"* and

211

upon this *"pétros"* I will build my church." Why does the verse distinguish between the two? The reason is that a specific meaning was communicated by using two different words. Some will present the argument that Jesus was speaking in Aramaic when he said this, which is true. Two facts, however, need to be considered. First, why did not the Holy Spirit simply transliterate an Aramaic word as was done in other cased when Peter was called Cehpus? The Holy Spirit led the writers to make this distinction. The second fact is that the Catholic Church accepts the Greek Canon and does not recognize an Aramaic canon. Would it be inconsistent to accept all the Greek Cannon, except for this verse?[136]

The *"pétra"* that is used here points to the confession that Peter made. "You are the Christ, the Son of the living God." This is in keeping with the question that Jesus asked Peter in verse 13: "Who do people say the Son of Man is?" The question was not who is Peter but who is Jesus. Peter's reply was revealed to him by God (v. 17). The revelation had to do with the divinity of Jesus. **It is upon that solid bolder** (*"pétra"*) that the church of our Lord Jesus Christ is built. Further, James McCarthy reminds us that Matthew was writing to a Jewish audience. He cites G. Campbell Morgan, who affirms that the word "rock" throughout Hebrew Scriptures, was always used symbolically to refer to God.[137] Such passages include 1 Samuel 2:2, Psalm 18:32, and Isaiah 44:8.

Peter himself stated that Jesus is the *"pétra"* when he said:

> See I lay in Zion a chosen and precious cornerstone,
> and the one who trusts in him will never be put to shame.
> Now to you who believe, this stone is precious. But to those
> who do not believe, The stone that the builders rejected has
> become the capstone and a stone that causes men to stumble
> and a rock that makes them fall (1 Peter 2:6-8).

The word used for stone in this passage is *"lithon,"* but, the word used for the "rock that makes them fall" is *"pétra."* This is the same word that Paul uses in 1 Corinthians 10:3,4 to refer to Christ:

> They all ate of the same spiritual food and drank of the
> same spiritual drink; for they drank from the spiritual rock
> that accompanied them, and that rock was Christ.

There is evidence in both the Old and the New Testaments that the symbolism of the rock referred to God and then to Jesus. It is important to nail down the truth that the Church is not built upon a man, **but upon Jesus Christ, the Son of the living God.**[138]

Bartholomew F. Brewer, a former Roman Catholic priest and author of *Pilgrimage from Rome*[139], makes the following observations regarding the Roman Catholic teaching that the church was built on Peter[140]:

1. Did Peter act as if he were the head of the church?

In Acts 8:14, the apostles sent Peter and John to examine Philip's ministry in Samaria. It was not Peter who sent anyone. He was sent by the apostles.

In Acts 10:25-26, when Cornelius fell at Peter's feet in reverence, Peter said "Stand up, I am only a man myself."

In I Peter 5:1, Peter calls himself "a fellow elder." There is no evidence that he considered himself as having authority over the other apostles.

2. Did the other apostles act as if Peter were the head of the church?

If Peter had been signaled by Jesus as the supreme pontiff, why did the apostles continue to debate as to who from their ranks would be the greatest? See Mark 9:34; Luke 22:24.

In Galatians 2:1-10, Paul describes his trip to Jerusalem to meet with the leaders (James, Peter, and John). Notice that he did not meet with Peter alone. As a result of this meeting, it was agreed that Paul and Barnabas would focus their ministry on the Gentiles. The leaders, including Peter, would go to the Jews.

In 2 Corinthians 12:11 Paul states: "In no way was I inferior to the most eminent apostles, even though I am a nobody." Could he have made that statement if Peter was the acknowledged vicar of Christ?

3. Whom do the epistles affirm as the head of the church?

Ephesians 1:22; 2:20-21; 5:23; Colossians 1:18; 1 Corinthians 3:11. These passages make it very clear that Jesus is the head of the church.

4. Who resolved the problem at the Jerusalem Council?

Peter or James? In Acts 15:13-20 Peter and Paul, as well as others gave testimony of what God had done among the Gentiles. It was James, however, who proposed the solution to the problem they were facing. The letter they sent to the Gentiles stated: "it pleased the Holy Spirit and us..." There is no mention of Peter making an authoritative proclamation to solve this problem.

5. Who rebuked Peter?

In Galatians 2:11-14, Paul rebuked Peter for his hypocrisy and bad influence he had on Barnabas. Peter ate with Gentiles, but when Jews appeared, he withdrew from the Gentiles giving the impression that he was still observing Jewish restrictions.

6. Who is the high priest of the church? .

In I Peter 3:18; Hebrews 7:26-27; Hebrews 9:25-28; and Ephesians 1:22, Christ is the high priest of the church. Ephesians 2:20 makes it clear that the church "is built upon the foundation of the apostles and prophets, Christ himself being the cornerstone."

From these portions of Scripture we learn that Peter was an apostle in his own right (1 Peter 1:1), but he was never elevated above others and he did not act as if he were the head of the church. The other apostles did not treat Peter as if he were the head of the church. Peter himself said that the Church is built on Jesus and the epistles affirmed this teaching. It was James and not Peter who proposed the solution to the problem discussed in the Jerusalem Council. Paul felt he had the liberty to rebuke Peter because of his inconsistent behavior of eating with the Gentile believers, but then withdrawing from them when other Jews showed up. Finally in the book of Hebrews we find the clear and authoritative doctrine that Jesus is the all sufficient high priest of the Church. The Church is built on Jesus Christ, the Son of the living God, and not on a man.

LESSON I

BAPTISM

One of the most important issues that need to be dealt with in the discipleship process has to do with baptism. The two principal aspects of this issue have to do with the age at which a person is baptized and the meaning of Christian baptism.

It is not unusual for a person with a Catholic background who has had an experience of salvation through faith in Jesus Christ to ask, "why should I be baptized again? Wasn't the first baptism valid?" These questions needs to be treated with sensitivity and integrity. An implication of this question is that the new believer's parents were sincere when they baptized him. Their sincerity needs to be accepted at face value. Undoubtedly, they wanted their child to relate properly to God from the very beginning. The parents need to be affirmed for this desire. But the question needs to be asked, is sincerity enough? There was a time when certain types of inoculations were administered to children on the belief that they would prevent certain diseases. Now we know that some of those inoculations had potential side effects that were worse than the illness they were trying to avoid. By the same token, the new believer's parents had the best of intentions when they had their child baptized, but in light of what the Bible teaches, infant baptism does not impart salvation to the infant and can give him or her a false sense of security regarding eternal salvation. The thing to do is to not condemn the parents for having baptized their child, but to not commend them for their good intentions and to invite them to study what the Bible says about infant baptism and about believer's baptism.

Biblical Texts The Catholic Church Uses

The Catholic Church uses several Scripture passages to support the practice of infant baptism. However, it needs to be pointed out from the outset that there is not a single Bible verse that explicitly teaches infant baptism. The Catholic Church uses the following passages:

Households That Were Baptized

The Bible records several households that were baptized. First, we find that Peter baptized Cornelius and his household (Acts 10:48). Then, we find that Paul and his fellow workers baptized Lydia and her household (Acts 16:15), the Philippian Jailer and his household (Acts 16:33), Crispus and his household (Acts 18:8), and the household of Stephanas (1 Corinthians 1:16). The argument that is presented is that if the "households" were baptized, it included the infants in these families and that this justifies the Catholic practice of baptizing infants. But is that what the Bible says? The Bible states that it was those who *believed* were baptized. The Philippian jailer "believed in God with his household." They heard the good news of salvation, placed their faith in Christ, and then were baptized. This pattern is found in the other instances cited in Scripture. Infants do not have the mental capacity to understand the gospel and to personally place their faith in Christ. The biblical teaching is that belief is a prerequisite for baptism (e.g., Acts 2:40; Mark 16:16).

Children that drew near to Jesus

The Catholic Church also cites Luke 18:16,17 to bolster its argument for infant baptism. In this passages, Jesus says: "Let the children come unto me, and do not hinder them for the kingdom of God belongs to such as these. I tell you the truth, anyone who does not receive the kingdom of God like a little child will never enter it."

In order to understand this passage more clearly, the context needs to be studied. As McCarthy points out, these were Jewish parents who brought their children for Jesus to lay hands on them and pray. And that is precisely what Jesus did. He *blessed* them but he did not *baptize* them.[141]

The truth of the matter is that this passage itself provides sufficient reason to oppose the Roman Catholic practice of baptizing infants to cleanse them of original sin. If we have to be like children to receive the kingdom of God, theirs is a simple, innocent faith that we as adults must have in order to receive Christ's saving grace.

Texts that speak about the new birth

The Catholic Church utilizes John 3:5 to support its argument that people receive grace through the sacrament of baptism. "I solemnly assure that no one can enter into God's kingdom without being begotten of water and Spirit." (New American Bible, Saint Joseph Edition).

What The Bible Teaches About Baptism.

Believer's Baptism

The Bible teaches that people need to believe in Jesus Christ before they are baptized.

Acts 2:41 states: "Those who accepted his message were baptized, and about three thousand were added to their number that day." This was the gospel message that Peter preached on the day of Pentecost. Upon hearing the message, they "cut to the heart" and said to Peter and the other apostles, "brothers, what shall we do" (Acts 2:37). Peter replied: "Repent and be baptized everyone of you, in the name of Jesus for the forgiveness of your sins" (v. 38). Those who were baptized were people who had the capacity to understand the message, repent of their sins, and make a personal decision to be baptized. This portion, along with other verses of the Bible (e.g., Mark 16:16; Acts 8:12), make it very clear that a person must make a personal decision to place his trust in Jesus as Savior before he is baptized. Infants cannot do this therefore, biblical baptism is reserved for those who can make the decision to receive Christ.

Baptism Is An External Symbol Of An Inner Reality

One of the clearest passages regarding the meaning of baptism is found in Romans 6:3-4, which states: "Or don't you know that all of us who were baptized into Jesus Christ were baptized into his death? We were, therefore, buried with him through baptism into his death, in order that, just as Christ was raised from the dead through the glory of God the Father, we too may live in a new life." Baptism is an external symbol of the inner reality. When we receive Jesus as our savior, we die to our past life and start living the new life that He has given us. Baptism by immersion, therefore, is a graphic picture of the burial and resurrection of Jesus. The literal meaning of the Greek word *baptizo* is to immerse.

Baptism Is An Act Of Obedience

Before ascending into heaven, Jesus gave his disciples His final instructions:

> All authority in heaven and on earth has been given
> unto me. Therefore, go and make disciples of all nations,

> baptizing them in the name of the Father, and of the Son,
> and of the Holy Spirit, and teaching them to obey everything
> I have commanded you. And surely I am with you always,
> to the very end of the age (Matthew 28:18-20).

The disciples followed the instructions of Jesus. In Acts 2:40 we read: "Those who accepted his message were baptized." In Acts 9:18 we read that after Saul had had that marvelous experience with Jesus, Ananias prayed for him and Saul "got up and was baptized."

Believer's baptism, therefore, is an external symbol of an inner reality (the new birth) and an act of obedience to Jesus, who commanded his followers to share the good news of salvation and to baptize those who would put their trust in Him. The study of the following biblical passages will shed further light on this doctrine.

John 3:5
Is Baptism Essential For Salvation?

The Roman Catholic Church has traditionally seen John 3:5 as corroborating the sacrament of water baptism. The church insists that when Jesus declares, "Unless one is born of water . . ." Christ is pointing to the need of water baptism as a sacramental conduit of God's grace through initial justification. As Karl Keating affirms, "Jesus said that no one can enter heaven unless he has been born again of water and the Holy Spirit (John 3:5)." [142] Consequently, when any of the approximately sixteen million infants baptized annually in North America by the Roman Catholic Church undergo the sacrament of baptism, the priest touches the water and invokes the coming of the Holy Spirit. The priest goes on to proclaim that those who are buried with Christ in the death of baptism are also raised to newness of life. The Roman Catholic Church defends this position by gathering the support of early church Fathers. [143] But is this the actual meaning of Jesus' words?

Several points must be made to bring this text into proper focus. First, historically, it is wrong to suppose that Jesus is talking about the practice of "Christian baptism" since such baptism as practiced by the church did not yet exist. It is more historically accurate to believe that when Jesus talked of "baptism" he probably had in mind the ritual cleansings performed in Israelite religion. The fact that Jesus rebuked Nicodemus for not being aware of "these things" (3:10) suggests strongly this "teacher of Israel" was being faulted for his failure to understand the "spiritual" significance of practices that were common in Israel's religious traditions, not for lacking clairvoyance in failing to foresee a future Christian practice.

The symbolism of water in connection with the work of God's Spirit is readily seen in the Old Testament. Several texts suffice to show that water is a symbol of the Spirit's work:

> **Psalm 51: 2,** "Wash me thoroughly from my iniquity, and cleanse me from my sin." While "water" is not expressly mentioned it is implied in the "washing." Note, however, that the psalmist is aware that his problem is internal (v.6). Such a work cannot be resolved through external libatif water. Furthermore, if a literal water cleansing is expected then it should be followed by a literal scrubbing with hyssop (v.7). Clearly, the language is metaphorical for the inner cleansing accomplished through God's Spirit.

> **Isaiah 1:16,** "Wash yourselves, make yourselves clean; Remove the evil of your deeds from my sight." Here it is clear that the cleansing is not a physical washing, but rather a radical change in behavior.

> **Jeremiah 33:8,** "And I will cleanse them from all their iniquity by which they have sinned against Me," Again the language of "cleansing" is symbolic for there never was a time when Israel was physically baptized. The crossing of the Red Sea cannot be the intended meaning here for that event was in the past.

> **Ezekiel 36:25-26,** "Then I will sprinkle clean water on you, and you will be clean; I will cleanse you from all your filthiness and from all your idols." Here, God uses the cleansing effect of water as synonymous with the regenerating work of His Spirit.

These texts suffice to show that literal water is never an active agent in bringing about the actual cleansing from sin or regeneration. The water is always symbolic of the Spirit's work. All of this suggests that to be born of "water and Spirit" as noted in John 3:5 may be Jesus' way of referring to the historic spiritual work of regeneration.

Second, that Jesus is not referring to water baptism as a condition of initial justification is overwhelmingly evident from the rest of John's gospel. As Norman Geisler and Ralph Mackenzie point out, "Furthermore, if baptism is specified here as a condition of salvation, then it is contradictory to everything else in the entire Gospel of John which says "that everyone who believes in him [Christ] might not perish but might have eternal life" (John 3:16; cf. vv.18, 36). What is more, all of the believe-only verses are not limited to this sermon. They are scattered throughout the whole of John's Gospel (e.g., John 5:24; 6:35; 7:38; 8:24; 9:35; 10:38; 11:26; 12:44-48; 20:31).[144] It is sheer eisegesis, driven by ideological presuppositions, to take a passage such as John 3:5, which is open to several interpretations and impose a questionable meaning upon it such that it directly contradicts what is the overwhelming teaching of the gospel. In doing so, as Geisler and Mackenzie note of the Catholic Church, it has read the sacramental ritual into the reality; it has confused the symbol with the substance.[145]

But if water baptism is not being described then what is its meaning? Several possibilities exist:

"Being born of water" may be a reference to the water of the womb, thus Jesus is saying that saved people are born biologically into the world, but spiritually into God's kingdom (cf. 3:4).

"Born of water" may be a symbolic way of speaking about the regenerative power of the word of God (Ephesians 5:26; 1 Peter 1:23).

As noted by the use of the "water" metaphor in the Old Testament when speaking of God's Spirit, "born of water" may be a synonym for "born of the Spirit." Consequently some translate the text as follows: "You must be born of water (even) the Spirit."[146]

"Being born of water" may be a reference to the baptism unto repentance practiced by John the Baptist (Matt. 3:2,11). In this case it may be that Jesus was acknowledging the insufficiency of repentance alone as symbolized by John's baptism. There is more to salvation than repentance for sin. The proactive regeneration of the person by the Spirit was also indispensable.

What should be noted in all the above possibilities is that nowhere is Christian baptism in view and certainly not baptismal regeneration.

220

Third, in solidifying our conviction that John 3:5 does not teach the necessity of water baptism we need only turn to the thief on the cross who was saved quite apart from any baptism (Luke 23:43) and Cornelius who was saved prior to his Christian baptism (Acts 10:45).[147]

Finally, appealing to church Fathers in support of a biblical doctrine can be problematic. Apart from the fact that only the Bible is inspired and infallible, the fathers are often contradictory in their doctrinal views. It is wrong to pick and choose isolated scraps of belief from this ancient theologian and that early bishop, all the while overlooking the many places where you disagree and how their beliefs fit into their comprehensive belief.

ENDNOTES

1 Adolfo Roberto, *Un Vistazo a La Doctrina Católica Romana (A Look at Roman Catholic Doctrine)* (El Paso: Casa Bautista de Publicaciones, 1984), 62.
2 Lausanne Agreement (1974), paragraph 2, cited in Paul B. Schrotenboer, *Roman Catholicism: A Contemporary Evangelical Perspective* (Grand Rapids: Baker Book House, 1987), 42.
3 Abbott, *Documents of Vatican II* - (New York: Guild Press, 1966), 117.
4 Ibid.
5 Ibid
6 John A. Hardon, *The Catholic Catechism*, (New York: Boubleday, 1981), 161.
7 Albert J Nevins, *Answering A Fundamentalist* (Huntington: Our Sunday Visitor, 1990), p. 25.
8 See Robleto, *Un Vistazo a la Doctrina Romana*, 53.
9 Ibid., p. 26.
10 Ibid., p. 29.
11 Ibid., p. 25.
12 Ibid., p. 50.
13 Paul G. Schrotenboer, *Roman Catholicism: A Contemporary Perspective* (Grand Rapids: Baker Book House, 1988), p. 54.
14 Abbott, *Documents,* 118.
15 John Calvin, *Institutes*, cited in Schrotenberger, *Roman Catholicism*, 47-48.
16 Ralph Michaels, *Share the New Life with a Catholic* (Chicago: Moody, 1975), 14.
17 This and the following arguments are presented by James McCarthy, *The Gospel According to Rome*, 281-309.
18 Pastoral letter of the bishops of Mexico, 1984, cited in Paul G. Schrotenboer, *Roman Catholicism* (Grand Rapids: Baker Book House, 1987), 39-40; Ricardo Ramirez.
19 Eric D. Svendsen, *Who Is My Mother?,* (New York: Calvary Press, 2001), 36.
20 H. Deenzinger and A. Schoumetzer, *Enchiridion Symbolorum* (Edition XXXIII. Barcelona, etc. Herder 1965), 503, cited in Stephen Benko, *Los Evangélicos, los Católicos y la Virgin María* (Evangelicals, Catholics, and the Virgin Mary) (El Paso: Casa Bautista de Publicaciones, 1981), 29.
21 Denzinger, 1880, cited in Benko, 29.
22 Benko, 29.
23 *The Catholic Catechism,* op. cit., 156.
24 Pius IX, *Ineffabilis Deus,* Denzinger 1641 (2803-4).
25 *The Catholic Catechism,* op. cit., 157. It needs to be pointed out that the passage in Genesis 3:15 states that the *offspring* of the woman would crush the serpent's head, not the woman herself.
26 Hardon, The Catholic Catechism, op. Cit., 157.
27 Abbott, *Documents of Vatican II*, p. 90.
28 For a more complete description of this and other traditions see Robleto, pp. 92-94.
29 Robleto, p. 96
30 Both José Borrás and Hocking make this point.
31 Duns Scotus, *Commentarium in Sententiarum*, III, 3,1,2, cited in *The Catholic Catechism,* op. cit., 160.
32 Pius XII, constitution *Munificentissimus Deus,* III, 44.
33 Ibid., 160.
34 Kenneth Woodward, "Hail, Mary," *Newsweek* (August 25, 1997), 49.

[35] Ibid., 49.

[36] Ibid., 51

[37] Felician, Catholic Almanac, 182

[38] Walter Abbott, *The Documents of Vatican II* (New York: The America Press, 1996), 92.

[39] Ibid

[40] Hardon, *Catholic Catechism*, op. cit., 166.

[41] Abbott, Documents of Vatican II, 94.

[42] Ibid

[43] Felician, *Catholic Almanac*, op. cit., 166.

[44] "Marian History: Visions and Truths," *Newsweek* (August 25, 1997), 54-55.

[45] Hardon, *Catholic Catechism*, 442.

[46] Felician, *Catholic Almanac*, p. 360

[47] Ibid, p. 366

[48] Adolfo Robelto, *Un Vistazo*, 110, 111.

[49] For a more extensive explanation, read Stephen Benko, *Los Evangélicos, los Católicos y la Virgen María* (El Paso: Casa Bautista de Publicaciones, 1981).

[50] Abbot, *Documents of Vatican II*, p. 88.

[51] See McBrien, *Catholicism*, pp. 71-72.

[52] Abbot, *Documents of Vatican II*, p. 91.

[53] Abbot, *Documents of Vatican II*, p. 91.

[54] See the *New Jerusalem Bible*

[55] Dr. David Hocking makes this point regarding Stephen in *"Mary, Purgatory, & The Pope,"* audio cassette, *Mission to Catholics,* P. O. Box 19280, San Diego, CA. 92119.

[56] José Borrás, *"¿Qué Creen Los Evangélicos Sobre Maria?"* (What Do Evangelicals Believe About Mary?), audiotape, Sammy Fuentes Evangelistic Association, 4910 Branscomb, Corpus Christi, Texas, 78411.

[57] Ibid., For and extensive discussion of this subject see, Eric D. Svendsen, *Who Is My Mother?,* (New York: Calvary Press, 2001), 79-105.

[58] Henry Denzinger, *The Sources of Catholic Dogma,* no. 2331, (St. Louis: B. Herder Book Co., 1957), 647.

[59] Eric D. Svendsen, *Who Is My Mother (Amityville, NY: Calvary Press, 2001), 232.*

[60] Ibid.

[61] Ludwig Ott, *Fundamentals of Catholic Dogma,* (Rockford, Ill.: Tan Books and Publishers, 1960), 205.

[62] Svendsen, op. Cit., 232.

[63] For a discussion of these options see Stephen Hartdegen, "The Marian Significance of Cana," *Marian Studies II* (1960), 87-88., cited in Eric D. Svendsen, *Who Is My Mother (Amityville, NY: Calvary Press, 2001), 175.*

[64] Svendsen, op. Cit., 175.

[65] Ibid., 176.

[66] Ibid., 176,177.

[67] McHugh, 365.

[68] *Against Heresies,* 3.16,7.

[69] *Dialogue II.*

[70] *Epist. 41,* See Irenaeus, *Against Herisies* 3.16.7.

[71] D. A. Carson, "John," *The Expositor's Bible Commentary,* (Grand Rapids: Zondervan, 1976), 173., cited in Svendsen, 191.

[72] Svendsen, 190.

[73] James G. McCarthy, *The Gospel According to Rome* (Eugene, Oregon: Harvest House, 1995), 188.

[74] Borrás, *¿Qué Creen Los Evangélicos Sobre,* María?

[75] Killgallon, *Life in Christ*, p. 155.

[76] Felician, *Catholic Almanac*, op. cit., 223

[77] Michael A. McGuire, *Baltimore Catechism No. 1*, (New York: Benzinger Brothers, 1942), p. 36.

[78] McCarthy, op. Cit., 55-57. McCarthy explains that "sanctifying grace" is a gift of the Holy Spirit initially given to individuals through the sacrament of baptism. Actual grace is a supernatural assistance to do good and avoid evil.

[79] John O'Brien, *The Faith of Millions* (Huntington, Ind: Our Sunday Visitor, Inc. 1974), 142.

[80] Killgallon, Life in Christ, p. 160. See also Baltimore Catechism No. 1, pp. 87-88.

[81] McGuire, *Baltimore Catechism No. 1, 87, 88.*

[82] Felician, *Catholic Almanac,* op. cit., 225.

[83] Council of Trent, *Canon 5 of the Decree Concerning The Sacraments.*

[84] Killgallon, *Life in Christ,* p. 167.

[85] Ibid., 90.

[86] McGuire, *Baltimore Catechism,* p. 90.

[87] Ibid., 92.

[88] James G. McCarthy, *Catholicism: Crisis of Faith*(Cupertino: Lumen Productions, 1991), 11.

[89] Killgallon, *Life in Christ,* p. 187.

[90] Ibid., 102.

[91] Felician, *Catholic Almanac,* op. cit., 227.

[92] Killgallon, *Life in Christ,* p. 198.

[93] Ibid., 120.

[94] Felician, *Catholic Almanac,* op., cit., 228.

[95] Felician, *Catholic Almanac,* op. cit., 230-231.

[96] Ibid.

[97] Ibid.

[98] Ibid., 228

[99] Abbott, *Documents of Vatican II,* 15

[100] James Killgallon, Gerard Weber, & Leonard Zeigmann, *Life in Christ* (Chicago: Acta Foundation, 1976), 131.

[101] Felician, *Catholic Alamanc,* 210

[102] Killgallon, *Life In Christ,* 155

[103] Ibid

[104] Ibid., 159-216

[105] Ibid., 217.

[106] Ibid., 218

[107] Ibid

[108] Knights of Columbus, *Sacramentals: Signs of Religious Value* (New Haven, Catholic Information Service, 1953), 21.

[109] Ibid., 23.

[110] Ibid., 21, 23.

[111] *Sacramentals,* Ibid., 18-19.

[112] Ibid, 19.

[113] Killgallon, *Life in Christ,* 219.

[114] Hardon, *The Catholic Catechism,* 554-555

[115] Ibid.

[116] Killgallon, *Life in Christ,* 139.

[117] Ibid., 141.

[118] Ibid., 142.

[119] Ibid., 143

[120] Ibid.

[121] Denzinger, 1562, 74, cited by Paul Schrotenboer, Roman Catholicism, 63, 64.

[122] James White, *The Roman Catholic Controversy* (Minneapolis: Bethany House Publishers, 1996), 42.

[123] For an interpretation of James 2 from a demonstrative perspective see *Westminster Theological Journal* Vol.   XLII, Spring 1980.

[124] Douglas Moo, *James*, TNTC (Grand Rapids: InterVarsity Press, 1985), 99.

[125] See Martin Farrell, *The New American Catechism* (Des Plains, Illinois: FARE, Inc., 1978), 96.

[126] Ibid.,. 96.

[127] For a discussion of this see Brewer, "The Fallacy of Catholicism," audiotape, Mission To Catholics, P. O. Box 19280, San Diego, CA., 92119.

[128] Hardon, The Catholic Catechism, 277.

[129] McBrien, 1144.

[130] Hardon, The Catholic Catechism, 276

[131] Hocking makes this point

[132] For a discussion of this, see Robleto, p. 110

[133] Op. Cit. McBrien, 1143. McBrien states: "This is not to say that there is no basis at all for the doctrine, but only that there is no clear biblical basis for it." See also Williams, Contemporary Catholic Catechism, p. 251

[134] Felician Catholic Almanac, op. Cit. 182.

[135] Abbot, Documents of Vatican II, p. 38

[136] See McCarthy, The Gospel According to Rome, 242,43.

[137] McCarthy, The Gospel According to Rome, 240,41.

[138] For an in-depth treatment of this doctrine read William Webster, The Matthew 16 Controversy: Peter and the Rock (Battleground: Christian Resources Inc., 1999).

[139] Bartholomew, F. Brewer, Pilgrimage from Rome(Greenville, SC: Bob Jones University Press, 1986).

[140] Brewer, The Primacy of Peter, op. cit.

[141] James G. McCarthy, The Gospel According to Rome, (Eugene: Harvest House Publishers, 1995), 324.

[142] Karl Keating, *Catholicism and Fundamentalism*, (San Francisco, Ca.: Ignatius Press, 1988), 178. See also Ludwig Ott, *Fundamentals of Catholic Dogma*, (Rockford Ill.: Tan Books and Publishers, 1960), 354.

[143] The Roman Catholic Church cites *The Epistle of Baranbas,* Justin, Tertullian, and Cyprian in support of infant baptism.

[144] N. L. Geisler and R. E. Mackensie, Roman Catholics and Evangelicals: Agreements and Differences, (Grand Rapids: Baker Books, 1995), 484.

[145] Ibid., 485.

[146] Since the phrase "born of water and Spirit" is governed by a single preposition (ejx udatoV kaiv pneuvmatov) the conjunction "and" (kaiv) is viewed as epexegetical thus, meaning, *that is to say.* Consequently the phrase can be translated "born of water *that is to say* the Spirit".

[147] Other texts that prove salvation is independent of Christian baptism include Acts 2:41; 8:13; 18:8. In 1 Corinthians 1:17 Paul makes a distinction between the Gospel and baptism, which is catastrophic for baptismal regeneration. Paul's statement borders on heresy if the sacrament of baptism is salvific and essential to the gospel.

PART FOUR

CONTEXTUALIZING STRATEGIES

CHAPTER EIGHT

DEVELOPING EVANGELIZATION STRATEGIES

Introduction: Rafael's Journey

One of the blessings we received while serving as missionaries in the Republic of Panama and teaching at the Panama Baptist Theological Seminary was that of fellowshiping with Rafael. He had grown up in a devout Roman Catholic home in Honduras. His desire to be a priest began when he served as an altar boy in the local parish. Having a bright mind helped him to memorize large portions of the Catechism manual. As an adolescent, he enrolled in a pre-seminary school. His admiration for his professors grew as he observed them and gained first-hand acquaintance of their devotion to the church and to the people they served. At the completion of his seminary training, Rafael was ordained to the priesthood.

As a parish priest, Rafael found a great deal of satisfaction officiating in the Mass and ministering to the people. One of his pet peeves, however, was the fact that many parents followed the Catholic Almanac's suggestions in naming their children at baptism. Some of the names were those of recognized saints while others were those of obscure personalities. To make matters worse, some parents would select only portions of a name found in the Almanac. For example, on the Day of the Immaculate Conception, some parents would simply select the name "Conception" for their son or daughter. Rafael would argue with the parents against giving their child a strange name that he or she would be stuck with the rest of their lives.

Initially, Rafael concentrated on his priestly duties without any doubts and reservations. As time went on, however, he began to question if he actually had the power to transform the bread and the wine into the actual body and blood of Jesus in the celebration of the Eucharist. When he would express these doubts, his bishop would tell him that he was wrong in questioning the teachings of the Catholic Church. Thinking that Rafael did not have enough work to challenge him intellectually, the bishop assigned him a task. The number of Evangelicals had been steadily growing in Honduras, so the bishop assigned Rafael the task of studying the Bible and developing approaches to refute Evangelical teachings with the Scriptures. Accepting the challenge, Rafael would spend many hours every week studying each of the Evangelical doctrines in the light of Scripture. His search, however took him in an unexpected direction. The more he studied the Bible, the more questions he had about his own Church. In addition to the Eucharist, he began to have questions about the biblical foundation for such Catholic doctrines as Penance, Confirmation, Baptism, the Eucharist, and the necessity of works to merit salvation. As he studied, his frustration grew because the seminary professors, whom he had admired as a student, kept utilizing the traditions of the Church as the foundation for these beliefs over against the Bible itself. As time went on, the more questions he raised, the more alienated he became from his superiors. Frustrated and confused, Rafael left the priesthood and moved from his native country to Panama.

One day as he traveled by train across the isthmus from Panama city to Colon, Rafael saw a North American man sitting across the isle reading his Bible. Unable to resist the temptation, Rafael leaned over and asked the man: "Do you understand that book?" The man responded: " With the help of the Holy Spirit, I continue to learn from it every day. What is most important is that the message found in this book changed my life completely." Rafael inquired how this was so. The man responded by sharing his testimony of conversion to Christ and then utilizing passages from Scripture that explain how people can receive the forgiveness of their sins and have the assurance of being right with God by placing their faith in Jesus as their personal savior. "That," replied Rafael, "is what I have been looking for all of my life. I was a Roman Catholic priest for many years, but I was not sure where I would go when I died." The man listened attentively, answered his questions with biblical passages, and never argued with him about his beliefs. By the time their trip ended, Rafael had prayed to receive Christ as his personal savior. Knowing that Rafael still had many doctrinal questions that needed to be answered, the man, who Rafael later found out was missionary Paul C. Bell, invited him to participate in weekly Bible studies. Every Tuesday evening, Rafael would show up at the missionary's home with Bible in hand and many questions in his mind. As he found biblical answers to his questions, Rafael's joy and confidence increased. After two years of study, Rafael felt a distinct call to serve as pastor in a church that had been started by the missionary. In addition to his pastoral duties, Rafael taught at the seminary for thirty years and was instrumental in training many for Christian ministry. It was always a delightful experience to hear him speak about "the journey that changed his life."

EVANGELIZATION STRATEGY LESSONS

Introduction

As we have noted throughout our studies in this book, many sincere, dedicated, well-intentioned Evangelicals have made serious mistakes while attempting to lead persons with a Roman Catholic background to a personal experience of salvation in Jesus Christ. One of the most common mistakes that some Evangelicals make is that of trying to get Catholics to make a decision to receive Christ on their very first visit. While it is true that some Catholics with whom the Lord is already dealing will be receptive on the first visit, the truth is that for the vast majority of them a relationship of trust will need to be established before they will be open to hearing a person's testimony and a presentation of a plan of salvation. A second mistake that some Evangelicals make is that of assuming that all Catholics are alike. This stereotypical image leads some Evangelicals to attempt to use the same evangelistic methods with all of them.

As a result of this, many Catholics are confused, if not offended, by the image of them that some Evangelicals reflect while trying to witness to them. Often this also results in Catholics simply not understanding what Evangelicals are talking about. A third mistake that some Evangelicals make is that of trying to prove that Roman Catholics are wrong in every thing they believe and practice. The assumption on the part of some Evangelicals is that if they can just convince Catholics that they are wrong, they will automatically become receptive to the Gospel message. In most instances, the opposite is true. Catholics often feel offended, threatened, and angry when their beliefs and practices, which they hold so dear, are criticized or attacked. A fourth mistake, which is related to this last one, is that some Evangelicals believe that they have to "straighten Catholics out" in every doctrinal point before they will become receptive to the gospel message. In so doing, they often concentrate on points that are important, but not essential for salvation. In order to be effective witnesses, Evangelicals need to focus on a *personal relationship of salvation in Jesus Christ.* This is the most significant issue that needs to be addressed. Many Catholics are just as sincere, dedicated, and devout as the most committed Evangelicals. The main point is that many of them have not received Christ as their personal savior. That needs to be the focus of our witness. A fifth mistake that many Evangelicals make is that they want Catholics to forsake all of their practices (e.g., their devotion to the Virgin Mary and the Saints) immediately after having made a profession of faith in Christ. What many Evangelicals do not know is that it takes time for Catholics, who have had a saving experience with Christ, to sort out these doctrinal issues as they study the Word of God.

In this chapter we will address these mistakes by presenting some positive evangelization strategies. Lesson J, "Building Witnessing Relationships," can be utilized as a training strategy to help Evangelical church members know how to cultivate friendships and communicate the message of salvation in relevant ways. Lesson K, "Approaches to the Various Catholic Groups," can help Evangelicals become aware of the different types of Catholics that there are and the different methodologies that are needed to communicate with each group. Lesson L, "Reaching Our Latin American Friends" can be useful in reaching this group as well as instructive in reaching other cultural groups.

LESSON J

BUILDING WITNESSING RELATIONSHIPS

Personal Evangelism is one of the most effective ways to lead people to a saving knowledge of Jesus Christ. It is necessary, therefore, to train the people in our churches to witness in an intelligent and confident manner. In this lesson we will review some of the most commonly used evangelistic approaches and will present a detailed plan for Relational Evangelism.

Types of New Testament Evangelism

As we study the New Testament, we find that there are many ways in which Christians witnessed to those who needed to hear the message of salvation. While they had *one* message, they communicated it in *many different ways* depending upon the background and spiritual needs of the prospects.

Visitation Evangelism - Planned Encounters

Acts 5:42 states: "And daily in the sanctuary, and in every house, they ceased not to teach and preach Jesus Christ." Visitation Evangelism has some distinct benefits.

1. Benefits of visitation evangelism

    a) Often, it reaches people who are not related to the church in any way. These are people who do not have friends or relatives who are church goers. Unless Christians go out of their way to meet them, they may never hear the message.

    b) This type of evangelism also reaches people which whom God is already dealing in some way. As we visit people in our neighborhood we will find those who are ready to hear the message of salvation because someone has already sown the seed of the Gospel or something is happening in their lives.

    c) This type of evangelism can also be helpful in that it can be systematic. In other words, a church can focus on different segments of its community until it has covered the entire community.

2. Obstacles to Visitation Evangelism

   a) One of the obstacles to visitation evangelism is that many church members are intimidated by the idea of going to the home of a stranger and seeking to talk to them about the Lord.

   b) Another obstacle is that there are many people today who are not very receptive to a total stranger coming into their homes and talking to them about a matter which is very personal.

3. Overcoming the Obstacles to Visitation Evangelism

   a) Train a special group for this task. Every church has a few people who are especially gifted in personal evangelism and can be that special task force (your Marines) who are willing to knock on doors and talk about the Lord. Methods such as "Continuing Witness Training" can be very helpful in this.

   b) Do cultivative work prior to a visitation effort. Some churches precede their visitation efforts with community events, direct mail, telephone surveys, special programs, etc.

   c) Use referrals. Some churches have a strong visitation program for those who have visited the church or who have been referred to them by church members or by service agencies. Visitation Evangelism is still a viable option for the local church. Often, however, new ways need to be found to establish prior contact with those who are to be visited.

Spontaneous Evangelism - Unplanned Encounters

The way in which Paul witnessed to Lydia is a good example of Spontaneous Evangelism. Acts 16:13 states that Paul met Lydia by a river side at Philippi. He did not meet her in a church nor did he make prior arrangements to witness to her. There at the river side the opportunity presented itself and Paul shared a gospel witness with her. Verses 14 and 15 state the Lydia listened attentively, received the message, and was baptized along with her household. The implication is that Paul had an opportunity to witness to the rest of the family.

1. Pre-requisites for Spontaneous Evangelism

    a) Availability to the Lord- People involved in Spontaneous Evangelism need to be available to the Lord. In other words, they need to be willing to share the message of salvation on the spur of the moment, whether this is a convenient time for the witnessing encounter or not.

    b) Sensitivity to the Prospect - People involved in Spontaneous Evangelism need to be sensitive to the S. O. S. messages that the prospect might be sending. Many times people are going through difficult experiences in their lives and need someone to talk to. Often by listening to them, the witness finds an opportunity to share the good news of salvation.

2. Preparation for Spontaneous Evangelism

    a) Prayer - The witness needs to pray that the Lord will work in the lives of the prospects as well as in his/her own life. In Acts 8 we have the description of the way in which Philip witnessed to the Ethiopian man. Was it a coincidence that Philip was just at the right spot at the time that the Ethiopian man was reading just the right passage from Isaiah? The evidence we find in Acts 8 is that the Holy Spirit was working in the life of the prospect as well as in the life of the witness. This was not a chance encounter but a divine appointment. As we pray, the Lord can guide us to the persons with whom He is already working in order that we might share the Good News.

    b) Relevance - We mentioned earlier that sometimes prospects sends distress signals. It is important that we have an idea of the types of experiences that the prospects are going through in order for us to know how to witness most effectively to them. In his book *Lifestory Conversations*, Fairchild points out that there are certain themes that people focus on as they try to get help or seek to communicate. Some of these are: (1) sorrows (e.g., illness, death of a loved one), (2) joys (e.g., accomplishments, happy events), (3) transitions (in work, residence, personal status, relationships), and (4) life transforming influences (events, persons who made a difference in their lives).

The suggestion which Fairchild makes is that we listen to people when they talk about these themes, share with them similar experiences which we might have had, and tell them how Jesus made a difference either by deepening our joy, being with us in the moments of sorrow, guiding us as we experience change, or providing an example for us to follow. In other words, we listen to *their* story, share *our* story, and utilize that as a bridge to tell *HIS* (Jesus') story. This approach allows us to minister to people when they are needing the greatest help, as well as present the message of salvation in a way that will be most relevant to their needs. Spontaneous Evangelism can be instrumental in reaching people who might not be reached otherwise.

Relational Evangelism - Repeated Encounters

Relational Evangelism involves sharing the Gospel with people with whom we have on-going contact.

1. New Testament Examples of Relational Evangelism

    a) Andrew led his brother Peter to the Lord (John 1:42)

    b) Philip brought his friend Nathanael to Christ (1:45)
        Cornelius gathered his entire household (family and close friends) to hear the Gospel (Acts 10:24)

2. Situations that require Relational Evangelism

    a) When there is lack of trust in the witness

There are situations in which the prospect simply does not know or trust the witness.

An illustration: Let us suppose that you are standing in one of the street corners in the city where you live and you are sneezing and coughing. All of a sudden someone whom you have never seen before stops, looks at you, and pulling out a little bottle without a label and with a green liquid in it says to you: "I notice you have a cold, take this, it will help you." Would you take it? Why not? Is it the bottle, the liquid, or the absence of a label? Now, suppose you are standing on the same street corner and your mother comes by and says: "I can tell that you have a cold." Then dipping into her purse she pulls out a little bottle without a label and with a green liquid in it and says: "Here son (or daughter) take this, this will help you." This, you would take. Why?

OBVIOUSLY THE DIFFERENCE IS IN THE RELATIONSHIP.

There are many situations in which people need to hear the gospel from someone whom they trust. It could be that due to their religious or cultural traditions they have an inherent distrust of Evangelicals. A relationship of trust will need to be established before they even hear the message of salvation, let alone invite Jesus Christ into their hearts.

b) When there is lack of knowledge of the Gospel

There are situations in which the prospect knows very little about the Bible. In these instances, it is going to take those repeated encounters for them to come to the point where they understand the message of salvation. These repeated encounters may be in the form of informal conversations or structured Bible Studies. These will be the times when the prospect will ask questions and need time to reflect before coming to the point of making a decision.

We have reviewed three types of personal evangelism practiced in the New Testament: Visitation, Spontaneous, and Relational. Because there are large numbers of persons (in some cases entire cultural groups) who do not have an Evangelical background nor a meaningful relationship with someone who is a Christian, we will develop an approach to the third type.

Utilizing Building Witnessing Relationships as an introduction, the material which follows can be helpful in assisting persons to develop a systematic approach to the cultivation of personal relationships, with the view to leading them to a saving knowledge of Jesus Christ.

The participants need to be encouraged to do the following:

1. Gain an understanding of the main concepts.
2. Prayerfully focus on some viable prospects.
3. Form a Support/Accountability Group.
4. Follow through on the activities which lead to the building of relationships and sharing of the Gospel.

A RELATIONAL EVANGELISM STRATEGY

In order to be effective in Relational Evangelism it is necessary to be deliberate and systematic. In other words, there are some people that we need to concentrate on and there are some activities that we need to be involved in. To facilitate this process, we are going to address five questions. The witness will need to work toward the objectives which are established by these questions.

Who Are My Prospects?

Often, people do not witness because they do not have close friends who are not Christians. Studies indicate that the longer that people are church members, the fewer friends they have outside the church. While there is a positive side to the fellowship which people experience in the church, the negative side is that they can become so isolated that they do not have a personal acquaintance with people who need Christ.

In order to overcome this isolation, it is helpful for church members to look around them and determine who the prospects are in their spheres of influence. Utilizing FORM 1 (found on the following page), church members can put some names under each of the categories: Relatives, Friends, Neighbors, and Fellow workers (or students). They do not need to fill in all the spaces, by those names whom the Lord leads them to include. Following the instructions on FORM 1, church members need to begin to pray regularly for those on their lists, at times during prayer meeting at church or in small groups.

FORM 1

PROSPECTS IN MY SPHERES OF INFLUENCE

FRIENDS

RELATIVES

ME

NEIGHBORS

CO-WORKERS

Instructions:

1. Write down the names that the Lord leads you to put in each square.

2. Begin to pray for them regularly.

3. Get a prayer partner and covenant to pray for each other's prospects.

At What Level am I Communicating With My Prospects?

When Jesus shared the Gospel with Nicodemus, he communicated at three levels:

Face to Face Level   (John 3:1,2)

The first part of the conversation was the getting acquainted phase. It was at this point that Nicodemus shared with Jesus that he had been observing Him and had arrived at a conclusion regarding Jesus' identity. Quite likely, Nicodemus told Jesus something about himself and about his religious pilgrimage because Jesus later makes reference to this (v. 10).

Conversation at the Face to Face level is important because it is the initial step in getting acquainted with people. It is often at this level that we learn the name of a person and perhaps something about the person's family, interests, occupation, etc.

Even though this is an important level of communication, it is very superficial. Unless we make a deliberate effort, we can know persons (for example, neighbors) for years without really knowing enough about them to have an idea of how to present the Gospel to them in relevant ways. Also, at this level, there has not been enough trust developed so as to overcome some of the barriers that might be in the hearts and minds of the prospects.

In order to cultivate a person's friendship, therefore, an effort needs to be made to deepen the level of communication. This may involve inviting that person to your home, to a recreational event (sports, drama, musical, etc.). The bottom line is that we need to spend time with people before we can get to know them better. The time of day, type of activity, and rate of progress of the friendship will depend a great deal on the personality and interest of the prospect.

Mind to Mind (John 3:3-13)

After communicating at the face to face level, Jesus communicated with Nicodemus at the Mind to Mind level. In other words, Jesus shared with Nicodemus some of the basic ideas about salvation. He told him that in order to see the kingdom of God, he needed to be born again. Jesus then answered questions about the nature of the new birth and even gave him an illustration.

Just like wind, which cannot be seen but whose effects can be felt, the new birth cannot be explained in human terms but its effects can certainly be observed. Jesus, therefore took time to explain the main ideas about the new birth and used examples from every day life in order to help Nicodemus understand what He was talking about.

It is at the Mind to Mind level that we can communicate to our prospects the basic ideas about the plan of salvation. Involving prospects in cultivative Bible Studies, inviting them to a film (e.g., the "Jesus" film) video, drama, or musical can begin to sow the seed of the Gospel in their minds. Often conversations in which we answer their questions and listen to their concerns can lend themselves to communication at the Mind to Mind level. At this point you may want to give the prospect a marked New Testament, a Gospel Tract, a good book which explains the Gospel, or an appropriate Christian Magazine. C.S. Lewis' book, *Mere Christianity,* for example helped him to find answers and understand the gospel.

Heart to Heart Level (John 3: 14-16)

From the Mind to Mind level, the conversation progressed to the Heart to Heart level. Here is where Jesus shared with Nicodemus straight from His heart. Here is where He told him that He was going to be lifted up on the cross and die (v.14). At this point Jesus shared with Nicodemus about the depth of God's love. He loved the world so much that He sacrificed His own Son! (v.16). It must have been a very solemn moment when Jesus shared with him what was on His heart.

IT IS AT THE HEART TO HEART LEVEL THAT THE GOSPEL IS COMMUNICATED MOST EFFECTIVELY. It is also important to know that WHEN WE SHARE WITH PEOPLE AT THE HEART TO HEART LEVEL ABOUT OTHER MATTERS, IT BECOMES EASIER TO SHARE WITH THEM ABOUT THE GOSPEL. When we take the time to get acquainted with people, we are in a position to learn about their needs, share the basic facts of the Gospel, and lead them to a personal decision to accept Jesus Christ.

LEVELS OF COMMUNICATION

LEVEL	PURPOSE	WITNESSING
FACE TO FACE	Get to Know People	Learn about Prospect
MIND TO MIND	Exchange Ideas	Basic facts - Gospel
HEART TO HEART	Communicate Emotions	Personal Decision

Instructions:

1. Take FORM 2 and transfer the names from FORM 1

2. Next to each of the names that you have written, indicate the level at which you are communicating "Face to Face," Mind to Mind" "Heart to Heart."

3. Spend time in prayer and ask the Lord to lead you to focus on one or two of them.

4. Spend time planning some activities that will help you to deepen your level of communication.

FORM 2

GETTING TO KNOW MY PROSPECTS

Name	Communication Level	Gospel Knowledge	Attitude	Lifestyle Changing

Friends

Relatives

Neighbors

Co - Workers

Where are They in Their Spiritual Pilgrimage?

The third important question which you need to address in Relational Evangelism has to do with the stage at which people are in their spiritual pilgrimage. In other words, how much do they know about the Gospel and what is their attitude toward the Gospel?

Different Levels Among New Testament People

In the New Testament, we find that people had different levels of understanding and were at different stages of readiness with regard to the Gospel.

1.   The Samaritan had much to learn about the Gospel, yet she was willing to hear the message of salvation.

2.   Nicodemus knew a great deal about the Old Testament, yet he had many questions regarding the new birth.

3.   The Rich Young Ruler apparently knew enough to ask about "eternal life," yet he was not responsive to Jesus' words.

Incorrect Assumptions On Our Part

1.   "Everyone is at the same stage of readiness"

At times, we become discouraged when people do not receive Christ after we have presented a Gospel witness. *It is important for us to know that people have differing levels of understanding and are at different stages of readiness.*

2.   "It Is All Up To Me"

At times, we act as if the witnessing task were all up to us! What about the free will of the person? What about the work of the Holy Spirit? When we assume that "if we just present the Gospel in the *right way* everyone is going to receive Christ right then and there," we are setting ourselves up for disappointment. We need to remember that even Jesus encountered people who refused His message and walked away. Many people are ready to receive the Lord while others are not. LET'S FIND OUT WHERE THE PEOPLE ARE IN THEIR KNOWLEDGE AND ATTITUDE REGARDING THE GOSPEL, AND LET'S DESIGN A STRATEGY THAT WILL ALLOW THE HOLY SPIRIT TO WORK IN THEIR HEARTS!

Stages Of Readiness

STAGES OF AWARENESS OF THE GOSPEL

STAGE I	STAGE II	STAGE III	A C C E P T
NO KNOWLEDGE	VAGUE KNOWLEDGE	BASIC KNOWLEDGE	

ATTITUDES TOWARDS THE GOSPEL

POSITIVE	+	+	+	C H R I S T
INDIFFERENT	=	=	=	
NEGATIVE	-	-	-	

People are at three stages regarding their knowledge of the Gospel:

Stage I " No Knowledge": They do not know any of the Gospel truths

Stage II "Vague Knowledge": They know very little about the Gospel

Stage III "Basic Knowledge": They know the main truths of the Gospel

Indicate the stage in which every person you are praying for is at this time.

There are three attitudes which people have toward the Gospel:

Negative Attitude: They are not open to hearing the Gospel

Indifferent Attitude: They are just not interested

Positive Attitude: They are open to hearing the gospel

Indicate the attitude toward the Gospel of every person for whom you are praying.

CONTEXTUALIZING STRATEGIES

1. Addressing the Knowledge Question

It is important to have an idea how much people know about the Gospel so that we can know what we need to do to help them to understand the basic truths regarding salvation. Do you remember the first question Philip asked the Ethiopian man? Was, "will you accept?" or "do you understand?" (Acts 8:30). For Philip it was very important that the Ethiopian man understand who Jesus was and how he could be saved by putting his trust in the Lord. After hearing the basic truths of the Gospel, the Ethiopian man received Christ (Acts 8: 32-37).

How can we help people to understand the basic truths of the Gospel?

a) By sharing our testimony (see Chapter 4)

b) By using a Gospel tract (one that is brief, explains the plan of salvation clearly, and calls on people to receive Christ).

c) By involving them in Bible Study (see Chapter 4)

2. Addressing the question of attitude

We have shared several ideas on how to help people to understand the basic truths of the Gospel in order that they might receive Jesus into their hearts. Remember there is a sense in which the attitude of people toward the Gospel can change as they study the Word of God. People who are initially indifferent may become interested as they are involved in Bible Study.

The strategy with those who have a negative attitude toward the Gospel needs to be different.

a) Find out why they have a negative attitude.
    - Unpleasant experience with a Christian
    - A mistake or sin in their lives
    - Misunderstanding of Christianity (see it as a list of don'ts)

b) Try to build a relationship with the person
    - Listen to the person
    - Show understanding
    - Invite him to participate in non-threatening (cultivative) activities
    - Pray a lot

Instructions:

1. Go back to Form 2

2. Under "Gospel Knowledge/Attitude" Briefly write (in pencil so you can update it) what you think his knowledge of the Gospel of each person is and his attitude toward the Gospel.

3. On the basis of this, and following the suggestions given, design a strategy to help this prospect know more about the Gospel and develop a more receptive attitude toward it.

What is Happening in Their Lives?

The fourth question that we need to address in Relational Evangelism is "What is happening in the lives of our prospects?" Several studies indicate that people who were previously resistant to the Gospel became receptive when they went through a crisis or major change in their lives. It is often during these lifestyle changes that people's lives are so shaken up that they try to find answers and to establish relationships that will help them cope.

Lifestyle Changes

1. Death of a spouse - this requires the greatest adaptation

2. Separation or Divorce - death of a relationship

3. Illness - personal, family member, close friend

4. Marriage - desire to build a strong foundation

5. Birth of first child - strong feeling of responsibility

6. Loss of job - disappointment, financial concern

7. Empty nest - when children have left home

8. Retirement - loss of job related self-worth

9. Other - experiences that require major adjustments

Strategy

1. Pray for them.

2. Look for opportunities to minister to them.

3. Spent more time with them.

4. Share Lifestyle Change Testimony (see above).

5. Involve them in a support group.

6. Involve them in Bible Study.

Instructions:

1. Go back to Form 2.

2. Under "Lifestyle Changes," write down the experiences that they might be going through which are similar to the ones listed above.

3. If they are going through one of these experiences (or similar ones), intensify your efforts and ministry.

4. Enlist people to help you pray for these persons (being careful to keep details and identities confidential).

How Can I Witness to Them?

After you have gotten to know something about the spiritual pilgrimage and needs of the prospects, you are in a better position to present the Gospel in a way that will be meaningful to their lives. Two things can help you to lead them to a saving knowledge of Christ.

Set Up a Support/Accountability Team

Do you know what makes programs like Weight Watchers so effective? More than the actual dietary products is the fact that the person trying to lose weight is not alone. There is a group that encourages the person and also to whom the person is (voluntarily) accountable (when the time comes to get on that scale). A SUPPORT / ACCOUNTABILITY TEAM can be tremendously helpful. Get 2 or 3 people to covenant to meet regularly, pray, and encourage one another as you seek to be more effective. The Lord can accomplish miracles through a group like this.

Follow a Methodical Plan

Many wonderful ideas and intentions fall by the wayside for lack of a methodical plan. Many potentially great witnesses just simply "don't get around to it." Prayerfully look at FORM 3 and either follow this one or develop a similar one. Please don't feel that you have to follow these steps in exactly the same order, each situation will be different. This plan can (and should) be changed in accordance with the needs and the response of each individual prospect. In some instances, you will be able to move much faster than in others. The important thing is for you to be intentional and methodical about cultivating the friendship and sharing a Gospel witness.

FORM 3

WITNESSING TO MY PROSPECTS

	Spent Time	Minister	Testimony	Recreational Events	Phone Visit	Cultivating Events	Bible Study	Witness	Decision	Attend Church

Name

Friends

Relatives

Neighbors

Co - Workers

Instructions:

1. **SPEND TIME** with prospect.

2. Find ways to **MINISTER** to prospect.

3. Share your **TESTIMONY** with the prospect.

4. Invite prospect to a **RECREATIONAL EVENT** (sports, drama, music).

5. **PHONE or VISIT** the prospect to stay in touch.

6. Invite prospect to a church- related **CULTIVATIVE EVENT**.

7. Involve the prospect in a **BIBLE STUDY**.

8. Share a gospel **WITNESS** with your prospect.

9. Encourage prospect to make a **DECISION** for Christ.

10. Invite prospect to **ATTEND CHURCH**.

Conclusion

Relational Evangelism is biblical and effective. There are people who will not be won to the Lord unless someone takes the time to build relationships with them, help them to overcome their lack of knowledge of the Gospel or negative attitude toward it, and minister to them when they are experiencing lifestyle changes.

This plan appears to be complicated, but is actually very simple. It simply involves five things:

1. Find out who your prospects are and begin to pray for them.

2. Determine at what level you are communicating with them and find ways to get to know them better.

3. Learn about their spiritual pilgrimages and help them to learn more about and develop positive attitudes toward the Gospel.

4. Find out if they are going through a crisis or transition in their lives and spend more time ministering to them.

5. Follow a plan to cultivate their friendship and share the gospel. It may take a short time or a long time, but remember that you are not alone. You are an instrument of the Holy Spirit as He does the work. Be flexible in the plan that we have outlined so that you can be sensitive to the leading of the Holy Spirit.

A young lady from another country went to America. Someone asked her how she had become a Christian, noting that she came from an area that is very resistant to the Gospel. Pointing to a Christian lady who had befriended her and ministered to her, the young lady said: "SHE BUILT A BRIDGE FROM HER HEART TO MINE AND JESUS CHRIST WALKED ACROSS." That's Relational Evangelism. GO OUT AND BUILD BRIDGES!

LESSON K

APPROACHES TO THE VARIOUS TYPES OF CATHOLICS

Introduction

There are many different types of groups within Roman Catholicism. There are those who follow the teachings of the Church with great devotion and attend Mass regularly. There are, on the other hand, those who consider themselves "Catholics of minimal obligation" (they were baptized and confirmed in the Church, married in the Church, and expect to be buried by the priest). There are also those who are Catholics in name only and hardly know the most basic teachings of the Church.

In order to lead our Roman Catholic friends to a personal experience of salvation in Jesus Christ, we need to know as much as we can about the various groups within the Catholicism in order to present the message of salvation in a way that is relevant to each group.

Types of Catholics

Traditional Catholics

Traditional Catholics are generally older persons who participated in the Catholic Church before the Second Vatican Council. Many of them make an effort to continue the traditional practices that are not observed in the same way today. Among these are the Mass in Latin, not eating meat on Fridays, and having a devotion to patron saints (e.g., St. Christopher). These Catholics show great reverence toward God and the authority of the Church. Generally they know more about the creeds and prayers prescribed by the Church than about the Bible itself. These people are against the immorality in society that is denounced by the Church and observe the sacraments more regularly than the other types of Catholics. Traditional Catholics are more prone to have altars and statues of saints in their homes and to observe the rites prescribed in the liturgical calender. They have some knowledge about the Rosary and participate in novenas and other rituals for those who have died. Many traditional Catholics are not in favor of the changes of Vatican II and some believe that the Catholic Church is becoming more like the Protestant Church every day.

253

B. Progressive Catholics

Progressive Catholics are generally younger than traditional Catholics and are more in favor of the changes of Vatican II. These changes include the Mass in the language of the people, more participation on the part of the laity in the Mass and activities of the Church, a greater emphasis in Bible reading both in church and in the homes, and a greater emphasis on ecumenism to the extent that they now call Evangelicals "separated brethren." As a result of these changes, progressive Catholics are more knowledgeable about the Bible and are more receptive to the idea of participating in Bible studies with Evangelicals and to visit Evangelical churches.

C. Charismatic Catholics

Charismatic Catholics have much in common with Progressive Catholics. Generally, Charismatic Catholics are very much in favor of the changes brought on by Vatican II and spend time reading the Bible and praying. In many countries Charismatic Catholics have conferences in which they listen to sermons and testimonies, sing joyfully, and pray to invite the Holy Spirit into their hearts. Some participate in *Life in the Spirit Seminars,* in which they utilize materials that are very similar to the *Four Spiritual Laws* and encourage the attendees to receive Christ as their personal savior.[1] As a result of this, many Charismatic Catholics affirm that they received Christ in their hearts and that they are filled with the Holy Spirit. Some of them are willing to attend Evangelical church services and to participate with great enthusiasm. One of the issues related to Charismatic Catholics has to do with their understanding of biblical doctrines. The fact that they are Charismatic does not mean that they are Evangelical in their doctrines. Many, for example, continue with their devotion to the Virgin Mary and participate in the Mass and in the sacraments according to the teachings of the Catholic Church.

Nominal Catholics

Nominal Catholics constitute the largest group of Roman Catholics. As the term indicates, these are Catholics in name only. Quite likely, they were baptized in the Church as infants and consider themselves Catholics, but seldom attend Mass and know very little about the doctrines and practices of their Church. Some of these can be considered "Cultural Catholics." They associate their culture with their religion. For example, they believe that to be Italian or Latin American (or whatever their national identity) is to be Catholic. This group attends church during important occasions such as baptisms, weddings, and funerals, but does not receive instruction and nurture from the Church.

Some of them have their own devotion to the Virgin Mary and the patron saints but do not relate this to the regular activities of the Church. Due to the fact that Nominal Catholics know very little about the Bible, they need to hear the basic truths of Gospel of Jesus Christ.

Syncretistic Catholics (Catholicism & Animism)

Syncretistic Catholics are persons who practice a mixture of Catholicism and Animism (Native Religions). They take images of the saints and use them in animistic practices such as divination, casting spells, witchcraft, communicating with the spirits of the dead, folk medicine, and seeking to protect themselves from evil spirits. This syncretism is the result of a blending of pagan, indigenous practices (local or imported from places like Africa) and Catholic beliefs that relate to the worship of saints.[2]

In many places, native people have simply adopted the name of a Catholic saint for their pagan deity and have continued to worship it under the name of that saint. In some places such as Chicastenango, Guatemala, indigenous people offer a goat on the steps of a Catholic Church in accordance with their pagan practices and then enter the Church and light up candles to the Virgin Mary and other saints.

How to Present the Gospel to Each Type of Catholic

Traditional Catholics

Traditional Catholics generally have a very limited knowledge of the Bible and are very concerned about the changes of Vatican II. They are generally not interested in attending Evangelical worship services, and are not very receptive when a person comes to their homes and tries to lead them to Christ on the first visit. It is absolutely necessary to establish a genuine friendship with them in order to witness to them. In their case, fellowship meetings in the homes is one of the most effective strategies. Also, due to their concern about the changes of Vatican II, it is important to focus on the living Christ who does not change and is the same yesterday, today, and forever. In other words, we should encourage them to put their faith in Christ who does not change.

Progressive Catholics

Due to the fact that progressive Catholics are very much in favor of the changes of Vatican II, they are more receptive to establish a friendship with

Evangelicals, to accept an invitation to attend meetings in an Evangelical church and to participate in Bible studies. Some of them, however, believe that there is actually very little difference between Evangelicals and Catholics because they sing similar hymns and choruses in their Churches. The greatest challenge is to guide them through Bible study to a clearer knowledge of the biblical doctrine of salvation and Christian discipleship. Some of them already consider themselves born again Christians. It is very important to begin with what they know and to lead them to a clear comprehension of the Christian life from a biblical perspective.

Charismatic Catholics

Because Charismatic Catholics have much in common with Progressive Catholics, much of what we have said about the latter applies to the former. What distinguishes them, however, is the fact that they affirm that they have received the Holy Spirit. There are two things that we must keep in mind as we relate to this group.

First, we need to be sure that they truly understand what the Bible teaches about salvation and the presence of the Holy Spirit. The fact that they have had an emotional experience does not mean in and of itself that they have received the Holy Spirit. Second, the fact that Charismatic Catholics claim to have received the Holy Spirit does not mean that they understand this or the other essential doctrines of Scripture. For example, when Charismatic Catholic continue their devotion to the Virgin Mary, they are allowing her to take the place of the Holy Spirit in their lives, for much of what the Catholic Church attributes to Mary is what Jesus said the Holy Spirit would do. It is helpful to invite them to participate with us in Bible study. The Holy Spirit said that He would lead us to all truth. It is essential that we emphasize that the Holy Spirit gives witness of the presence of Christ in our lives. When they study the Bible, Charismatic Catholics can evaluate their experience in the light of Scripture.

Nominal Catholics

The fact that Nominal Catholics know very little about the doctrines and teachings of the Catholic Church indicates that we do not need to spend a lot of time on that subject. Also, the fact that they are Catholics in name only, does not mean that they will be very open to developing friendships with Evangelical Christians and to attend church with them. If we do not treat them with respect and we criticize their religious practices, they will feel obligated to defend them even though they are not active in a Catholic church. In other words, what will cause them to resist will not be their beliefs but their fears and prejudices. It is very important, therefore, to avoid criticizing their saints, the Virgin Mary, or other devotions. What we need to do is establish genuine friendships and involve them in Bible studies that focus on their daily needs and pave the way for the sharing of the gospel message.

Syncretistic Catholics

Due to the fact that Syncretistic Catholics practice a mixture of Catholicism and Animism, they are also Nominal Catholics and know very little about the teachings and practices of the Catholic Church..[3] With them, it is also pointless to spend a great deal of time dealing with the traditional teachings of the Roman Catholic Church.

Because they are involved in animistic practices, it is necessary to approach the witnessing task from the standpoint of spiritual warfare. In other words, we need to spend time fasting and praying before we attempt to witness to them. They need to know what the Bible teaches about salvation. They also need to become convinced that God is powerful enough to liberate and protect them from all evil forces in the universe. For them, the decision is not just to accept biblical doctrines intellectually, but to abandon their evil practices and place their complete trust in Jesus Christ, who has all authority in heaven and on earth.

Conclusion:

As we can observe through this study, there is great diversity regarding the various types of Catholics. These are broad categories which may overlap at times. It is helpful, nonetheless, to be aware of the different types of Catholics in order that our witness might be more focused. Two additional categories are "Liberal Theologians" (who question the ancient doctrines of the church and "Liberation Theologians" (who focus on liberating the poor and are indifferent to many doctrinal issues).[4] Each group has its own characteristics. It is important to take these into account and to design appropriate strategies to present the gospel in a way that makes sene to each group and relates to their specific needs. The following chart presents this information in a succinct manner.

CONTEXTUALIZING STRATEGIES

	Bible Knowledge	Questions	Approach
Traditional Catholic	Some	Changes in the church's traditional practices	Focus on the unchanging Christ
Progressive Catholic	More	What's the meaning of changes in Second Vatican Council?	Affirm changes; use as open doors for Bible study
Nominal Catholic	Almost none	Relate more to personal devotions:the saints, the Virgin Mary	Involve them in Bible study. Show how a personal faith in Christ can make a difference in daily life.
Cultural Catholic	Almost none	These relate to cultural identity and the practice of Roman Catholicism. "To be Italian is to be Catholic".	Long term Bible study. Show how a personal faith can make a difference.
Charismatic Catholic	Generally good	What is the difference between Catholics and Evangelicals?	Make sure they have a biblical understanding of "recieving Christ". Involve them in discipleship Bible studies

LESSON   L

REACHING OUR LATIN AMERICAN FRIENDS

Introduction

Latin Americans are responding more to the Evangelical message today than any other time in their history. Andrés Tapia asserts that in the last 25 years, the number of Evangelicals in Hispanic America has tripled and that by the year 2010, they will constitute a third of the population on this continent.[5] In Brazil, more than half a million persons are joining Evangelical churches every year. In 1990, a third of the population of Guatemala was Evangelical, and the projections are that early into this new century the Evangelical population will reach fifty percent.[6] Samuel Escobar adds that Evangelicals have grown from 15 million in the decade of the 60's to at least 40 million in our day.[7] According to the Brazilian Catholic bishop Boaventura Kloppenburg, Latin America is becoming Protestant more rapidly than Central Europe did in the sixteenth century, the time of the Protestant Reformation.[8]

The Hispanic American population in the United States is also showing great receptivity to the gospel message. Two studies that have been done by Catholic researchers, reveal that in the last fifteen years a million Hispanic Americans have left the Catholic Church and have identified themselves as Protestant (mainly Evangelical) or as members of a sect. These studies indicate that every year, between 80,000 and 100,000 Hispanic Americans are following this trend.[9] It is calculated that today 23 percent of the Hispanic American populace in this country is non- Catholic.[10]

The fact that Hispanic people are responding to the Evangelical message in a marvelous way does not mean that the task has been easy or that it will be in the future. Besides, we should recognize that, even if the projection becomes reality , namely that by the year 2010 a third of the Hispanic Americans will have accepted the Evangelical message, the fact will remain that two thirds of the Hispanic American population would still need to have a personal relationship with Jesus Christ.   How will we respond in the future when someone asks us what we did with the great opportunity that God gave us to win Hispanic people in our generation?

In order to fulfill the Great Commission in the Latin American context, it is necessary for us to give attention to a few factors which are very important. First, we should be well acquainted with the socio-religious context of the Latin American people. Second, we should know the doctrines and principal practices of the predominant religion, Roman Catholicism. Third, we should design evangelistic strategies that are adapted to the context in which they live. Finally, we should design strategies of discipleship that take into account the religious background of new believers and that guide them to a new understanding of the Lordship of Christ in their lives, their families, their communities, and their churches.

The Latin American Socio-Context

There is great cultural, linguistic, political, economic, and religious diversity among the Latin American people. Although Spanish is the predominant language (except in Brazil), several languages of European origin are spoken (such as Portuguese, French, German, and Italian), in addition to the 250 indigenous languages.[11] **In spite of the diversity, there are certain values which the majority of the population holds in common.**

Writers such as Miguel de Unamuno, Samuel Ramos, Santiago Ramírez, María Elvira Bermúdez, and Octavio Paz assert that among the values of the Latin American society are found: (1) the importance of personal dignity, (2) the importance of family unity (both nuclear and extended), (3) a profound feeling of spirituality, (4) the freedom to express their emotions, (5) love of art and music, (6) the importance of celebrating the victories of life, (7) a desire to be respectful and decent persons and (8) the importance of friendship.[12]

Although we know that these values are found in different degrees in different groups and individuals, it is important to note that we have much in common with people in this context, even when these belong to other religious groups.

Attitudes of Evangelicals

With this in mind, it is important that Evangelicals think about the things that they have in common with the persons that surround them, even when these persons do not form a part of the religious group to which they belong. For example, because of the profound interest in the unity of the family, today there is great concern in the hearts of parents resulting from the ravages caused by the practices of modern society. What would happen if we took time to get to know our neighbors and colleagues (in school or work) and ministered to them with our friendship, testimony, Bible studies, and our financial resources? In other words, the common value we have pertaining to the family can be a tunnel through which we establish a friendship and communicate the gospel of our Lord Jesus Christ.

One of the things that makes the Evangelical task difficult is that they focus on the differences they have with persons who are not Evangelical. As a result, they feel apprehensive, and it is hard for Evangelicals to know how to relate to them. On the contrary, if Evangelicals think about all the things that they have in common, they will find many ways to cultivate friendships and to present the gospel to them. These persons are fellow human beings who face many of the challenges that we encounter, feel many of the emotions that we feel, who experience many of the sufferings that we experience, have many of the personal aspirations and aspirations for their families that we have, celebrate many of the victories that we celebrate, feel many of the anxieties that we feel, and have many of the needs that we have.

The Teachings of Jesus Christ

Our Lord Jesus Christ took into account the religious background and the needs of the people when he presented the message of salvation to them. For example, to the Samaritan woman who went to draw water from the well, Christ offered her the water of life. To Zacchaeus, who was hated by the people, the first thing Christ did was to offer him fellowship. To the religious leader, Nicodemus, who had not found satisfaction in the law, Christ spoke to him of the new birth. By means of His words and example Jesus, taught his followers to:

1. To love their neighbor as ourselves (Matthew 27:37-40)

2. To minister in their needs to those who are to us (Luke 10:30-40 [The Good Samaritan])

3. To forgive others (Matthew 18:21-22)

4. To love their enemies and to pray for those who persecute them (Matthew 5:43-48)

Although it is true that in the past relations between Catholics and Evangelicals have left much to be desired, it is also very true that there are two reasons why Evangelical Christians ought to reexamine their attitudes toward Catholics: (1) Christ commanded them to love others; (2) Some Catholics are showing more friendship to Evangelical Christians.[13]

In order to be able to evangelize, it is important that we have the spirit of Christ. In the past, a good number of Evangelical Christians have been more interested in proving that Catholics are wrong than in guiding them to a personal saving encounter with Christ.

Basic Principles

When preparing ourselves for this task, there are certain rules that we ought to follow:

1. We should utilize a plan for continual prayer. No amount of knowledge in and of itself will bring persons to the feet of Jesus; only the power of the Holy Spirit.

2. We should strive to know well the doctrines of the persons whom we want to evangelize

3. We ought to show respect toward the beliefs of these persons even though we may not be in agreement with what they believe.

4. We ought to distinguish between the official doctrines of the Catholic Church and what these persons, in particular, believe.

5. We ought to use the Bible as our only authority. At the same time, we ought to distinguish between what is biblical and what is traditional in our own religious practices

6. We should recognize our own prejudices against these persons who hold to different beliefs.

7. We should cultivate a spirit of love and compassion.

8. We ought to help persons to discover for themselves what the Bible says regarding salvation.

9. We ought to concentrate first on the matter of salvation.

Conclusion:

As we know, there is a great cultural and religious diversity in Latin America. By following the example of Jesus Christ, we should strive to know the groups or person with whom we wish to share the message of salvation. At the same time, we should be aware of the fact that, as human beings living in the same region of the world, there is much that we have in common with them. Again, like our Lord Jesus Christ, we ought to adapt the presentation of the message to the specific needs of each person. Upon undertaking this glorious task, we ought to have in mind that which the apostle Peter advised: "Always be prepared to present a defense with meekness and reverence before the one who asks a reason for the hope that is in you." (I Peter 3:15).

ENDNOTES

1   *Word of God, Life in the Spirit Seminars* (Ann Arbor: Servant Books, 1979).

2   See, Tetsunao Yamamori and Charles Taber, *Christopaganism of Indigenous Christianity?*(Pasadena: WilliamCarey , 1975) , Domingo Fernández, *Superstición Africana en América*(Miami: Logoi Inc., 1973), Eugene Nida, *Understanding Latin Americans* (Pasadena: William Carey, 1974).

3   Officially the Roman Catholic church opposes these practices (See Nevins, *Answering A Fundamentalist* p. 106). The fact that so many who call themselves Catholics practice this form of syncretism leads one to believe that either there has been an absence of strong discipleship or the people have willfully disobeyed the church.

4   For a fuller discussion of some of these categories see Kenneth S. Kantzer, *"Church on the Move,"* Christianity Today, (November 7, 1986).

5   Andrés Tapia, *"Why is Latin America Turning Protestant?"* Christianity Today (April 6, 1992), 28.

6   Thomas S. Giles, *"Forty Million and Counting,"* Christianity Today (April 6, 1992), 32.

7   Samuel Escobar, *"A New Reformation,"* Christianity Today (April 6, 1992), 30.

8   Tapia, op. cit., 28.

9   Rev. Ricardo Chávez, spokesman of the Catholic Conference of California, *"The San Jose Mecury News,"* Feb. 28, 1990, 12A.

10 "Catholic Leaders Worried Over Loss of Hispanics to Protestant Churches," *The Atlanta Journal and Constitution,* May 14, 1989.

11 Eugene Nida, *Understanding Latin Americans*(Pasadena: William Carey Library, 1974), 5.

12 Nida, 9.

13 Let us listen to what the Roman Catholic priest William says: "In the past, we Catholics have not treated other Christians well. We have treated them as doubtful Christians with the same ardor with which we treated the Communists. We have taught that their churches were false churches simply because we acknowledge one church and one unity, the one established by Rome. A peaceful coexistence is what we are hoping for from now on." *Contemporary Catholic Catechism,* 96.

CHAPTER NINE

DESIGNING CONGREGATIONAL STRATEGIES

Introduction: Maria's New Family

After years of observation and concern, I decided to attempt to fashion a congregational style that would minimize the traditional and cultural obstacles that Catholics encounter when they visit typical Evangelical churches. When a church inquired if I would be their pastor, I discussed with the leaders the vision I had for a culturally relevant congregation in a predominantly Roman Catholic community. They were gracious enough to agree to try this experiment. Without going into detail here, I will mention briefly some of the changes we made in what was a very traditional congregation.

First, we agreed that we would enter the sanctuary in a spirit of reverence and worship. Instead of talking with our fellow church members, we would spend time in silent prayer preparing our hearts for the worship service while the organ played soft music. Second, we agreed that we would not greet visitors individually and publically, but would give a general welcome and would greet one another while a song was being played. We stressed that visitors needed to feel genuinely welcomed and loved. Third, we agreed to use a screen in which to project choruses and hymns so that our visitors could easily follow and participate. Fourth, we agreed that our Sunday morning sermons would be positive and uplifting. We stressed that we would never say anything critical or negative about other religious but would focus on pointing people to Christ. Fifth, we agreed to give the invitation to make a decision for Christ differently. Instead of calling on people to stand up and come forward, we would ask everyone to bow in prayer. We would then ask those who wanted to receive Christ to raise their heads, look at the pastor, pray a prayer led by the pastor, and then fill out a card with information so the pastor or someone else from the church could visit them and converse with them about their decision. We also said that after the service we would have a brief reception for those who wanted to converse with the pastor. Finally, we decided to place the announcements, which would be very brief, at the end of the service so that the service could flow naturally without interruption.

Not long after we implemented these changes, we were visited by a lovely Peruvian family who had recently arrived in our area. Samuel, Maria, and their two children had been visited by a member of our church who had spoken to them about the need to have a personal experience of salvation with Jesus Christ. After preaching an evangelistic sermon, I asked those who wanted to invite Jesus into their lives to look up at me while the others remained with their heads bowed. Both Samuel and Maria looked up at me, prayed a prayer with me, and listened attentively as I gave them brief instructions. At the conclusion of the service, both of them stayed for our reception. They said that the service and the sermon had touched them deeply and they wanted to know more about their walk with the Lord. I invited them to join our new believer's class that evening. They asked: "Do you attend church at night also?" They agreed, however, to come to the class.

At the class, Maria said that she had opened her heart to Jesus and had a peace she had never experienced before, but she still had many questions. She explained: "The reason my name is Maria is that my mother is strongly devoted to the Virgin Mary." Then she asked: "If I continue to come to this church, will I have to hate the Virgin Mary?" I answered: "No, where did you get that idea?" She said that she had some Evangelical co-workers in Peru who told her that everything related to Mary was idolatry and paganism and that she needed to "get rid of Mary" if she was going to be "a Christian." I told her that in our discipleship class for new believers we would deal with this doctrine in a few weeks, but that in the mean time, she needed to know my position regarding Mary. I told her that Mary had to have been a very special and consecrated person for God to have chosen her to give birth to His son. I also told her that there is much in Mary's life that we need to emulate such as her obedience, her sacrificial spirit, her faith, and her commitment to point people to Christ. She agreed that she would continue to attend the class and would look forward to the time when we dealt in more detail with this doctrine. Initially in class we dealt with such topics as the assurance of salvation, the importance of Bible study, believer's baptism, biblical confession, the Lord's supper, and the nature of the New Testament Church.

As we studied, our church fellowship became very meaningful to this family. She was a school teacher and he was a physical therapist. The jobs that they had been offered, however, did not materialize. Upon finding this out, our church members stepped in, provided free lodging and food for them, helped them to get a car, assisted them in finding new employment, and simply loved them. After attending church for six months, they decided to follow Jesus in believer's baptism. When Maria walked down the steps of the baptistry she told me: "The night before getting married I couldn't sleep because I was so excited, and last night I couldn't sleep either. This is such a marvelous experience." When Samuel and Maria shared with their families in Peru what they had done, their families became extremely upset. Maria explained that Samuel's parents had wanted him to become a priest, and Maria's family had wanted her to become a nun. Now they were very disappointed that they "had abandoned the religion of their family." For a long time their family would not answer their letters. We encouraged them to continue to love their families, to refrain from criticizing and pressuring them, and to continue praying for them. After a few months, their oldest son was going to have a birthday and Maria invited her parents over. They agreed to come on the condition that they not be expected to attend the Evangelical church. When they arrived, they were deeply touched by the love that was evident in this family and the fact that both of their grandchildren were so respectful of them and prayed before eating and going to bed. This prompted the grandparents to say to Maria: "This religion can't be all that bad if it produces these results in your family." They then became much more open to conversing about the Lord.

A year later, both Samuel and Maria felt the call of God into Christian ministry. With the help of our congregation, they both went to study at an Evangelical seminary. Samuel is now the pastor of a church and Maria is the children's ministry director. They both love the Lord dearly and continue to grow in their Christian experience. Some time ago I asked Maria: "What is you view of Mary now that you have studied the Bible?" She replied: "I still have a deep appreciation for Mary. I am truly inspired by her example, but she did not die for my sins. My supreme devotion is to the Lord. I pray to Him only."

Listening to her testimony and seeing what the Lord has done in the life of this couple and their children has truly inspired me. I am also comforted by the fact that I have learned from the mistakes I made while seeking to minister to Nora years earlier. I shutter when I think of the fact that I could have also turned this wonderful couple off with the insensitive approach to witnessing and discipleship that I had in the past. I am also very encouraged by the role that our culturally sensitive congregation played in ministering to this couple. We need many more congregations like this one.

CONGREGATIONAL STRATEGY LESSONS

Even though many of the changes that have taken place in the Roman Catholic Church since the Second Vatican Council such innovations as the Mass celebrated in the language of the people, increased participation on the part of the laity, and contemporary (praise type) music, the fact remains that many Roman Catholics encounter very significant differences in Evangelical congregations. One of these differences has to do with the concept of church that is found in each of the two groups. For many Catholics, the church is the sanctuary in which they worship. This has implications for the different items (e.g., statues, paintings, candles, holy water) that they find in their churches as well as the attitude with which people enter the church. Often practices that are very meaningful and dear to Evangelicals (e.g., having a wonderful time of fellowship before the worship service starts) can be interpreted by Catholic visitors as indications of irreverence. Among some of the other differences is the fact that in most countries, Catholics worship in historical cathedrals and sanctuaries located in the most prominent parts of the city. Starting Evangelical churches in small, modest buildings is often a challenge in areas that are predominantly Roman Catholic.

Another challenge stems from the fact that when Catholics join Evangelical churches, they have voids in their lives which Evangelical congregations do not fill. These voids stem from some of the religious practices that former Roman Catholics used to have such as the baptism of their babies, their children's First Communion, getting together as a family to commemorate the anniversary of the death of a family member, and having special celebrations during Lent, Christmas, and other special days.

Yet another challenge is encountered by Catholics when they visit Evangelical churches and they are asked to stand up, give people their name, and even say a few words. In their desire to make them feel welcome, some Evangelical church leaders intimidate and alienate their Catholic visitors. Other practices such as having too many congregational songs, having worship services that are very informal, and putting pressure on people to make a public decision cause many Catholic visitors to feel very uncomfortable and reluctant to return.

In Lesson M "The Concept of Church" we address the concept that many Catholics have of the church. In this discussion we emphasize the fact that ultimately it is not the historicity or majesty of the buildings that attracts people, but true Christian love, redeeming relationships, and a spirit of servanthood. While it is important to have the neatest, most attractive houses of worship possible, we make some suggestions on how to minister to a person's spiritual needs in order to lead them to Christ.

In Lesson N, "Biblical Ceremonies for Socio-Religious Acts," we attempt to help Evangelicals to have a better understanding of the religious events that are important to Roman Catholics. At the same time, however, we challenge Evangelicals to design ceremonies that are *truly biblical* and *culturally relevant.* These functional substitutes can not only fill the spiritual/social voids of former Catholics but contribute to their spiritual growth as well as to their ability to reach their loved ones for Christ.

In Lesson O, "Contextualized Worship Services," we help Evangelicals to evaluate their services from the perspective of their Catholic friends. In other words, what do the things we do in our worship services mean to our Catholic friends? What do we need to do differently in order to avoid unnecessary social and traditional barriers? The answers to these questions can lead to the designing of worship services that truly honor God while at the same time communicating in a positive manner to our Catholic visitors. These lessons can contribute to the establishment of contextualized strategies for congregational development.

LESSON M

CONCEPT OF THE CHURCH

Introduction

It is very important that we know the concept that many Roman Catholics have regarding the church. This has implications for the methodology that we use to win them to Christ and to encourage them to join a congregation in which they can continue to learn about the Word of God and grow in their faith.

Catholic Concept of the Church

The Church is the Sanctuary (the Building)

Although the Catholic Church does not officially teach that the church is the building, in a certain sense the concept of many Catholics with regard to the church is like that of the Jews in the time of the Old Testament; that is to say, that the church is the sanctuary. This concept has various important implications.

1. The Architecture

One implication is that the architecture and the beauty of the sanctuary give validity to their religion. Large and impressive cathedrals and sanctuaries inspire a sense of confidence in many Catholics. They feel that the "true church" is the one that possesses the greatest and most beautiful buildings. In many cases, these Catholic cathedrals are found in the center of the city and are used for the ceremonies (weddings, funerals, etc.) of the most prominent persons in social and political spheres. There is a feeling in the hearts of many Catholics that their religion is the "official" religion because their sanctuaries have all the signs of acceptance, recognition, and respect. In contrast to this, many Catholics have the impression that the small and humble buildings of many Evangelical groups reflect a lack of religious validity. If these Evangelical groups really were the "true church," they would have impressive buildings. Some Catholics have the bias that the historicity of Catholic sanctuaries (cathedrals) shows that theirs is the true religion. In Latin America, Catholics not only have large and impressive sanctuaries, but many of these were built during the time of the Spanish conquest. In other words, the presence of these sanctuaries, for many Catholics, provides evidence that their religion has been the official religion of Latin America and of their country for several centuries. In contrast to this, many Catholics see Evangelical churches as buildings which have been built recently and which lack a historic base that gives validity to the religion which they profess. Some of the Catholics ask themselves: "Why should I identify myself with one of these new sects when my family has belonged to a religion which has been recognized officially for centuries?"

The Church Is Where God Is

Another concept that many Catholics have is that the presence of God is in the sanctuary. This concept has several implications.

1. The presence of God and the sacraments

In accordance with Catholic doctrine, the presence of God is related to the sacraments. When the Eucharist is celebrated, for example, Catholics not only remember the death and resurrection of Jesus, but they believe that the bread and wine turn into the body and blood of Christ. This makes Christ present bodily as well as spiritually. It is for that reason that Catholics speak about the adoration of the Host, because for them it is the adoration of Christ.

2. The presence of God and the sacramentals

The sacramentals are the material and symbolic things that help the Catholics express and practice their faith. The most used sacramentals are the wardrobe of the priest, the cross, the sign of the cross, holy water, images, paintings, altars, candles, medallions, and incense. It is the belief of many Catholics that God becomes present through sacramentals. For example, the sign of the cross and Holy Water sprinkled on the coffin in a funeral assures the bereaved that the deceased loved one has the blessing of God. Lighting a candle and praying before a statue in the sanctuary gives Catholics the feeling that they are communicating with someone who is present at that very place and that this saint or this virgin will convey their petition to God.

It is very important that we be aware of the fact that many Catholics associate the presence of God with what they can *see* (images, the architecture of the sanctuary), *hear* (music), *touch* (medallions), *taste* (the Host), and *smell* (incense). In other words, religious experience for them appeals to their five senses.

The fact that Catholics believe that the presence of God resides in the sanctuary leads them to have a sense of reverence. It is for that reason that they remain silent, kneel to pray, and that many women cover their heads.

How to Overcome Preconceived Ideas with Regard to the Church

In view of the impressive buildings that Catholics have, their feeling of history with regard to their buildings, and the concept that they have concerning the presence of God in their sanctuaries, Evangelicals have great obstacles to overcome in getting Catholics to visit their services and feel at home in their church buildings. Although we cannot (or should not) build great cathedrals and fill them with images so that they may feel comfortable, there are many things that indeed we can do related both to the physical aspect of our buildings and the spiritual aspect of our worship.

Having the Most Adequate Buildings Possible

Evangelicals have the conviction that God does not dwell in houses made by human hands, but in the hearts of believers. This, however, should not prevent us from acquiring and maintaining the most adequate buildings possible for the glory of God. Church buildings should be as clean and as attractive as possible. Later, we will talk about spiritual factors that help people to respond to the gospel. It is important, however, that when Catholics visit us they leave with the impression that we have made an effort to provide a favorable environment in which to gather and worship God.

Paying Attention to Symbolism

Although as Evangelicals we do not believe that there ought to be images in the sanctuary, the truth is that what we do have conveys messages in symbolic ways. Such things as altar cloths on the pulpit and on the Lord Supper's table, flower arrangements, flags, the arrangement of the furniture on the platform, and the paintings in the baptistry and on the walls have symbolic value. One of the things that we ought to ask is, "What does this mean for Catholics when they visit Evangelical churches?" Church buildings poorly cared for and poorly decorated (e.g., faded pictures and worn-out flags) can communicate to visitors that Evangelicals do not pay much attention to the environment in which they gather to worship God.

Providing a Spiritual Environment

Although it is true that the large and impressive buildings of Catholic churches appeal a great deal to the cultural, historic, and aesthetic taste of Catholics, it is also true that, in the final analysis, it is not the *buildings* that minister to the people, but the *spiritual environment* that they find in the church. Several studies that have been done about the reason persons have responded to the gospel and have joined Evangelical churches reveal that the most important factors were the sincere fellowship, a genuine environment of spirituality, informative and edifying sermons, relevant Bible studies, inspiring worship services, and compassionate pastoral care. Evangelicals, therefore should not feel defeated when they do not have impressive buildings. They should do the best that they can, but at the same time, they should be conscious of the fact that they have much to offer to people who do not know Christ as their personal savior. It is also important to be aware of the concept that Catholics have with regard to the church, so that Evangelicals can reach and disciple them in a more effective manner. After winning them for Christ, we should help them to understand the biblical concept of the church.

Biblical Teaching Concerning the Church[1]

Due to mistaken concepts that many people have with regard to the church, it is beneficial that we first define what the church is.

What the Church is Not

The church is not an organization with a centralized government. It is not a uniform but united body. It is not an institution that saves people since the one who saves is Christ. It is not perfect, since it is composed of human beings. It is not an end in itself, but the means by which others may know God. It is not a building, but the people who make up the church.

What the Church is

The Bible describes the church so that people may know its nature and its mission. It literally means "the ones called out" to a society of believers redeemed by Christ and united mutually by the bonds of faith and love. This is a very important concept in the New Testament. That is why the term "church" appears 109 times. In 17 of these passages, it refers to all the people of God scattered throughout the globe, but in the rest of the passages it refers to the local church, a group of believers geographically located in a place as a spiritual family.

1. The Church is the body of Christ - In the first place, the church is presented as the body of Christ. With such a figure, a common life that one shares with Christ is emphasized (Romans 12:5; Ephesians 4:4).

2. The Church is a group of believers - The church is presented as a society of believers in Christ, redeemed by the action of God so such believers are characterized as being chosen, redeemed, reborn, and sealed (Ephesians 1:3-13).

3. The Church is an organism, with Christ as the head - Christ is the head of the church. In other words, the church is His body (Ephesians 1:22-23). He governs it by the Holy Spirit and his Word. The analogy of the relationship between a husband and wife is applied to the church (Ephesians 5:23 and Philemon 2:7)..

4. The Church is the family of God - The Bible describes the church as "the family of God" (Ephesians 2:19-22). This family has God as its father and one another as brothers and sisters. The analogy of a loving, caring, mutually supportive family portrays what the church should be.

5. The Church has an intrinsic nature - Although imperfect because it is composed of human beings, it contributes decisively to elevate dignity. For example: it is the sanctuary of the Most High; Christ works inside the church and the Holy Spirit is present, guiding and empowering believers. It is the hope of the fallen race. This happens because it was founded by Christ with the expressed promise of victory (Matthew 16:18).

The concept of the church, therefore, does not need to change in every generation or epoch. It is permanent, like its founder. Its purpose and relationship with God remain the same for every generation. What does change - and it is advisable that it be this way - are the methods of adaptation to a changeable social reality.

Conclusion:

The Bible clearly teaches that the church is the body of Christ and not the building. Nevertheless, when dealing with our Catholic friends, it is important that we understand the concept that they have of the church. This should motivate us to maintain our buildings as clean and as attractive as possible. At the same time, we should manifest the true characteristics of the church which honors Christ, such as love, fellowship, Christian service, biblical preaching, inspiring worship, and effective discipleship. This will help visitors to feel welcome and to recognize that the true church is the one that honors Christ with its actions and it teachings.

LESSON N

BIBLICAL CEREMONIES FOR SOCIO-RELIGIOUS ACTS

Introduction:

Special events in the life of a cultural group provide opportunities to establish close friendship ties and to communicate the message of salvation. In Latin America, for example, there are many opportunities for celebrations. This includes both the rites of passage (like births, confirmations, and weddings) and the celebration of days with social, political, and religious significance. The Catholic Church has known how to make good use of these special days by giving them religious significance and enhancing the identification of the people with the church. In order to understand the nature and significance of these days, we will begin with a description of the way in which they are celebrated. Later, we will speak in more detail about the way in which we can plan activities for festive days. Even though we will focus primarily on Latin American festivities, this principle can be applied to other cultural groups in different parts of the world.

Religious Celebrations

In the life of the Latin American, there are many opportunities to celebrate. These celebrations can be divided into two categories: 1) *socio/religious* celebrations and 2) *personal celebrations*. Although these can be divided to facilitate an analysis , the truth is that these are so interwoven that they cannot be totally separated. That is to say, personal celebrations have religious as well as social implications.

A.   Celebrations Related To The Liturgical Year

The liturgical calender focuses on key events in the life of Christ. During these special days, Catholics are instructed to read the Bible and pray. This provides a magnificent opportunity for Evangelicals to invite their Catholic friends to participate in Bible studies related to the themes that are emphasized during these special seasons of the Liturgical Calender.

Advent

The Advent period begins four weeks before the birthday of Christ. During the first two weeks, the Second Coming of Christ as Judge and Lord at the end of the world is celebrated. From December 17th to the 24th, the emphasis changes to an anticipation of his birth in the celebration of Christmas. Recommended Bible readings: passages that refer to the Messiah.[2]

Christmastide

The Christmastide period opens with the Feast of the Nativity, December 25, and lasts until the Sunday after Epiphany[3] (January 6). The Baptism of the Lord, observed on the Sunday following Epiphany, marks the end of Christmastide.[4]

Lent

The penitential season of Lent begins on Ash Wednesday, which occurs between February 4 and March 11, depending on the date of Easter. It has 6 Sundays and 40 weekdays. The climactic last week is called "Holy Week." The last three days (Holy Thursday, Good Friday, and Holy Saturday) are called the *Paschal Tridum.*[5]

Scripture readings: Baptismal and penitential passages

Eastertide

Eastertide, whose theme is resurrection from sin to the life of grace, lasts for 50 days, from Easter to Pentecost. Easter, the first Sunday following the vernal equinox, occurs between March 22 and April 25. The final phase of Eastertide lies between the Feast of Ascension of the Lord and Pentecost. It stresses anticipation of the coming of the Holy Spirit and the action of the Holy Spirit.[6]

Scripture Readings: Acts of the Apostles and the Gospel of John.

Ordinary Time

Ordinary time includes the period of time between Christmastide and Lent. It also includes all the Sundays after Pentecost, through the last Sunday of the liturgical year. The overall purpose of this season is to elaborate on the theme of salvation history.[7]

Celebrations related to the sacraments

a) **Baptisms** - The baptism of a baby in not only a religious ceremony, but also a social one as well. After the baptism, family members and friends get together to celebrate this important event in the life of their family.

b) **Confirmation** - After having received instruction in Catechism, a child is ready to receive the sacrament of Confirmation. Generally, children are dressed in white and, as in baptism, the family gathers to celebrate this event.

c) **Weddings** - Matrimony is considered a sacrament which is the reason why it is celebrated in the church. At the same time, this is a social act that is celebrated by the family and friends with great joy.

d) **Anointing (Last Rites)** - The sacrament of Extreme Unction (now known as "Prayer for the Sick") is utilized not only to prepare the person for death, but to pray for the person's healing. Because in most cases the person is gravely ill, family and friends usually gather due to their love and concern.

Un-official Celebrations

There are certain types of celebrations that do not appear in the Liturgical Calender but are observed in the various communities with the approval of the priest.[8]

a) **Christmas Celebrations**

1) **Posadas** - In some Latin American countries, people have the tradition of doing a re-enactment of Joseph and Mary's search for lodging in Bethlehem. A couple dresses up like Joseph and Mary and, accompanied by a group, go from house to house singing and looking for lodging. By prior agreement, the people in the homes refuse to give them lodging until they get to the designated home, where the couple, as well as the group, are invited in to participate in singing, eating and drinking hot chocolate or coffee.[9]

2) **Placing The Baby In The Manger** - This celebration is one in which family members and special friends are invited to a home to participate in the placing of the "baby Jesus" in the manger. In preparation for this, the inviting family usually sets up a very elaborate manger scene with small statues of people and animals. At the appropriate moment, a designated person places the small doll representing Jesus in the manger. This is followed by the serving of refreshments and fellowship.

3) **The Three Kings** - On the 6th of January, there is the celebration which commemorates the arrival of the Three Kings. This is usually accompanied by the giving of gifts following the tradition of the gifts brought by the Wise men to the baby Jesus. Children usually look forward to this day as they do to Christmas day.

b) Holy Week Celebrations

1) **Processions** - In many places, people participate in processions during Holy Week in which they carry large statues of Jesus on the cross and of Mary. Generally, these are accompanied by groups of people, some of whom are playing instruments. The mood of these processions resemble that of funeral marches. People focus on the suffering of Jesus and of Mary in these parade-type processions.

2) **Stations of the Cross** - In some countries, people participate in a pilgrimage to visit the stations of the cross, meditating on the various aspects of the suffering of Jesus as he made his way to the place where he was crucified. (For more information on this, see Lesson D)

3) **Crucifixion Dramas** - During lent, people present dramas that depict the crucifixion of Jesus. In some countries, people allow themselves to be nailed to a cross where they remain for a brief moment and then are brought down and given medical attention. Those who do this are motivated by a desire to gain favor with God.

Socio/Cultural Celebrations

As we have reviewed the celebrations in the lives of Roman Catholics, undoubtedly, we have found that Evangelicals have many things in common with Catholics. At the same time there are significant things in which, due to their convictions, Evangelicals differ with Catholics . These differences, however, should not lead Evangelicals to separate themselves completely from their Catholic relatives and friends. Jesus said: "I do not pray that you will take them out of the world, but, that you will keep them in the world" (John 17:15). He also said: "You are the light of the world" (Matthew 5:14).

In order to do the will of our Lord, Evangelicals need to look for ways to fellowship with Catholics without violating their Evangelical convictions. This has implications for our personal lives as well as for our churches.

Personal Celebrations

Many of the personal celebrations can be classified as ceremonies of transition (rites of passage). These relate to the transition from one stage of life to another. These include births, birthdays, weddings, Father's Day, Mother's Day, funerals, and anniversaries (related to weddings or the departure of a loved one). These celebrations are of great importance, for they provide the opportunity to express gratitude to God and to loved ones. These are times when family members gathers to fellowship, express their love, spend happy moments together, and communicate their values to the new generation.

Celebrations in The Homes

Celebrations in the homes present an opportunity to cultivate friendships which paves the way for us to communicate the gospel to our relatives and friends.

Some time ago, I preached a week-end revival in an urban church during which time seventy five persons made a profession of faith in Jesus. When I enquired why we had had such a good response, I was informed that about 60 of these had been brought by one of the church members. She lives in an apartment building and has a wide variety of activities ranging from birthday and anniversary celebrations to welcoming new people in the apartments, visiting the sick, and ministering to people in need. After developing friendships, she invites them to a Bible study in her apartment. As a result of this, by the time people come to church with her, they have already made a decision to receive Christ .

When my wife and I moved to another city, we found out that we were the only Evangelicals in our community. When Independence Day came around, we were invited to a block party. At first we were a bit hesitant, knowing that very likely some of the people might get drunk. After praying, we decided to go. This gave us the opportunity to meet many of our neighbors. As a result of this, I was able to lead one of my neighbors to a personal experience of salvation in Jesus Christ. Several of the ladies in our community invited my wife to have a Bible study in our community. This resulted in the conversion of one lady and in the strengthening of the faith of most of the other ladies. One of them who was forsaken by her husband accepted our invitation to join us for Christmas dinner along with her two daughters. She never forgot our kindness during a time when she was really hurting.

My wife was won to the Lord as a young woman, when she attended a birthday party in her community. Her mother was very zealous about her Catholic faith, even though she did not attend church. While at the party, along with her sister and brothers, my wife listened attentively as an invited guest gave his testimony of how he had come to have a personal faith in Jesus Christ. When this guest asked if there were some who were interested in knowing more about Jesus, the young woman who is now my wife, along with her siblings, indicated an interest. While participating in a neighborhood Bible study, all four of them came to a personal faith in Christ.

A church that is reaching many nominal Christians with a Catholic background has trained its members to plan picnics and invite relatives and friends. In these picnics they don't "preach the gospel" or have "Bible studies." Instead, they have wholesome fun and deepen their friendships. This usually leads to other opportunities to converse with them about spiritual matters and then involve them in Bible studies.

As we can see, there are many opportunities to cultivate friendships and prepare the soil for sharing the message of salvation. These celebrations in the homes can become the bridge many people need to overcome obstacles of prejudice, lack of information, and timidity.

Dynamic Equivalent Celebrations

As we have already noted, many events that Catholics celebrate take place at church. These celebrations are not only expressions of their faith but opportunities to fellowship and strengthen family ties. Due to the Evangelicals' understanding of the Word of God, there are some Catholic practices in which they cannot participate. For example, we cannot be Godparents in the baptism of an infant because this is not what the Bible teaches. At the same time, it is important for us to be aware of the fact that there are many social events in which we can participate. In addition to this, there are some celebrations that can be both *socially appropriate* and *biblically sound*. Missiologists call these "dynamic equivalents" or "functional substitutes."[10] Let's explore some of these.

Equivalents For The Sacraments

1) Dedication of babies instead of baptism

For a Catholic couple, the dedication of their baby is a religious and social event. Due to the doctrine of original sin held by the Catholic Church, Catholic believe that if children die without being baptized they will go to Limbo. Parents believe that it is their obligation to baptize their child and to celebrate this event. When they become Evangelical Christians, there is a void in their lives if they do not have the opportunity to do something with religious significance and to celebrate the event with their families.

The dedication of a baby provides the opportunity for parents to express their gratitude to God, dedicate their baby to God, and celebrate with the family and the congregation. It is an opportunity not only for the baby to be dedicated, but also the parents, the grandparents and even the church members to commit themselves to provide the environment that will contribute to the child's spiritual development. In addition to celebrating at church, the couple can have a celebration at home to which family members and friends can be invited. The greater the dignity that is given to the dedication and the greater the significance that it has for the church, the more it will bless the parents and their relatives.

2) Profession of Faith in place of Confirmation

When the children of Catholic parents receive the sacrament of Confirmation the family celebrates the event and takes pictures so that this will be an unforgettable experience. Often, when the children of Evangelical parents make a public profession of faith, a few people take notice but there are no celebrations at church or at home. What if there were a celebration at church and at home to commemorate this significant event? Would it not give us an opportunity to invite family members and friends and to share with them the meaning of making a personal decision to receive Christ?

3) Memorial Service Instead of Praying for the Dead

Many Catholics have the practice of observing the anniversaries of the death of their loved ones by getting together and praying for their souls. The

Bible does not teach that Christians should pray for the souls of those who have died. When anniversaries come around, some former Catholics feel confused and sense a void in their lives, believing that they should be doing something to commemorate their departed loved ones. A memorial service held at church or at home acknowledging the anniversary and celebrating the life of the loved one can be done in such a way that it is culturally appropriate and biblically sound. This can provide an opportunity to share the gospel with family members and friends, focusing on the hope we have of seeing our loved ones in heaven.

4) Prayer for the sick instead of Last Rites

When a relative is seriously ill, family members call the priest to perform the last rites. Even though the Catholic Church now calls this rite "Prayer for the Sick," the truth remains that it is considered a sacrament which in itself imparts grace. Because this practice is unbiblical, we need to find a way to minister both to the person who is ill as well as to the family. When Evangelicals visit the home and pray for the person who is critically ill, read portions of Scripture, sing appropriate songs (if requested), and minister to the family, they are filling a void that is very real in the lives of many people.

5) Dedication of the Home, not just the House

Some Catholics have the custom of inviting the priest to come, sprinkle holy water, and bless their houses. For some syncretistic Catholics, it may even have the meaning of casting out evil spirits from the house. Evangelicals generally do not dedicate their houses. It could be a very meaningful experience for a family that has purchased a new house to dedicate themselves, as well as their home, to the service of the Lord. A dedication service similar to the one that is celebrated for church buildings could be very meaningful and fulfilling. Unchurched family members could be invited and this could provide an opportunity to share the gospel with them.

Equivalents For Socio/Religious Celebrations

There are ceremonies that are somewhat similar, yet, may have a different biblical focus. In these instances it will be very helpful to make sure that these are culturally relevant, yet, biblically sound.

1)   Weddings - Even though the wedding ceremony is somewhat similar, there is a spiritual dimension that needs to be evident in an Evangelical wedding ceremony. This starts with the counseling of

the couple, witnessing to them if they have not received Christ, praying for the ceremony, and conducting it in such a way that will honor God and present a witness of the difference Christ can make in the life of a couple.

2) Funerals - Funerals are often an opportunity to minister to the family and to present the message of salvation. This can be done in several ways. First, there should be words of comfort for the loved ones. They should be reminded that they are not alone. Loved ones should be comforted by the songs, the Bible readings, the prayers, the sermon, and the caring fellowship. Second, there should be words of assurance. Based on the words of Jesus, we can assure the family that their loved one (if he or she accepted Jesus as savior) is in heaven with the Lord (John 5:24; John 14). Third, there should be pastoral care. When an Evangelical minister takes time to visit the person who is ill, to visit the family after the person has died (to comfort and to assist with funeral and other necessary details), officiates in the funeral service, and then goes to visit the family after the service at the cemetery, this touches the family deeply. Many families have been won to the Lord as a result of the ministry they have received in the funeral of a loved one.

3) Holy Week - Holy week is the time of year when people with a Catholic background focus the most on spiritual matters. They have more religious fervor at this time than at any other time or the year. We have already mentioned the types of activities in which they participate during the Lenten season. We do want to point out that this is a marvelous time to have a series of sermons on the Seven Last Words of Jesus, to have dramas, to have Friday afternoon services and to have other activities that focus on the suffering and death of Jesus. Many have responded to the gospel message while participating in these types of special events.

Conclusion:

Celebrations provide marvelous opportunities to cultivate friendships with family members, friends, neighbors, and work associates. They build bridges for the communication of the gospel. Understanding the spiritual and social significance of these celebrations is absolutely essential. Once we know this, we can pray that God will give us the creativity and dedication it takes to plan celebrations and events that are culturally appropriate, yet thoroughly biblical, in order that we might communicate the message of salvation.

LESSON O

CONTEXTUALIZED WORSHIP SERVICES

Introduction

For many Roman Catholics, attending an Evangelical worship service may be a new and at times an intimidating experience. Despite the fact that some of the more innovative Catholic Churches now sing hymns and choruses, involve more lay people, and have more Bible reading than previously, there are still enough differences in Evangelical worship services to cause visitors to be apprehensive and confused. There are, therefore several things that need to be done to reduce some of the points of tension and enable visitors to find the worship experience meaningful and inspiring. These things relate to the setting in which the service is held, programs for the children, the purpose of the service, the recognition of visitors, the announcements, the length of the service, the music, the preaching, the relevance of the sermon topics, the redemptive note of the message, and the invitation.[11]

The overall environment in the worship service

Roman Catholics are accustomed to an environment of reverence and silence prior to the start of the worship service. Many parishioners go to their pews, kneel, and pray in preparation for the Mass. Some of them, absolutely cannot believe the "market place" environment that they see in Evangelical churches prior to the start of the worship service. People are laughing, talking in a loud voice, and moving around during the time that the prelude is being played. While Evangelicals view this as a time of fellowship and rejoicing, many Roman Catholics view this as a sign of irreverence and lack of respect for the sanctuary.

Evangelicals who expect to lead many nominal Roman Catholics to a personal experience of salvation in Jesus Christ and to disciple them in the context of a Bible believing church need to be sensitive to their Roman Catholic visitors' feelings and take the steps that are necessary to promote a spirit of reverence in their worship services.

Having said this, we must point out that the Evangelical worship service does not need to be a replica of the Catholic Mass. Quite the contrary, it could be a culturally relevant and dynamic worship service. Kirk Hadaway describes this type of service when he states:

285

> This character is somewhat difficult to describe, but the terms usually employed are "exciting," "celebration, " "electricity," and "spirit of revival." Whatever terms are used, anyone who has worshiped in many growing congregations will agree that the worship experience sets these churches apart.[12]

The worship service does not have to be spectacular to capture the attention of the people. There is something, however that happens in the lives of the people when they have participated fully in a worship service. That "something which happens" makes a difference in the way in that people feels towards God, others, their responsibilities, and life in general.[13] The person has worshiped when he can say like Jacob: "Truly the Lord is in this place" (Genesis 28: 16). There are key factors that contribute so that worship can be a positive factor in the growth of the church.

The setting in which the service takes place

The setting in which the worship service takes place contributes towards making this is an inspiring experience or hinders it. Some churches have the resources to acquire elegant buildings with all the amenities. Others do not have the same resources. This does not mean, however that nothing can be done to improve the setting in which the service takes place. There are many things that can be done. In some cases the sanctuary can be painted. In other cases changes need to be made to improve the lighting in the sanctuary. Perhaps some churches need to change the seating arrangement so that the people can enter and leave more easily. The fundamental question that should be asked is, what impression do visitors receive when they come to our church? Sometimes the members became accustomed to seeing doors or walls that need painting but for the visitors this is a sign of negligence and perhaps, low morale. While it is true that many churches have very limited resources, it is also true that in many cases the church members' houses are much more attractive than the place where they meet to worship to God. Three areas that absolutely demand attention are the nursery, restrooms and parking facilities. Numerous studies indicate that parents are deeply concerned that the nursery be clean and that the workers be competent. This may determine whether they return, regardless of the music, the preaching, and the other aspects of the worship service. A recent study of travelers done by a petroleum company station indicated that the service travelers appreciate the most is the provision of clean restrooms. New comers expect the same in the churches they visit. Adequate parking is also and absolute must. Church members must be willing to park farther away from the building in order to provide space for visitors.

While church members might be more persistent, visitors may not be willing to spend a great deal of time looking for a place to park. These matters are extremely important in communicating to visitors that we are truly happy to see them. It is important, therefore, to pay attention to the place in which worship occurs so that everything will contribute toward making it an uplifting experience for the members as well as for the visitors.

The purpose of the service

One of the factors that contributes toward making the worship service a meaningful experience is defining the purpose of the service. There are so many spiritual needs that sometimes people expect each worship service to minister to the members of the church and well as the visitors simultaneously. This confuses the members of the church. Sometimes, when they bring visitors, the pastor preaches doctrinal sermons and when there are no visitors the pastor preaches beautiful evangelistic sermons.

A good number of churches that are contextualized have decided that the Sunday morning worship will focus primarily on evangelism. In some cultures the Sunday evening service has the greatest number of visitors and can be designated as the visitor friendly service. The important thing is not the hour but the fact that the pastor and the members have come to an agreement on the primary purpose of each service. The members will, therefore, know when they can expect doctrinal and other sermons that contribute toward Christian maturity and when they can safely invite visitors to hear evangelistic sermons. While it is true that everyone should find every service inspiring, it is also true that when the primary purpose of each service is known, the results will be much greater.

The welcoming of visitors

Many contextualized churches give special attention to the way in which the visitors are treated. For those of us who have been Evangelical Christians for a long time it seems very appropriate to ask visitors to stand up, to give their name, to receive a visitor's card and to give us an opportunity to welcome them to the service. Sometimes when we visit a sister church we feel comfortable standing up, giving a fraternal greeting, and expressing our happiness for the opportunity to be there. Some studies, however, indicate that one of the greatest fears that people have is that of speaking in public. What happens, then, when new people come to our worship services? Many visitors feel uncomfortable, fearful, and intimidated when we ask them to stand up and speak to the congregation. At the very least, they feel uncomfortable that they are being asked to stand up while everyone is looking at them. This is especially true for Roman Catholics who are not accustomed to being welcomed, let alone being singled out during the Mass.

In many instances, they may want to come, observe, and later decide if they would feel comfortable there. But if we direct the attention of the entire congregation to them, it is quite unlikely that they will return.

There are perhaps two purposes that we have in mind when we ask people to stand up: (1) we want to express our joy that they are visiting us; and (2) we want to take their name and address to visit them or send them a letter. Could this be done without our causing discomfort or embarrassment for our visitors?

There are several ways in which we can express our joy for their presence. One of them is to make a general comment simply welcoming all our visitors. Some churches have the custom of singing a hymn of welcome and of greeting members as well as visitors without requesting that the visitors stand up or say something. Some churches have people at the door of the church that greet the visitors, give them information (e.g., Sunday School class), give them a visitor's card, and help them to find a seat. Some churches reserve seats closest to the entrance for the visitors so that they will not feel embarrassed while searching for a seat especially when the service has already begun. The way in which visitors are welcomed varies from one culture to the other. The rule to follow, however is: people need to feel comfortable when they visit our church.

There are numerous ways to get information from our visitors. One way is for the members that have invited the visitor to fill a card with their name and address. Another way is for the ushers at the door to welcome them and to get this information. It is important to keep in mind that many unchurched people are apprehensive when they are requested to fill a card. Some may think that they are being enrolled in the membership or some other group of the church. It is important, therefore, to be sensitive toward these fears that the visitors have and do everything in such way that they have such a positive and uplifting experience that they will want to visit us again.

The announcements

There are several questions that need to be asked with regard to the announcements. One of these is, what type of announcements should be made during the worship service? If one is speaking about a worship service designed especially to minister to the visitors, it is recommendable that only announcements of general interest be made. The announcements that have to do with the organizations of the church (e.g., Sunday School teacher's meetings) should be placed in the bulletin or should be made during the Sunday School hour. This spares visitors from having to listen to many announcements that are not of interest to them. Another question is, in what part of the program should the announcements inserted? In many worship services a lengthy period of announcements squelches the spirit of worship. Some churches make the announcements before the worship service starts. Other churches make the announcements after the invitation. This will need to be decided in accordance with local customs. We should be careful, however, not to allow the period of announcements to interrupt the spirit of worship that has been cultivated in the initial part of the service.

The length of the service

The length of worship service varies between one culture and another. In some cultures if the Sunday morning worship service is not over by twelve o'clock the congregation gets restless and some begin to leave. In other cultures the members are not in a hurry to finish the service at a certain hour. There are two factors, however, that we should consider. First, in many cities the lifestyle is such that the people are guided by the clock. If the people have become accustomed to activities that move at a rabbit's pace and the service moves at the pace of a tortoise, they will easily become bored. Second, generally Catholic visitors are not accustomed to lengthy worship services. They usually attend for one hour maximum. We are not suggesting a particular length for worship services. What we are saying is that we should pay attention to the way in which time is utilized.

There are several things that can be done so that the service moves at a comfortable pace. First, as we have already mentioned, we can limit the announcements to only those that are of general interest. Second, we can utilize more ushers to take up the offering. If the number of ushers is doubled the time of the offering can be cut in half. Third, we can reduce the time it takes for a person who finishes speaking or singing at the pulpit and the time it takes for the other person to get up and start walking toward the pulpit. Again, we are not suggesting here that the service should be conducted in an accelerated manner. What we are saying is that in a dynamic service everything is organized in such a way that there is enough time for worship, the message of the word, the invitation, and the other activities that are of vital importance. In other words, a dynamic service moves in an inspiring and sure way toward its culminating point without interrupting the spirit of worship. The people feel that one activity leads to the other and that each a contributes to the glorious experience of the worship.

The music in the worship service

Music plays a very important part in the worship service. It is especially through the music that our spirits are elevated to worship God. There are several factors that make possible for the music to contributes in a positive way to the worship experience.

First, culture influences the type of music that is utilized in the worship service. There are hymns that have been a great source of inspiration for many people throughout the years. When a group, however, depends totally on hymns that were written many decades ago (or hymns whose music represents a culture of the distant past) there is a great probability that the worship service is not going to be as dynamic as it could be he. Generally, it takes time for a group to write its own hymns and to utilize the instruments that are utilized in its own culture. While we should be careful that these hymns and choruses are doctrinally correct, there is a higher degree of involvement when the congregation sings the hymns that reflect its own culture. From time to time, there are debates about the instruments that should be utilized in church. In each case, the believers, without a doubt, will need to utilize their judgement to determine what instruments contribute to worship and are not a stumbling block because they are associated with anti-biblical practices. The study of the Old Testament reveals that a great variety of instruments were utilized to worship to God.

Second, the participation of the congregation in the music contributes to the worship experience. We should, however, be mindful of the fact that often Catholic visitors feel uncomfortable if there is an excessive amount of congregational singing. They are not accustomed to singing many songs and to using a hymn book. Some contextualized churches have paid attention to this in the preparation of their worship service (especially in what they have designated as "seeker friendly services"). In these instances, churches reduce the number of congregational songs and include a larger number of solos and choral groups. Some of these churches also print simple hymns in the bulletin so that the visitors will not have to spent time searching for these hymns in the hymnal and trying to decipher how the stanzas are sung. Again, the objective is that of reducing the tension on the part of the visitors so that they may have a positive experience and feel the desire to return.

Music plays an indispensable in the worship. When music is contextualized to the culture and the needs of the people it becomes a valuable element in worship.

Planning The Preaching

The focal point of the worship service is the preaching of the Word of God. Although the styles of preaching vary, there are certain things that characterize preaching in the churches that they are contextualized. Some of these characteristics are: (1) the contextualization of the topics of the message; (2) the redemptive tone in which the message is presented; and (3) the communication of the vision to the church in the message.

The relevance of the sermons

Many pastors of contextualized churches, preach messages that are relevant to the lives of the people. These pastors have taken the time to know the problems, anxieties, and aspirations of the people in the communities they are trying to reach with the gospel. These pastors have asked the following questions: (1) What is the worldview of these people? In other words, what concepts do Roman Catholics have regarding a supreme being, the purpose of the life, and how a person attains salvation?; (2) What voids are there in the soul of these people that could be fulfilled with the gospel?; (3) What challenges do these people face is it their daily life at home, in their communities, and in their jobs for which the word of God has an answer?; and (3) What are the needs of these people that can serve as a bridge through which the gospel can be communicated.? In an earlier chapter we mentioned the fact that Jesus adapted the presentation of the message to the needs of his listeners (e.g., Nicodemus, Zaccheus). The pastors of contextualized churches try to do the same. When the people leave the church after the service, they feel that they have heard a message from God that relates to their daily lives. The pastors of contextualized churches preach messages that are relevant to the lives of the people.

The redemptive tone of the sermons

Another characteristic of the sermons preached by pastors of contextualized churches is that they have a redemptive tone. There are preachers who believe that they are preaching the gospel when they denounce sin and tell the people how sinful they are. It is true that the Bible has much say about sin, but that is only part of the message. Roman 6: 23, for example, says that "the wages of the sin is death." If we continued reading, we realize that "the gift of God is eternal life in Jesus Christ our Lord." The good new is that God has made provision for the sin of humanity in Jesus Christ and that if we accepted him, we have abundant life now (John 10:10) and the glorious assurance of eternal life (John 3:16). The word "gospel" itself means good news.

The pastors of contextualized churches preach the good new of salvation. They do not just speak about the sin, but emphasize the glorious truth that in Jesus Christ we have liberation from the power of sin. The redemptive tone of the message not only says to human beings that they are sinners but that they can conquer sin. They not only show people their condition but teach them how they can be different. The redemptive message gives people a new vision of what they can be if Christ is in their heart. Instead of leaving the service with a feeling of guilt and defeat for what they have done, people who hear redemptive messages leave the service with a new optimism that with the help of the Lord their lives will be different. This is especially true of Roman Catholics who take a legalistic approach to religion and feel all the while that they cannot measure up. The text "I can do all things through Christ who strengthens me," needs to become the motto of new believers in Christ. Sermons preached in contextualized churches have a redemptive tone. The members invite their friends with confidence because they have the assurance that they are going to hear to uplifting sermons. A word of caution should be given here: *Evangelical preachers should never use to pulpit to criticize, ridicule, or make fun of Roman Catholics, their beliefs, or their practices.* There is nothing that is more devastating than for a family member or friend to bring a Catholic to an Evangelical church only to hear that type of message. That is not preaching the gospel of Jesus Christ and it is certainly not done in His spirit.

The invitation to respond

For the many Evangelical Christians, the invitation given at the end of the sermon is of great importance. Theologically the invitation is based on the fact that Jesus invited to the people to follow him. On many occasions this invitation was given in public. Giving the invitation, therefore, is based on the conviction that the people need to make a public decision to receive Christ as savior.

In the memory of many Evangelical Christians there are scenes of the moment when invitation has been given in Billy Graham evangelistic crusades. It is an unforgettable experience to see hundreds of people go forward in a stadium indicating their desire to receive Christ as their savior. This type of direct invitation has been utilized effectively in many places. There are settings, however, in which a public invitation in a church building or a stadium does not have the same results. As we have said in one of the previous chapters, there are certain contexts in which there is a need to cultivate friendships, present the message gradually, give an opportunity for people to respond to the gospel in their homes, and prepare them to share their decision in a worship service.

Some contextualized churches encourage people to receive Christ in their heart but do not ask them that to make their decision public immediately. In a church that met in a school auditorium that did not have a center aisle, the pastor had adapted his methodology for giving the invitation. Upon concluding the message, the pastor asks all of the people to bow their heads, and spend a moment reflecting on the message they have just heard. He then asks those who want to receive Christ to look up and focus their attention on him. When the people do this, he spends a moment speaking to them about the meaning of receiving Jesus Christ as savior. From the pulpit, he prays for them. After this, he asks that the people to take a card that has been included in the bulletin or that is on the back of the pew ahead of them. He instructs them to fill out that card and promises that during that week a minister from the church will visit them and talk in more detail about the decision that they have made. In their homes, the minister answers their questions and helps them to understand the plan of salvation. After this, the minister enlists them in the new believers' class. It is not until the time of their baptism that the new converts stand before the congregation and give their testimony of salvation. In a community where response to the gospel message had been very limited, this pastor has succeeded in winning thousands to the Lord. The method of giving the invitation has contributed significantly to this success. This is especially true in some settings in which Roman Catholics are reticent to go to the front in a sanctuary because they feel that there is where the presence of God is (in the Altar) and they are not worthy to be there.

We are not saying here that this is the only method that should be used. This is being utilized as an example of the contextualization of the invitation in a specific place. In order to achieve this type of contextualization we needed to distinguish between the principle and the method. The principle is that the people should have the opportunity to make the decision to receive Christ in their heart. This decision has dimension that go beyond individual experience. The way in which the invitation is given has to do with the method and not the principle. The pastor, that we mentioned, believes that it is at the baptism that the new believer makes a public profession of faith in Jesus Christ. Others,

293

perhaps may do this differently. Within this principle there is variety as to the sociocultural form that is utilized. Christ, for example, did not give the invitation while the piano was playing and the choir was singing. This is an adaptation that has be done in more recent years. There is nothing which certifies that this method of giving the invitation is necessarily more biblical. What is important, however, is that the principle be followed (to give people and opportunity to respond to the voice of the Lord) and that the method be adapted (the specific way of giving the invitation) to the local context so that the greatest possible number comes to have the glorious experience of receiving Christ as their savior.

The worship service is an important factor that contributes to the growth of the church. In order for the worship service to be truly dynamic, attention needs to be given to the setting in which the service takes place, the definition of the purpose of the service, the way in which the visitors are welcomed, the way in which the announcements are made, the duration of the service, the music, and the preaching. This requires much prayer, planning, and dedication. When the people leave the worship service with the firm conviction that they have been in the presence of the Lord, not only will they return, but they will enthusiastically invite others to participate in this spiritual feast. A dynamic worship service contributes to the growth of the church. An understanding of Roman Catholic teachings, practices, and attitudes can help Evangelical churches plan their services in such a way as to minister to, inspire, and evangelize those who need to receive Christ as personal savior.

ENDNOTES

[1]   This section was taken from discipleship material in Daniel R. Sánchez, Jorge Pastor, *Evangelicemos A Nuestros Amigos* (Let's Evangelize Our Friends), (Birmingham: Woman's Missionary Union, 2000).

[2]   Foy A. Felician, *Catholic Almanac* (Huntington: Our Sunday Visitor, 1977), 285.

[3]   *Epiphany means the manifestation of God to the Gentiles* (the wise men from the East). See Williams, *Contemporary Catholic Catechism*, 37.

[4]   Ibid, 285

[5]   Ibid,. 285

[6]   Ibid, 285-259

[7]   Ibid.,. 286

[8]   Ricardo Ramírez, *Fiesta, Worship and Family* (San Antonio, Texas: Mexican American Cultural Center, 1981), pp. 11, 25.

[9]   M, Celestine Castro, M. C-M., *Posadas* (San Antonio: Mexican American Cultural Center).

[10] See Ralph D. Winter, *Perspectives On The World Christian Movement*(Pasadena: William Carey Library, 1992), D-177 and Tetsunao Yamamori and Charles Taber, *Christopaganism of Indigenous Christianity?*
(Pasadena: William Carey , 1975), 184-91..

[11] For a more extensive discussion of this subject see, Daniel R. Sánchez, *Iglesia: Crecimiento y Cultura* (Church: Growth and Culture), (Nashville, TN: Convention Press, 1993), pp. 139-42.

[12] Kirk Hadaway, *Church Growth Principles,* (Nashville, TN: Broadman Press, 1991) p. 62.

[13] Anne Ortlund, *Up With Worship* (Glendale, Ca: G/L Publications, 1975).

INSTRUCTIONS FOR THE LEADER

This book can be taught in a variety of ways. Often flexibility is needed in order to accommodate busy schedules and numerous responsibilities. The important thing is to allow sufficient time for the participants to learn and apply the concepts which are presented in this seminar. The following formats are presented for your consideration:

I. **Individual Study Format**

II. **Seminar Format**

    Five Sessions (1 ½ hours each)

    A. **Bible Study – 20 minutes**
    B. **Group Activity – 30 minutes**
    C. **Practical Instruction – 40 minutes**

III. **Church Training Format:**

    Ten Sessions (50 minutes each)

    A. **Bible Study and group activity – 25 minutes**
    B. **Practical Instruction – 25 minutes**

IV. **Combination Worship Service – Church Training Format**

    A. **Use Bible studies as outlines for sermons**
    B. **Use Church Training format for the other material**

V. **Retreat Format:**

    Seven Sessions (2 hours Friday evening; 5 hours Saturday)

    A. **Group Activity – 20 minutes**
    B. **Practical Instruction – 40 minutes**

BIBLIOGRAPHY

Walter Abbot, S.J., *Documents of Vatican II*, ed., (New Jersey: New Century Publisher, 1966).

José Borrás, "Catholicism Today And Our Mission Task," *Baptist Witness in Catholic Europe*, (Rome: Baptist Publishing House, 1973).

Bartholomew F. Brewer, *Pilgrimage from Rome*, (Greenville, SC: Bob Jones University Press, 1986).

Foy A. Felician, *Catholic Almanac*, (Huntington, IN: Sunday Visitor, 1992).

Austin Flannery, O.P., *Vatican Council II*, (New York: Costello Publishing Company, 1975).

John A. Hardon, *The Catholic Catechism*, (New York: Boubleday, 1981).

James Killgallon's *Life in Christ*, (Chicago: Acta Foundation) or other similar catechism.

Richard P. McBrien, *Catholicism*, (San Francisco: H Paper & Row, 1981).

Michael A. McGuire, *Baltimore Catechism No. 1*, (New York: Benzinger Brothers, 1942).

James G. McCarthy, *The Gospel According to Rome*. (Eugene: Harvest House Publishers, 1995).

Ralph Michael, *Share the New Life with a Catholic*, (Chicago: Moody, 1975).

Albert J. Nevins, M.M., *Answering A Fundamentalist* (Huntington: Our Sunday Visitor, 1990).

Eric D. Svendsen. *Who Is My Mother?*, (Amityville: Calvary Press, 2001).
Evangelical Answers: A Critique Of Current Roman Catholic Apologists (New York: Reformation Press, 1999).

Philip J. Scharper, *Meet the American Catholic*, (Nashville, Broadman Priest).

Paul G. Schrotenboer, *Roman Catholicism: A Contemporary Evangelical Perspective*, (Grand Rapids: Baker Book House, 1988).

James R. White, *The Roman Catholic Controversy*, (Minneapolis: Bethany House Publishers, 1996). *Mary-Another Redeemer?* (Minneapolis: Bethany House, Publishers, 1988).

William Webster, *The Matthew 16 Controversy*, (Battleground, WA: Christian Resources Inc., 1999).

Gerald Williams, *The Contemporary Catholic Catechism*, (Des Plains, IL: FARE, Inc., 1973).

Made in the USA
Lexington, KY
20 January 2014